REFERENCE ONLY

Essays and Studies 2014

Series Editor: Elaine Treharne

The English Association

The objects of the English Association are to promote the knowledge and appreciation of the English language and its literature, and to foster good practice in its teaching and learning at all levels.

The Association pursues these aims by creating opportunities of co-operation among all those interested in English; by furthering the recognition of English as essential in education; by discussing methods of English teaching; by holding lectures, conferences, and other meetings; by publishing journals, books, and leaflets; and by forming local branches.

Publications

The Year's Work in English Studies. An annual bibliography. Published by Blackwell.

The Year's Work in Critical and Cultural Theory. An annual bibliography. Published by Blackwell.

Essays and Studies. An annual volume of essays by various scholars assembled by the collector covering usually a wide range of subjects and authors from the medieval to the modern. Published by D.S. Brewer.

English. A journal of the Association, *English* is published three times a year by the Association.

The Use of English. A journal of the Association, *The Use of English* is published three times a year by the Association.

Newsletter. A *Newsletter* is published three times a year giving information about forthcoming publications, conferences, and other matters of interest.

Benefits of Membership

Institutional Membership

Full members receive copies of *The Year's Work in English Studies*, *Essays and Studies*, *English* (3 issues) and three *Newsletters*.

Ordinary Membership covers *English* (3 issues) and three *Newsletters*.

Schools Membership includes copies of each issue of *English* and *The Use of English*, one copy of *Essays and Studies*, three *Newsletters*, and preferential booking and rates for various conferences held by the Association.

Individual Membership

Individuals take out Basic Membership, which entitles them to buy all regular publications of the English Association at a discounted price, and attend Association gatherings.

For further details write to The Secretary, The English Association, The University of Leicester, University Road, Leicester, LE1 7RH.

Essays and Studies 2014

War and Literature

Edited by
Laura Ashe and Ian Patterson
for the English Association

D. S. BREWER

ESSAYS AND STUDIES 2014
IS VOLUME SIXTY-SEVEN IN THE NEW SERIES
OF ESSAYS AND STUDIES COLLECTED ON BEHALF OF
THE ENGLISH ASSOCIATION
ISSN 0071–1357

First published 2014
D. S. Brewer, Cambridge

D. S. Brewer is an imprint of Boydell & Brewer Ltd
PO Box 9, Woodbridge, Suffolk IP12 3DF, UK
and of Boydell & Brewer Inc.
668 Mt Hope Avenue, Rochester, NY 14620–2731 USA
website: www.boydellandbrewer.com

ISBN 978–1–84384–381–8

A CIP catalogue record for this book is available
from the British Library

This publication is printed on acid-free paper

Contents

List of Illustrations

Notes on Contributors

Laura Ashe is Associate Professor in English and a tutorial fellow of Worcester College, Oxford. She is the author of *Fiction and History in England, 1066–1200* (2007) and co-editor of *The Exploitations of Medieval Romance* (2010). She is now writing the new *Oxford English Literary History vol. 1: 1000–1350*.

Joanna Bellis is the Harry F. Guggenheim Research Fellow at Pembroke College, Cambridge, working on war literature from the fourteenth to the sixteenth centuries. Her current projects include a critical edition of John Page's eyewitness poem *The Siege of Rouen*, and a monograph on accounts of the Hundred Years War in medieval and early modern literature, provisionally entitled *The Word in the Sword: Writing the Hundred Years War, 1337–1600*.

Catherine Clarke is Professor of English at the University of Southampton. A specialist in medieval literature and culture, her publications include the monographs *Literary Landscapes and the Idea of England, 700–1400* (2006) and *Writing Power in Anglo-Saxon England: Texts, Hierarchies, Economies* (2012). She has a particular interest in depictions of civil war in earlier medieval England, especially in the context of the twelfth-century 'Anarchy'.

Mary A. Favret is Professor of English and Gender Studies at Indiana University. Her most recent book is *War at a Distance: Romanticism and the Making of Modern Wartime* (2010). Her scholarly interests currently include reading as a visual practice, the affective force of numbers, and the novels of Jane Austen.

Rachel Galvin is an Andrew W. Mellon Postdoctoral Fellow at Johns Hopkins University, and holds a Ph.D. in Comparative Literature from Princeton University. She is currently writing a book titled *Poetry and the Press in Wartime* and co-editing a volume of essays, *Auden at Work*, with Bonnie Costello. Galvin is the author of a book of poems,

Pulleys & Locomotion (2009), and the translator of *Hitting the Streets* by Raymond Queneau (2013).

Ian Patterson is a Fellow and Director of Studies in English at Queens' College, Cambridge. He is the author of *Guernica and Total War* (2007) and translator of Proust's *Finding Time Again* (2004). He has published on war and pacifism and is now working on a new assessment of writing and left-wing politics between 1929 and 1950, and writing an analysis of contemporary literary culture through a hostile critique of Ian McEwan's work.

James Purdon is a Research Fellow in English at Jesus College, Cambridge. His published work includes articles on Joseph Conrad, on espionage fiction, and on the British cultural response to national electrification. He is currently preparing a book about state information systems and modernist narrative.

Mark Rawlinson is Reader in English at the University of Leicester. He has published extensively on the cultures of modern warfare, including *British Writing of the Second World War* (2000). Current work includes editing a series of anthologies of war plays for Methuen, writing a book of literary criticism provisionally titled *The Future of First World War Poetry*, and finishing a book on narratives of the Second World War after 1945.

Susanna A. Throop is Assistant Professor of History at Ursinus College. A cultural historian of the crusading movement in twelfth- and thirteenth-century Europe, she is the author of *Crusading as an Act of Vengeance, 1095–1216* (2011) and co-editor with Paul Hyams of *Vengeance in the Middle Ages: Emotion, Religion and Feud* (2010). She is currently co-editing *The Crusades and Visual Culture* with Elizabeth Lapina, Laura J. Whatley, and April J. Morris.

Katie Walter is Lecturer in Medieval English Literature at the University of Sussex. She is the editor of *Reading Skin in Medieval Literature and Culture* (2013), and (with Mary C. Flannery) *The Culture of Inquisition in Medieval England* (2013), and has a forthcoming monograph on the mouth in medieval traditions.

Carol Watts is Professor of Literature and Poetics in the Department of English and Humanities at Birkbeck, University of London. Her books include *The Cultural Work of Empire: The Seven Years' War and the Imagining of the Shandean State* (2007). Her work on loyalist calligraphy, first funded by a Leverhulme grant, is part of an ongoing project on refugees and the state during the American revolutionary war.

Tom F. Wright is Lecturer in English Literature at the University of Sussex. He has published articles on Thomas Carlyle, Ralph Waldo Emerson and Bayard Taylor, and is the editor of *The Cosmopolitan Lyceum: Lecture Culture and the Globe in Nineteenth-Century America* (2013).

Andrew Zurcher is a Fellow and Tutor at Queens' College, Cambridge. He teaches and writes on early modern English poetry, prose, and drama, with particular emphases on legal history and culture, material texts, and rhetoric. His books include *Spenser's Legal Language: Law and Poetry in the English Renaissance* (2007); *Shakespeare and Law* (2010), and *The Faerie Queene: A Reading Guide* (2011).

Preface

LAURA ASHE AND IAN PATTERSON

WAR WAS THE FIRST subject of literature; at times, war has been its only subject. In this volume, some contributors reflect on whether war will also be the last subject of literature, the reality that defeats representation. Yet if war resists artistic mimesis, it is also dependent upon it. Art's idealisation of war and of warriors, and its subordination of individual lives to an aesthetic of higher ideals, drives the repetitive destruction of people and peoples, of cultural and physical landscapes. Such idealisations are not destroyed by the writing of disillusionment, even when literature seeks directly to condemn conflict. The individual re-emerges in the act of writing, and the author's self-expression becomes ironically heroic, given life and importance by the very conflict it strives to disavow. Indeed, as several of our contributors show, the act of war writing in any context is a conjuration of awe, in which scale tends to overwhelm all clarity of moral judgement. The oppositions presumed to be inherent to war – the two armies or causes; or the corrupt generals and betrayed soldiers; or the distanced attackers and suffering civilians – are mirrored in the ambiguities of war writing, which can never discard either its potential for celebration, in the triumph of literary achievement if nothing else, or its immanent capacity for horror, in the cost to those who lived and died before they were traduced in writing. These pressures are not confined to self-conscious war writing; in many places and times, literature *not* about war is made to be about its refusal to write about war. Ezra Pound's famous paraphrase of Sextus Propertius insists without conviction on the primacy of love, that other great subject of literature – but war will, must, overwhelm it: 'The primitive ages sang Venus, | The last sings of a tumult, | And I also will sing war when this matter of a girl is exhausted.'[1] Pound's classicising self-deprecation is vicarious but charming; the poem is moving; but it was written in 1917. Pound's Propertius' turns of borrowed sincerity and insincerity are eloquent in their shaping of what is not said, cannot be said – or which

---

1   Ezra Pound, *Homage to Sextus Propertius* (1917), in *Personae* (New York, 1926), 216.

Pound does not wish to say. But if war and writing have always existed in an uneasy, even disingenuously corrupt, interrelation, then the twentieth century's global conflicts and acts of genocide move literature into newly dangerous territory. In 1919 Wyndham Lewis claimed that 'new subject matter has found for Art. That subject matter is not war, which is as old as the chase or love; but modern war.'[2] 'After Auschwitz', notoriously, literature has entered a new phase, in which the rhetoric of inexpressibility fights its own battle with the urgent necessity of representation, record and recognition. History is composed of wars; but war as a phenomenon is dangerously resistant to adequate historicisation. War literature may be the essential response to this conundrum.

Sometimes, indeed, literature has almost qualified as war carried on by other means. Writing about war, or in war, or because of war, or against war takes as many forms as war itself (though not many books take a hundred years, quite), and any attempt to survey the field would be patchy at best. No attempt is made to do that here. War changes as technology changes as culture changes, and literature reveals a great deal about the way these changes happened and what they meant. But not content with its role, literature also has wars of its own, battles of the books, wars of succession, ancients versus moderns, wars for cultural territory, hot wars and cold wars. Conflict and competition are so endemic to all areas of our culture these days that it is hard to imagine an alternative, but then even putative alternatives have tended to adopt another form of war. The class war rhetoric of the left, the war to end wars to end wars, provides another, sometimes subterranean, instance of war in literature over the last two hundred years or so, particularly in the twentieth century. But whether mimetic or metaphorical, literature that concerns itself overtly or covertly with the real pressures of war continues to speak to issues of pressing significance, and to provide some clues to the intricate imbrication of war with contemporary life.

2   *Daily Express* 5877 (10 February 1919).

I
Ideologies

Acts of Vengeance, Acts of Love: Crusading Violence in the Twelfth Century

SUSANNA A. THROOP

For Jonathan Riley-Smith

IN OCTOBER 1099, following the conquest of Jerusalem, First Crusade forces led by Duke Godfrey of Bouillon laid siege to the city of Arsuf, about fifteen miles north of modern Tel Aviv. According to the early-twelfth-century chronicler Albert of Aachen, the city's defenders attempted to distract Godfrey by crucifying one of Godfrey's men, Gerard of Avesnes. They placed him on the city walls within sight of the siege forces. Dying yet still able to talk, Gerard begged Godfrey to avenge his suffering and death. Godfrey told Gerard that, unfortunately, he could not avenge him; diverting men to do so would cost them the city. Furthermore, he added, 'Certainly if you have to die, it is more useful that you alone should die than that our decree and be violated and this city remain always unsafe for pilgrims. For if you die to the present life, you will have life with Christ in heaven.'[1] With that Gerard was left to his fate, while the crusaders continued to assault the city.

The assault failed dramatically, prompting reflection on the potential causes of God's disfavour. In particular, Godfrey's response to Gerard's request for vengeance was called into question. Arnulf of Chocques, the newly appointed patriarch of Jerusalem, roundly condemned Godfrey not only for abandoning Gerard to his fate, but especially for failing to avenge his death. Arnulf described Godfrey's actions as 'treachery and hardheartedness . . . impiety . . . base filth of all crimes'.[2]

Yet Godfrey's decision not to avenge Gerard was based on both military strategy and contemporary religious belief. From Godfrey's perspective, diverting men to avenge Gerard would have been poor tactics:

1   Albert of Aachen, *Historia Ierosolimitana*, ed. Susan Edgington (Oxford, 2007), 488.
2   Ibid., 492.

the city would have been lost, making prior deaths meaningless; more
men would have died in the short term; more pilgrims would have suffered persecution in the long term; and Gerard's own life would not
have been saved. At the same time, Albert of Aachen framed Godfrey's
response in religious, as well as strategic, parameters. To leave pilgrims
to suffer would have been a grave sin, and to break an oath made before
God equally so. Besides, Gerard's soul was not at stake. Indeed, his soul
was fortuitously positioned. In the eyes of many contemporaries, to die
on crusade was to ascend directly into heaven as a martyr,[3] and to die in
a manner so clearly reminiscent of Christ's own death would have surely
carried additional spiritual value. It would seem, then, that Godfrey's
response was wise in both temporal and spiritual terms.

Yet, according to our chronicler, Arnulf of Chocques clearly found
Godfrey's response (or lack thereof) morally unacceptable. This was
surely in part because the failure of the assault could be read as God's
punishment for the sins of the crusaders, prompting a search for the
particular sins that had prompted divine sanction. This kind of search
often led crusaders either to focus on generic, unspecified sins,[4] or to
identify commonplace and virtually universal sins, like pride or greed.[5]
What is striking here, and apparently inexplicable, is the conclusion
that it was Godfrey's failure to take vengeance in particular that was
problematic. In fact, it was more than problematic – it was 'impiety' and
'hardheartedness'. How can we make sense of this?

In our search for understanding, it hardly helps that 'vengeance' remains an explanatory word used with little hesitation to explain why
people do things. As Friedrich Nietzsche noted more than a century
ago, 'the word "revenge" is said so quickly it almost seems as if it could

3   This was a popular belief rather than an official theological or doctrinal position. See H. E. J. Cowdrey, 'Martyrdom and the First Crusade', in *The Crusades
and Latin Monasticism, 11th–12th Centuries* (Aldershot, 1999), 46–56; Caroline
Smith, 'Martyrdom and Crusading in the Thirteenth Century: Remembering
the Dead of Louis IX's Crusades', *Al-Masaq* 15.2 (2003), 189–96.
4   The idea that military failure was an expression of God's judgement was often expressed through the formulaic expression *de peccatis exigentibus hominum*;
see Elizabeth Siberry, *Criticism of Crusading, 1095–1274* (Oxford, 1985), 72.
5   For pride, see Heinrich Hagenmeyer, ed., *Epistulae et Chartae ad Historiam
Primi Belli Sacri Spectantes* (New York, 1973), 157. For greed, see Baldric of
Bourgueil, *Historia Jerosolimitana*, Recueil des Historiens des Croisades, Historiens Occidentaux 4 (Paris, 1879), 19.

contain no more than one conceptual and perceptional root'.[6] It is still generally presumed that we all know what 'vengeance' means and that the term itself does not require any further explanation.

This presumption sometimes rests on a belief in a deep-rooted biological need for vengeance that transcends time, space and culture. As Jared Diamond wrote in a 2008 article for *The New Yorker*,

> . . . the thirst for vengeance is among the strongest of human emotions. It ranks with love, anger, grief, and fear, about which we talk incessantly. Modern state societies permit and encourage us to express our love, anger, grief, and fear, but not our thirst for vengeance. We grow up being taught that such feelings are primitive, something to be ashamed of and to transcend.[7]

For Diamond, although such feelings are not shameful, they are nonetheless primitive in the sense that they predate our current Western cultures (and perhaps all human cultures). Vengeance, for Diamond and those who agree with him, is not a concept or construct, but rather a 'thirst', an undeniable desire so strong that it is believed a threat to social order. The key tools with which states repress the desire for vengeance, Diamond goes on to explain, are 'their associated religions and moral codes', which presumably includes Christianity.

Diamond is not alone in his conclusions. Yet at the same time, out of the public eye, scholars have continued to demonstrate that the words used for vengeance, the different emotions associated with vengeance, the moral value of vengeance, the ways in which a desire for vengeance may be expressed or sanctioned, have all varied dramatically from culture to culture.[8] Nonetheless, alongside all the scholarship discussing the diversity of vengeance in human cultures, assumptions about vengeance, especially about its 'unChristian-ness' and its implicit distance from Christian love, have remained.

For example, historians of the crusades long dismissed primary source

6   Friedrich Nietzsche, 'Human, All Too Human', in *On the Genealogy of Morality*, ed. K. Ansell-Pearson and trans. C. Diethe (Cambridge, 1994), 131.
7   Jared Diamond, 'Annals of Anthropology – Vengeance is Ours: What can Tribal Societies Tell Us about Our Need to Get Even?', *The New Yorker*, 21 April 2008.
8   A place to start is Raymond Verdier, ed., *La Vengeance: etudes d'ethnologie, d'histoire et de philosophie*, 4 vols. (Paris, 1980–84).

references to the idea that crusading was perceived as an act of vengeance in the twelfth century. Such references were regarded as idiosyncratic and erroneous; in the words of Carl Erdmann, the enormously
influential father of the modern study of crusading ideology, these references were 'an obvious improvisation suggestive of how immature the
idea of crusade still was'.[9] Those scholars who did acknowledge the idea
of crusading as vengeance often explained it as the mark of lay influence
on the crusading movement. Jonathan Riley-Smith asserted that the
First Crusaders 'thought, as there was always the danger they would, in
family and feudal terms and embarked upon a blood feud in which they
found it hard to distinguish between peoples they identified as "enemies
of Christ"'.[10] For Riley-Smith and others,[11] while crusading was seen as
an act of vengeance by some, it was not seen as such by all; more specifically, certain kinds of people (namely the laity) perceived it to be based
on certain kinds of factors (namely secular ideas and trends). If any
portion of the Bible contributed to the idea, it was the Old Testament.[12]
Riley-Smith also hypothesised that the growing influence of educated
clergy on the twelfth-century crusading movement led to the eventu-
al disappearance of the idea of crusading as vengeance in the textual
evidence.[13]

   This approach made sense, in large part, because the quest to identify
the goals of crusaders has frequently relied on an implicit binary distinction between the secular and the spiritual. While some historians have
argued that secular factors like the desire for wealth or fame motivated
crusaders, others have asserted that spiritual factors such as the desire
for forgiveness and salvation were predominant.[14] Although many now

---

9   Carl Erdmann, *The Origin of the Idea of Crusading*, trans. M. W. Baldwin and
W. Goffart (Princeton, 1977), 116.

10   Jonathan Riley-Smith, *The First Crusade and the Idea of Crusading* (London,
1986), 154.

11   Jean Flori, *Croisade et chevalerie* (Brussels, 1998), 188–9, 234; Peter Partner,
God of Battles: Holy Wars of Christianity and Islam (London, 1997), 81–2.

12   John Gilchrist, 'The Lord's War as the Proving Ground of Faith: Pope
Innocent III and the Propagation of Violence (1198–1216)', in *Crusaders and
Muslims in Twelfth-century Syria*, ed. M. Shatzmiller (Leiden, 1993), 65–83; Ma-
rie-Madeleine Davy, 'Le Thème de la vengeance au Moyen Âge', in *La Vengeance*, ed. Verdier, IV, 125–35.

13   Riley-Smith, *First Crusade*, 49, 55, 154.

14   See the historiographical discussion of Norman Housley, *Contesting the
Crusades* (Oxford, 2006), 75–98.

have rejected the idea that individuals were only moved either by 'secu-lar' or 'spiritual' motivations, the implicit binary has lived on in the way we think about specific ideas of crusading. From such a perspective, although both 'secular' and 'spiritual' ideas (such as, for example, blood-feud or the imitation of Christ) played important roles in the crusading movement, nonetheless each kind of idea was based on relatively dis-tinct traditions and constructed, utilised and appreciated by relatively distinct actors and audiences.

In this essay I will explain how the construction of the twelfth-cen-tury idea of crusading as an act of vengeance – an idea rooted, expressed and seemingly appreciated in both 'secular' and 'spiritual' texts – desta-bilises the persistent dichotomy of 'secular' and 'spiritual' in crusade studies. First, although the idea of crusading as vengeance certainly was influenced by lay ideas and emotional responses, in the texts it was most visibly influenced by ecclesiastical themes and religious sentiment. The New Testament as well as the Old factored into the ideology, and edu-cated Church leaders like St. Bernard of Clairvaux and Pope Innocent III used the idea enthusiastically – and not only when they were ad-dressing the laity. Second, the idea of crusading as vengeance actually did not die out during the twelfth century in the face of a firmer Church message, as Riley-Smith hypothesised. In fact, the idea appears in lat-er twelfth-century sources with greater frequency, suggesting that its popularity, perceived utility, or both, had grown. As I discuss the main cultural themes that served to make 'crusading as an act of vengeance' understandable for twelfth-century contemporaries, I will particularly emphasise the way in which the idea of crusading as vengeance rested on the belief that vengeance was a morally necessary act of love for God and fellow Christians.

'Vengeance' is, of course, a modern term, and before going further, it is worth pausing to clarify its usage here. The medieval terms that I translate as 'vengeance' are *vindicta, ultio* and *venjance*. The three terms were used relatively interchangeably by medieval writers; *vindicta* and *ultio* were both used to translate parallel terms from other languages like *nâqam* in Hebrew, and *venjance* was used to translate *vindicta*.[15] It would be impossible to claim that the three terms were perfect synonyms in the

---

15   In the Latin Vulgate, *nâqam* was translated as both *vindicta* and *ultio*. For a discussion of *nâqam* see H. G. L. Peels, *The Vengeance of God: The Meaning of the Root NQM and the Function of the NQM-texts in the Context of Divine Revelation in the Old Testament* (Leiden, 1995).

twelfth century, or that they equate perfectly with the modern meaning of 'vengeance' (if that itself can be securely established). My best work-ing definition for the concept embodied in *vindicta*, *ultio* and *venjance*, based on close reading of twelfth-century crusading sources, is 'violence (both physical and nonphysical) driven by a sense of moral authority, and in certain cases divine approbation, against those who are believed to question that authority and/or approbation'.[16]

'Love' is an equally tricky term, and the medieval terminology and meanings in question also require clarification. In the twelfth century, medieval thinkers had at least three different Latin terms that could all be translated as 'love' or even (in the right context) 'Christian love': in particular *dilectio*, *amor* and *caritas*.[17] The term that most concerns us here is *caritas*, the Latin root of the modern English 'charity'. Christian love was the love that one should have for God and fellow human beings, in-cluding not only one's family and friends but also, ideally, one's enemies.[18] It was (and for many Christians still is) the most important Christian virtue; it was believed to bind individual Christians to God and to their fellow Christians, and to inspire virtuous actions. A wealth of texts from the New Testament and the Church Fathers placed love at the heart of the faith for twelfth-century Christians. As we shall see, many of the same texts explicitly argued for violence and war motivated by love.[19]

But before we can turn to the connection between crusading, venge-ance and love, we need to clarify the connection between crusading and vengeance. How could crusading (an act of external aggression) be understood to be an act of vengeance (a reaction to another's prior words or actions)? One of the first Christian thinkers to outline a theory of just warfare, St. Augustine, strongly underlined that for a war to be just, it not only could but must be retributive: '[J]ust wars ought to be

16   Susanna A. Throop, *Crusading as an Act of Vengeance, 1095–1216* (Alder-shot, 2011), 12.

17   That said, *caritas* was always translatable as 'Christian love' and was recog-nised, at least in theological terms, as superior to both *amor* and *dilectio*.

18   For a brief overview of the historical development of the concept, see Mirko Breitenstein, 'Is there a Cistercian Love? Some Considerations on the Virtue of Charity', in *Aspects of Charity: Concern for One's Neighbour in Medieval Vita Religiosa*, ed. Gert Melville (Berlin, 2011), 57–62.

19   The best overview of this corpus remains Jonathan Riley-Smith, 'Crusad-ing as an Act of Love', *History* 65 (1980), 185–9. A related survey of charity in canon law is Lars-Arne Dannenberg, 'Charity and Law: The Juristic Implemen-tation of a Core Monastic Principle', in *Aspects of Charity*, ed. Melville, 11–28.

defined as those which avenge injuries.'[20] At the most basic level, then, vengeance was an appropriate descriptor whenever the crusades were framed as responses to unprovoked external injury, i.e. when they were framed in terms of an Augustinian just war.

The crusades were frequently described in precisely this way. From the Latin Christian perspective, the First Crusade (1096–99) was a response to a number of unprovoked attacks on what was perceived to be Christendom: Seljuk assaults on and their threat to the Christian Byzantine empire, especially the city of Jerusalem.[21] Pope Eugenius III summoned the Second Crusade (1146–49) after the crusader city of Edessa was taken by Zengi on Christmas Eve, 1144.[22] In his calls for the Third Crusade (1189–92), Pope Clement III reportedly invoked the destruction of the armies of the Latin Kingdom of Jerusalem at the Horns of Hattin, and the subsequent loss of Jerusalem to Salah al-Din in 1187.[23] Outrage at purported atrocities committed against Christians in the Levant accompanied each of these calls to arms.

Yet contrary to what we might expect, twelfth-century writers who employed the idea of crusading as vengeance did not rely exclusively or even predominantly on the need to avenge such external 'injuries'. Instead, they relied on perceived obligations that elided the idea of vengeance with the activity of crusading: the need to avenge both sin and crime, in particular the sin/crime of rebellious disbelief in Christianity symbolised by the crucifixion, and the need to avenge those whom one was supposed to aid. Christian love was pivotal for both obligations in crusading rhetoric. First, it was the essential marker of right intention, that made violence against sin and crime just, and

20   Augustine, *Quaestionum in Heptateuchum*, liber VI, 10 (cited and trans. H. E. J. Cowdrey, 'Christianity and the Morality of Warfare during the First Century of Crusading', in *The Experience of Crusading 1: Western Approaches*, ed. Marcus Bull and Norman Housley (Cambridge, 2003), 177).

21   Admittedly, many of the European primary sources discuss the 'Muslim conquest' of Jerusalem in general terms and it is often unclear which specific conquest is meant (if, indeed, any specific conquest is meant). Nonetheless, for example, see Orderic Vitalis, *Historia Ecclesiastica*, ed. Marjorie Chibnall, 6 vols. (Oxford, 1969–80), V, 4.

22   For example, see *Gesta Stephani,* ed. K. R. Potter and R. H. C. Davis (Oxford, 1976), 27.

23   For example, see Otto of St. Blasien, *Chronici ab Ottone Frisingensi episcopo conscripti continuatio auctore . . . Ottone Sancti Blasii monacho*, Monumenta Germaniae Historica, Series Scriptores 20 (Hanover, 1868), 319.

even morally meritorious. Second, Christian love defined and framed the relationships that created an obligation to aid and, consequently, for vengeance.

The assumption that vengeance was God's response to persistent 'evil' played a substantial role in twelfth-century crusading rhetoric. It was a commonplace for twelfth-century Christians that God would punish wrongdoers in their midst; that punishment was described with the terminology of vengeance. Sometimes God took vengeance on wrongdoers directly, but at other times Christian authorities were supposed to seek vengeance on his behalf. The New Testament verse strongly associated with vengeance upon wrongdoers by Christian authorities was Romans 13:4: 'For he is God's minister to thee, for good. But if thou do that which is evil, fear: for he beareth not the sword in vain. For he is God's minister: an avenger to execute wrath upon him that doth evil.'[24]

It was this authority which meant that angry violence, if perpetrated by a proper authority against wrongdoers, could be perceived as Christian. The key was that such violence was to be undertaken in the spirit of love. As the legal theorist Anselm of Lucca wrote in the eleventh-century treatise *De caritate* ('On love'),

> just as Moses the lawgiver by divine inspiration allowed to the people of God an eye for an eye, a tooth for a tooth, and so forth to repress the ungodliness of the peoples, so we will and applaud that princes should exercise vengeance against the enemies of the truth according to zeal, to a purpose of divine love and the duty of godliness.[25]

Anselm of Lucca was not innovating; the need for violence to be governed by right intention, specifically the right intention of *caritas*, was a point made many centuries earlier by St. Augustine.[26] Not surprisingly, then, the twelfth-century legal compilation ascribed to Gratian emphasised it too, claiming that vengeance taken for communal (not personal) injuries by a proper authority (temporal or spiritual) was justified, because it was motivated by the love of God and the Christian

---

24 'Dei enim minister est tibi in bonum. Si autem male feceris, time: non enim sine causa gladium portat. Dei enim minister est: vindex in iram ei qui malum agit.' Douai-Rheims Vulgate Bible: www.drbo.org.
25 Anselm of Lucca, *De caritate* (cited and trans. Cowdrey, 'Christianity and the Morality of Warfare', 179).
26 Riley-Smith, 'Crusading as an Act of Love', 185.

community.[27] Such vengeance aimed at the ultimate correction and thus salvation of the wrongdoer; as Bishop Ivo of Chartres wrote in 1094, one who seeks to 'push [another] away from the bad and pull him to the good' does not persecute, but rather loves, the other individual.[28] Thus, with a nod back to St. Jerome, 'to punish crimes for God is not cruelty but piety'.[29] Significantly, while we might perceive a conceptual gulf between 'punishment' and 'vengeance', twelfth-century writers on the crusades did not; the terms were largely interchangeable.[30] And since God himself would take vengeance on wrongdoers, failing to take vengeance on wrongdoers placed Christians themselves in turn at risk of divine vengeance: 'God is vehemently offended when we hesitate to attack and avenge the [sins] of some people; we provoke the divine patience to anger.'[31]

Guibert of Nogent thus used Zechariah 12:6 to explain the events of the First Crusade: '[T]herefore *they devoured all the people to the right and to the left in a circle* [means that] while over here the elect, whom the right hand signifies, are incorporated into the piety of Christianity, over there the reprobates, who are known to pertain to the left, are devastated with deserved vengeance of slaughter.'[32] From this perspective, the Muslims were the 'reprobates', and the vengeful violence directed at them was fully deserved. Another chronicler opened his account of the First Crusade with a general description of events, noting that '[God]

27 Gratian, *Corpus Iuris Canonici*, ed. A. E. Richteri, 2nd edn, 2 vols. (Leipzig, 1879), I, col. 956.

28 Ivo of Chartres, *Panormia*, VIII, 36, 'Ivo of Chartres: Work in Progress – Panormia VIII', project.knowledgeforge.net/ivo/panormia/pan_8_1p4.pdf. For more on Ivo of Chartres and love, see Bruce C. Brasington, 'Lessons of Love: Bishop Ivo of Chartres as teacher', in *Teaching and Learning in Northern Europe, 1000–1200*, ed. S. N. Vaughn and J. Rubenstein (Turnhout, 2006), 129–47.

29 Ibid., VIII, 21. Here Ivo referred to Homily 22 on Psalm 93 by St. Jerome; see *The Homilies of Saint Jerome*, trans. Sister Marie Liguori Ewald, 2 vols. (Washington, 2010). Indeed, Haymon d'Auxerre depicted saints themselves taking vengeance 'for charity' (Philippe Buc, 'La Vengeance de Dieu: de l'exégèse patristique à la réforme ecclésiastique et à la première croisade', in *La Vengeance, 400–1200*, ed. Dominique Barthélemy, François Bougard and Régine Le Jan (Rome, 2006), 451–86; 456).

30 Throop, *Crusading as an Act of Vengeance*, 11–15.

31 Gratian, *Corpus Iuris Canonici*, I, col. 926.

32 Guibert of Nogent, *Dei Gesta per Francos*, ed. R. B. C. Huygens, Corpus Christianorum, Continuatio Mediaevalis 127A (Turnhout, 1996), 304.

changes kings and times: he corrects the pious, that he might advance
them; he punishes the impious, that he might set them straight'.[33] The
crusaders themselves were meting out this divine punishment. As another early-twelfth-century chronicler explained, 'detestable Saracens,
permitted by divine justice, had crossed the borders of the Christians
and invaded the holy places; they murdered the Christian inhabitants,
and polluted the holy objects abominably with their filth, but after
many years they rightly endured the vengeance they deserved from the
arms of the northern peoples'.[34]

At first glance, this view of a crusade seems fallacious. How could
Muslims, an external enemy outside the boundaries of Christian society, be perceived in the same way as persistent wrongdoers dwelling
within Christian society? Part of the answer is that while we might see
a firm boundary between internal criminal justice and external warfare,
that boundary was not always recognised by twelfth-century western
European writers, for whom the borders to Christendom were themselves an affront. Some wars could, by their nature, resemble the punishment of criminals; such wars were just wars, in Augustinian terms,
and actions against criminals were described in virtually the same
terms as those used to describe just war. In his late-twelfth- and ear-
ly-thirteenth-century penitential handbook for confessors, Thomas of
Chobham made the comparison quite explicit, explaining that 'just as
it is necessary for princes to kill evildoers through just judgement, thus
it is necessary to kill through just war'.[35]

Crusade chroniclers also made explicit use of this parallel between
the punishment of criminals and warfare. In the early twelfth century,
Ralph of Caen described Tancred and his brother William fighting on
the First Crusade. Ralph carefully noted that 'this was certainly not
judged a battle by them, but punishment; nor [was it] a conflict against
enemies, but as if vengeance taken up concerning those condemned for
capital offenses'.[36] Other accounts went even further in justifying the
parallel, describing Muslims as criminals in detail. Perhaps the most
vivid example comes from the *De expugnatione Lyxbonensi*, an account

33   Baldric of Bourgueil, *Historia Jerosolimitana*, 9.
34   Orderic Vitalis, *Historia Ecclesiastica*, V, 4.
35   Thomas of Chobham, *Summa Confessorum*, ed. F. Broomfield (Paris,
1968), 430.
36   Ralph of Caen, *Gesta Tancredi in Expeditione Hierosolymitana*, Recueil des
Historiens des Croisades, Historiens Occidentaux 3 (Paris, 1866), 623.

of the successful conquest of Lisbon in 1147 during the Second Crusade. A rousing sermon is recorded as having been delivered to the crusaders, again echoing Ivo of Chartres and Jerome:

'But now, with God inspiring you, you bear arms with which murderers and plunderers should be wounded, the devious controlled, the adulterers punished, the impious lost from the earth, the parricides not allowed to live, nor the sons of impiety to go forth. You therefore, brothers, take up courage along with these arms . . . Deeds of this kind are the duty of vengeance which good men carry in good spirit . . . *It is not cruelty but piety for God.*'[37]

This was not war against external enemies; this was vengeance against wrongdoing and crime, undertaken as a duty for the 'common good' of Christendom, in the spirit of love.

The other part of the answer is that crusading rhetoric suggested that Muslims were guilty of a broader, more significant wrong: rejecting Christ and the Christian faith. The sermon from *De expugnatione Lyxbonensi* suggests Muslims were not only 'murderers and plunderers'; they were also 'impious' and 'sons of impiety'. *Impii* (impious) was a label frequently applied; other crusading texts referred to Muslims as *reprobi* (reprobates), *rebellantes* (rebels), *desfaes* (unfaithful), and *mescreans* (miscreant, criminal, but also, more literally, 'misbelieving').[38]

In crusading sources these terms were also used for heretics, and even at times for Jews, and many at the time wondered if Muslims were, in fact, heretics.[39] There was a clear distinction in canon law regarding violence towards non-Christians in the twelfth century. From the perspective of canon law, Muslims were outsiders who should not be attacked unless they were actively attacking Christendom. Jews were believed to be passive and subordinate, and were not to be persecuted with violence unless they rebelled against Christian society. In contrast, heretics who refused to recant were always subject to violent

37   *De expugnatione Lyxbonensi*, ed. C. W. David and Jonathan Phillips (New York, 2001), 80.

38   See Throop, *Crusading as an Act of Vengeance*, 93–5 and *passim*.

39   For example, see Peter the Venerable, *Liber contra Sectam sive Haeresim Saracenorum*, ed. J. Kritzeck, *Peter the Venerable and Islam* (Princeton, 1964), 227. For a more general discussion of these issues, see Dominique Iogna-Prat, *Order and Exclusion: Cluny and Christendom face Heresy, Judaism, and Islam*, trans. G. R. Edwards (Ithaca NY, 2002), 265–365.

punishment, since by their very refusal to accept orthodox belief and
practice they were undermining Christian society and its common
good, and rebelling against legitimate Christian authorities; to be a
heretic was *ipso facto* to be a criminal. Thus heretics were always legitimate targets of vengeance; it therefore mattered substantially whether
Muslims were considered to be heretics or not.

Despite the careful distinction between Muslims, Jews and heretics
in canon law outlined above, crusading texts blurred the lines between
all three groups, suggesting that they were in crucial ways the same. This
perceived similarity centred upon Jerusalem and the crucifixion. The
narrative unfolded that the Jews had wrongly killed Christ, the Muslims
were oppressing Christianity and the Christians were seeking vengeance
– all in Jerusalem. Indeed, some texts went further and incorporated
Muslims into the Christian historical narrative alongside the Jews, thus
implying that they were responsible for the crime of the crucifixion:

> God gave his body to the Jews,
> in order to set us free from prison;
> they wounded him in five places,
> he who underwent death and suffering.
> Now you are ordered against the [Muslims],
> and the rebellious and bloody people
> have done much with their shameful arms:
> now return to them their recompense![40]

Despite the apparent illogic of this cause and effect sequence (at least to
modern eyes), the number of sources representing this narrative structure – Jews crucify Christ, crusaders take vengeance on Muslims – must
encourage us to take it seriously as an essential ingredient of crusading
ideology.

This sense that targets of crusading violence somehow shared responsibility for Christ's death, even if only in part, was intensified by
the immediacy of the crucifixion in the texts. Frequently the crucifixion was depicted as happening both eternally and presently, and as
though immediately present to the crusaders; as Guibert of Nogent de-

---

40 'Chevalier, mult estes guariz', in *Les Chansons de Croisade*, ed. J. Bédier and
P. Aubry (Paris, 1909), 9. See also *La Chanson d'Antioche*, Old French Crusade
Cycle 4, ed. Jan A. Nelson (Tuscaloosa, 2003), 53 and 289; Baldric of Bourgueil,
Historia Jerosolimitana, 102.

scribed it, the First Crusaders entered battle outside Antioch in 1098 with 'the son of God hanging crucified for them before their eyes'.[41] Additionally, sources described crucifixion re-enactments – actions that mimicked the crucifixion, sometimes literally as in the case of Gerard of Avesnes – which demanded vengeance. In numerous texts, all three groups (Jews, Muslims and heretics) appear implicated in various such re-enactments,[42] and accused of rebellious disbelief.[43] This suggests to me that by means of its eternal significance, the crucifixion had anachronistically come to represent the perceived crime of wilful, deliberate infidelity, of deliberately betraying God, of consciously seeking to undermine Christian society. As Ralph of Caen explained, '[each crusader] was a shedder of unclean blood, pouring out guilty blood: you who tore Christ to pieces in all his limbs, accept in [your own] members the recompense'.[44] As this passage succinctly and vividly communicates, violence against Christians and Christendom (in contemporary idiom, the 'body of Christ') blurred with violence against Christ's actual body.

In many ways, the prominent role of the crucifixion in twelfth-century crusading accounts is unsurprising. It is now a historical commonplace that the twelfth century saw the rise of affective devotion towards the crucified Christ. Moving away from early medieval images of the Christ Triumphant, twelfth-century theologians and artists drew attention to the humanity of Christ, and, in turn, the intense physical agony of the crucifixion. Whether in the mass, on the walls of their churches, in their own private meditations, in sermons and stories, in religious dramas or embodied in blood relics, medieval Christians 'saw' Christ crucified on a daily basis. Some reported visions of the crucified Christ that cannot be regarded as metaphorical.[45]

In seeing the crucifixion, individuals were moved to love for God and fellow Christians, and to actions expressing that love. That was indeed the recognised purpose of meditation upon the crucifixion in text,

---

41   Guibert of Nogent, *Dei Gesta per Francos*, 191.
42   For example, see *La Chanson d'Antioche*, 196.
43   For further discussion see Throop, *Crusading as an Act of Vengeance*, 105–7.
44   Ralph of Caen, *Gesta Tancredi*, 697.
45   There is an extensive literature on this, including Sara Lipton, '"The Sweet Lean of His Head": Writing about Looking at the Crucifix in the High Middle Ages', *Speculum* 80 (2005), 1172–1208; Jeffrey Hamburger, 'The Visual and the Visionary: The Image in Late Medieval Monastic Devotions', *Viator* 20 (1989), 161–82; Rachel Fulton, *From Judgment to Passion: Devotion to Christ and the Virgin Mary, 800–1200* (New York, 2002).

word or image. As Peter Lombard expressed it in the twelfth century, in the crucifixion 'we are shown a sign of such love that we are moved and enflamed to the love of God, who did so much for us'.[46] Or, as one twelfth-century preacher exclaimed, 'the image of the crucifix is now depicted in church so that we, seeing that our Redeemer voluntarily endured poverty, infirmity, taunts, spitting, beating [and] death for our salvation, may be more and more inflamed to love Him in our hearts'.[47]

What actions were supposed to be prompted by this kind of love? There was a long-standing tradition of seeking to imitate Christ's life and suffering in order to express such love; this, known as the *imitatio Christi*, dates back at least to St. Augustine, and has its own connection to the crusading movement.[48] By the later Middle Ages, the love inspired by meditation on the crucifixion was supposed to encourage charitable acts within one's own community.[49] Yet as Riley-Smith explained in a pivotal article, love also led to crusading, in part because crusading was the administration of correction to wrongdoers, ultimately for their own good, and as an expression of appropriate hatred for sin.[50]

The texts add to this that the human targets of crusading violence had themselves failed to love God appropriately, had indeed rejected God; the crucifixion stood as an affective symbol of that rejection and failure. The Muslims were 'the enemies of the cross of Christ, who ought to be his sons'.[51] Similarly, Albert of Aachen described the Muslims as

46   Peter Lombard, *Libri Quattuor Sententiarum*, IV, 19 (cited and trans. Richard Viladesau, *The Beauty of the Cross: The Passion of Christ in Theology and the Arts from the Catacombs to the Eve of the Renaissance* (Oxford, 2005), 91).

47   Ralph Ardens, *Homiles*, 55 (cited and trans. Giles Constable, 'The Ideal of the Imitation of Christ', *Three Studies in Medieval Religious and Social Thought* (Cambridge, 1995), 197).

48   For the connection between *imitatio Christi* and the crusading movement, see William J. Purkis, *Crusading Spirituality in the Holy Land and Iberia, c.1095–c.1187* (Woodbridge, 2008).

49   Ellen M. Ross, *The Grief of God: Images of the Suffering Jesus in Late Medieval England* (Oxford, 1997), 24–5 and 45; R. N. Swanson, 'Passion and Practice: The Social and Ecclesiastical Implications of Passion Devotion in the Late Middle Ages', in *The Broken Body: Passion Devotion in Late-Medieval Culture*, ed. A. A. Macdonald, H. N. B. Ridderbos and R. M. Schlusemann (Gröningen, 1998), 1–30.

50   Riley-Smith, 'Crusading as an Act of Love'.

51   Peter of Blois, *Conquestio de Dilatione Vie Ierosolimitane*, ed. R. B. C. Huygens, Corpus Christianorum, Continuatio Mediaevalis 194 (Turnhout, 2002), 84.

'the offspring of adultery' and Christians as 'legitimate sons'.[52] Muslims were *desloiaus* ('disloyal'),[53] while crusaders were those 'who loved God and held him dear'.[54] One Latin chronicler boldly imagined the Muslim leader Kerbogha's mother making the point explicit to her son before Antioch. In the chronicler's imagination, she warned him that 'of their invincible God the prophets say: . . . *I will sharpen my sword as lightning, and my hand will snatch justice, I will return vengeance on my enemies, and retribution on those who hate me* . . . This God is angry at our people, because we do not hear his voice, nor do we do his will'.[55]

It is important to recognise that this textual rhetoric existed in the context of a stark conceptual dichotomy.[56] In theological terms, on the axis between Christian faith and non-faith there was little room for neutrality; one loved God or one did not, with clear consequences either way. As Bernard of Clairvaux expressed it,

it is certain that if [a man] should not return immediately to the love of God, it is necessary that he know that not only is he now nothing, but nothing at all, or rather, he will be nothing for eternity. Therefore that man [should be] set aside; not only now should he not be loved, moreover he should be held in hatred, according to this: *will I not hate those who hate you, Lord, and will I not languish over your enemies?*[57]

52 Albert of Aachen, *Historia Ierosolimitana*, 410. Later in the century, Henry of Huntingdon also described the First Crusaders as 'sons of God' and the Muslims as 'sons of the devil', echoing 1 John 3:10: *Historia Anglorum*, ed. Diana Greenway (Oxford, 1996), 436, 437.
53 *La Chanson de Jerusalem*, Old French Crusade Cycle 6, ed. Nigel R. Thorp (Tuscaloosa, 1992), 73.
54 *La Chanson d'Antioche*, 49
55 Robert of Rheims, *Historia Iherosolimitana,* Recueil des Historiens des Croisades, Historiens Occidentaux 3 (Paris, 1866), 728.
56 It is also important to recognise that the medieval reality did not always reflect the uncompromising nature of this dichotomy. Interfaith communities existed around the Mediterranean, and if 'tolerance' is not always an appropriate word to describe conditions within those communities, relatively peaceful 'coexistence' is nonetheless frequently demonstrable.
57 Bernard of Clairvaux, *Sermones super cantica canticorum*, ed. J. Leclerq and H. M. Rochais, S. Bernardi, *Opera omnia* 1–2 (Rome, 1957–58), II, 82, citing Psalms 138:21.

Or, in pithier terms, 'it is Christ who says: *he who is not with me, is against me, and he who does not unite with me will be scattered*'.[58]

If loving violence could be a response to perceived wrongdoing, it could also be a response to fellow Christians in distress. It was recognised that, sometimes, aiding fellow Christians entailed committing acts of violence; as one early-twelfth-century chronicler noted, '[I]t is a horrible thing, brothers, it is a horrible thing that you extend a rapacious hand towards Christians; it is a lesser evil to brandish your swords against Saracens. Indeed, it is a good thing, since it is charity to lay down your lives for your brothers.'[59] This loving violence undertaken to help fellow Christians was described as vengeance, and appears to have been considered equivalent to, or at least synonymous with, *auxilium* ('aid'), the military support owed to family, friends, lords and comrades-in-arms. When describing First Crusaders rushing to engage at the battle of Dorylaeum, Albert of Aachen stated they were going to 'aid and avenge the Christians'.[60]

The conceptual linkage between vengeance, aid and love was intensified by the use of familial terms for major figures – eastern Christians were brothers, God the Father was described as a father and lord, Christ as a brother, lord, or comrade, and Jerusalem or the Church as a mother. Indeed, perhaps above all God himself, in the person of Christ, required such helpful vengeance, motivated by love and framed in the language of social relationships. In sheer numerical terms, the number of references to the need to avenge one's beloved father/lord/brother Christ dwarf all other stated motivations for crusading. In qualitative terms, although some of those references are perfunctory and concise, others are among the most dramatic and emotionally-charged passages in the textual evidence. According to the chronicler Baldric of Bourgueil, a sermon preached before the First Crusaders took Jerusalem contained the following exhortation: 'I say to fathers and sons and brothers and nephews: for if some stranger struck one of your own, would you not avenge your blood? How much more should you avenge your God, your father, your brother, whom you see blamed, proscribed, crucified; whom you hear crying out and forsaken and begging for aid?'[61] In a similarly dramatic passage written later in the century, Peter of Blois declared

---

58   Peter of Blois, *Conquestio*, 83, citing Matthew 12:30 and Luke 11:23.
59   Baldric of Bourgueil, *Historia Jerosolimitana*, 15.
60   Albert of Aachen, *Historia Ierosolimitana*, 132.
61   Baldric of Bourgueil, *Historia Jerosolimitana*, 101.

that 'the blood of Naboth cried out, the blood of Abel cried out from the ground for vengeance, and found vengeance. The blood of Christ clamours for aid, and does not find anyone to help.'[62] To fail to meet the duty to aid and avenge – the obligations of love – was to invite shame before fellow Christians, and guilt before God. As a Second Crusade source stated, quoting St. Ambrose,

> The mother church cries to you as though with limbs chopped off and face deformed, she seeks the blood and vengeance of her sons through your hands. She cries out, indeed she cries out! . . . *He who does not drive back injury from his brothers and associates, although he is able to, is as much to blame as the man who strikes the blow.* Therefore you, good sons of the mother church, drive back the hostile force and the injury.[63]

As noted earlier, this was a binary ideology: one must love, and take vengeance appropriately, or fail to love and to avenge, and in so doing deserve vengeance oneself.[64]

If we now return to the story of Gerard of Avesnes with which we began, it may appear differently to our eyes. By not taking vengeance, Godfrey betrayed the relationship of Christian to Christian, demonstrating a lack of appropriate love, and arguably calling into question his own identity as a Christian. Even the descriptor 'impiety' and the phrase 'base filth of all crimes' are comprehensible, since by rejecting the obligation to express love, Godfrey aligned himself instead with those who failed to love properly – those who were incessantly referred to as the *impii*, and were perceived to be criminal in their refusal properly to love God and Christian society. In failing to take vengeance, Godfrey failed to love; he thus failed as a Christian.

It becomes clear, too, how the history of the idea of crusading as an act of vengeance undermines our certainty that the secular and the spiritual were discrete in crusading ideology. The idea of crusading as

---

62   Peter of Blois, *Conquestio*, 83; the references to Naboth and Abel are evocative in the context of land ownership, treachery and family relations: see 1 Kings 21 and Genesis 4.

63   *De expugnatione Lyxbonensi*, 78, with a reference to St. Ambrose, *De officiis*, 1.36.

64   Notable examples of divine vengeance on those who refused to crusade – that is, to take vengeance for God – can be found in Gerald of Wales, *Itinerarium Kambriae*, ed. J. F. Dimock (London, 1868), 113 and 126.

vengeance was frequently expressed by Church writers – indeed, most of the evidence presented here is ecclesiastical in nature – and it made use of the Bible and Christian Fathers, as well as more recent theological developments, such as the compilation of Gratian. Yet it was not purely a religious or spiritual ideology; it drew upon the bonds of family relationships, contemporary understandings of social obligations and the language of law and order; and it found expression in a wide range of texts, including in particular, vernacular literary epics. Similarly, and perhaps even more significantly, the history of the idea of crusading as an act of vengeance weakens any attempt to see a firm and perpetual gulf between Christian love, on the one hand, and violence and vengeance, on the other.

Coda

During the presidency of George W. Bush (2001–9) the world heard much of the same rhetoric described above: the need to fight 'evildoers' and an 'Axis of Evil'; descriptions of harm done to innocents who deserved to be freed from repression; the justness, indeed righteousness, of war in retaliation against such injuries, and even the term 'crusade' itself. All of this came from a man who publicly affirmed his belief that God had wanted him to be president, and had given him a divine mandate in the aftermath of 9/11.[65] We learned of confidential reports headed with Bible verses,[66] and rifle casings engraved with the same.[67] Nor is war the only context for such reflections of the past; similar sentiments also remain evident in many Americans' attitudes towards other ethical and political issues, such as capital punishment.[68]

65   Graham Maddox, 'The "Crusade" Against Evil: Bush's Fundamentalism', *Australian Journal of Politics and History* 49 (2003), 398–411.
66   Robert Draper, 'And He Will Be Judged', GQ.com (June 2009), 84–94: abcnews.go.com/images/ThisWeek/Politics%20GQ%20June2009.pdf.
67   Joseph Rhee, Tahman Bradley and Brian Ross, 'US Military Weapons Inscribed with Secret "Jesus" Bible Codes', ABC News.com (18 January 2010): abcnews.go.com/Blotter/us-military-weapons-inscribed-secret-jesus-bible-codes/story?id=9575794#.UcL-d-fVCYY.
68   Timothy Gorringe, *God's Just Vengeance: Crime, Violence and the Rhetoric of Salvation* (Cambridge, 1996).

Peril, Flight and the Sad Man: Medieval Theories of the Body in Battle

KATIE L. WALTER

IN ITS MOST BASIC TERMS, war depends upon getting men to risk their bodies, to override the instinct to flee danger so as to preserve life, and instead to stand and fight, and if necessary, to fight to the death. The means by which this is achieved can be understood variously as the effects of the noble virtue of courage at one end of the spectrum, and the despicable hardening of men into beasts at the other. The Middle Ages has not shaken off its reputation as a violent, conflict-ridden age (a view not without some justification), nor has it put to rest the charge that its codes of chivalry existed to keep violent men in check. Yet learned, Latinate treatises in this period (on natural philosophy, and on governance, among other subjects) confront the difficult ethics of war, and how it is men are brought to engage in battle and sacrifice their lives in its cause. The answers these treatises offer draw on complex understandings of human physiology and psychology. Towards the end of the fourteenth century and into the fifteenth, some such treatises, like Giles of Rome's widely influential *De regimine principum*, are translated into vernacular languages or are drawn on by vernacular authors writing on war and chivalry.[1] This essay focuses on these learned ideas about physiology and psychology as they appear in a set of late medieval English writings on war, principally those translating or reworking (in whole or in part) Giles's *De regimine principum* and Vegetius' *De re militari*. Taken together, these vernacular works offer a theory of the body in battle that is predicated on an (ethical) interrelation of body, affect and cognition, and that encompasses those responses sometimes excluded from accounts of medieval chivalry: fear, compassion, grief and, most crucially, sadness.

*

1   I therefore cite from Middle English translations of Latin treatises where they exist. I have lightly modernised the orthography of Middle English quotations, replacing þ with 'th' and ȝ with 'gh', 'y', etc., as appropriate.

Giles of Rome, in his thirteenth-century treatise *De regimine principum*, follows Aristotle in understanding peril to be present in three specific contexts: in sickness, at sea and in war.[2] Giles defines peril in order to model what an ethical response to it looks like: peril requires *fortis* or courage. Since courage, in the words of his fourteenth-century English translator John Trevisa, stands 'more principalliche in peril of werre [*war*] and bataille than in othere pereles', Giles's ethics are ultimately modelled on the courage required to face the prospect of death brought about through violent conflict:[3]

> [since] alle the dedes of bataille ben in peril of deth, neuere man is fortys [*courageous*] and bold werryour but he be in som wise dredles [*fearless*] of peril of deth. And as the philosofer [*Aristotle*] meneth, iii Ethicorum [*Book III, Nichomachean Ethics*], it longeth to hym that is fortis and a good werryour to drede not to die wel in bataille. And it is iseid that a man deyeth wel in bataille whanne thei fighten right-fullich, and for the contre he setteth hymsilf rightfulliche and bodili-che to perel of deeth for som greet profit of the comynte [*community*]. And if a man loueth bodiliche lyf more than thei scholde, he wol lightliche chese a foul flight.[4]

For medieval thinkers following Aristotle – Giles, but also Albertus Magnus and Thomas Aquinas – courage is displayed and tested primarily,

2   *The Governance of Kings and Princes: John Trevisa's Middle English Transla-tion of the 'De regimine principum' of Aegidius Romanus*, ed. David C. Fowler, Charles F. Briggs, and Paul G. Remley (New York, 1997), 63.
3   Ibid., 63. It is important to note that there are differing models of virtues, in which courage is understood differently: Aristotle's restriction of courage principally to military combat is in contrast with the Stoic understanding of courage as one of the four cardinal virtues. Medieval scholastics are engaged in harmonising these positions. See Jörn Müller, 'In War and Peace: The Virtue of Courage in the Writings of Albert the Great and Thomas Aquinas', in *Vir-tue Ethics in the Middle Ages: Commentaries on Aristotle's 'Nichomachean Ethics'*, 1200–1500, ed. István P. Béjczy (Leiden, 2008), 77–100.
4   *Governance of Kings*, 401. The importance of legal grounds for war is em-phasised here, and is a preoccupation of much writing on war: see, for example, Walter of Milmete's treatise in *Political Thought in Early Fourteenth-century Eng-land: Treatises by Walter of Milmete, William of Pagula, and William of Ockham*, ed. and trans. Cary J. Nederman (Tempe, Ariz., 2002), 50.

and perhaps only truly, in 'peril of deth'.[5] In the *Nichomachean Ethics*, Aristotle also specifically suggests that true courage in war is formed in relation to others, in the conviction that one fights justly, and for the greater good. Giles's use of the *Nichomachean Ethics* – which was widely quoted in treatises on war and governance in the Middle Ages – supports scholarly understandings of the role played by love in chivalric sacrifice: the man who displays courage in the face of death does so because he loves the 'comynte' – the community, his country, his sovereign – more than his own 'bodiliche lyf' (that is, life in the body, life in this world).[6] Conversely, love for life in the world will mean a man 'dredeth the swerd that benemeth [*destroys*] the lyf'.[7] In the running of battle, such excessive love for life will cause a man to turn coward and flee.

Getting men to risk their 'bodily life', then, has been understood to be achieved through chivalric culture's sanctification of violent death, in which risking the body becomes a mode of sublime enjoyment.[8] Indeed, *The Book of the Fayttes of Armes and of Chyualrye* (written by Christine de Pisan and translated into English by William Caxton in the fifteenth century, and drawing on both Aristotelian and Vegetian lore) asserts that, for the man who is well taught in the arts of war, 'fere ne drede of fyghting is to him nothing [. . .] but rathre is to hym as a ioye & a delyt'.[9] Fighting, even perhaps the very fear of fighting, is here

---

5 On the views of Albertus Magnus and Thomas Aquinas on courage, see Müller, 'In War and Peace'.

6 Aristotle, *Ethica Nicomachea* (*Nichomachean Ethics*), trans. W. D. Ross in *The Basic Works of Aristotle*, ed. Richard McKeon (New York, 1941), 935–1112; 975. The importance of common profit is stressed in Book III of *De regimine principum*: see *Governance of Kings*, 397; *The Book of the Ordre of Chyualry* stresses sacrifice for the sake of chivalry as the highest honour: *The Book of the Ordre of Chyualry, trans. and printed by William Caxton from a French version of Ramón Lull's 'Le Libre del orde de cauayleria'*, ed. Alfred T. P. Byles, EETS o.s. 168 (London, 1971 [1926]), 37. See also L. O. Aranye Fradenburg, 'Pro patria mori', in *Imagining a Medieval English Nation*, ed. Kathy Lavezzo (Minneapolis, 2004), 3–38. In Fradenburg's account, it is 'sacrificial jouissance' that is understood to provide chivalry's 'raison d'être'. Love for the sovereign, for the 'common weal', is the basis for a process whereby '[s]acrifice does its best political work by sublimating (into existence) an elite within the community': 7.

7 *Governance of Kings*, 120.

8 Richard W. Kaeuper, *Holy Warriors: The Religious Ideology of Chivalry* (Philadelphia, 2009), 120–30 and *passim*; Fradenburg, 'Pro Patria Mori', 7.

9 *The Book of Fayttes of Armes and of Chyvalry; translated and printed by William Caxton from the French Original by Christine de Pisan*, ed. A. T. P. Byles,

understood as pleasurable – a joy, a delight. Yet what Giles makes clear in *De regimine principum* is that enjoying fighting is not the same thing as being courageous: what counts as courage is the capacity to choose to abide in battle despite the prospect of death. In medieval psychological theory, problematically, abiding does indeed have to do with loving, and so enjoyment is its necessary corollary (we seek to remain in those things in which we experience joy). Such is the peril of war, however, that by nature a man should abhor and run away from it. How, then, do we explain the mechanism by which a man is prepared not only to fight, but to fight to the death? One solution to this paradox is that the courageous knight is driven by sadomasochistic urges;[10] the other, which I will explore in this essay, is that *sadness* is the necessary counterpart of joy in forming courage in battle. This is not to deny the possible co-presence of joy and fear (or pleasure and pain) in modes of risking the body, but it is to include within it grief for the suffering and loss of life, personal and otherwise, which it entails.

The importance given to sadness in medieval understandings of courage is one generated in part from the scholastic reception of Aristotle in the thirteenth century. As Jörn Müller describes, Aristotelian courage not only has to do with 'confident attacking' but also with enduring fear (that is, fear of future evils), and *tristitia* (that is, 'pains and sorrows already present').[11] As medieval commentators observe, this claim for the centrality of both fear and *tristitia* to courage seems incompatible with Aristotle's other assertion that a virtuous action must, by definition, bring enjoyment: can it be true that the courageous man, in enduring fear and pain, experiences them as pleasurable?[12] The scholastic Albertus Magnus tries to resolve this problem with the example of the martyr: by making a distinction between the pain felt in the body and the spiritual joy experienced in the martyr's mind, Albert finds a way, through looking to the 'ends' of action or experience, for pain and joy to coexist, but not to touch each other. However, Thomas Aquinas, rejecting the idea that pain in the body is not felt in the mind, argues instead that courage is precisely the act of enduring (*sustinere*) sadness (*tristitia*) that is apprehended in the soul and painfully felt (*dolorosa*) in

EETS o.s. 189 (London, 1937 [1932]), 33; see also 39.

10   See Fradenburg, 'Pro patria mori', esp. 24–30.

11   Müller, 'In War and Peace', 93.

12   See *Governance of Kings*, 26–7.

the body.[13] Müller argues that courage, for Aquinas, is therefore 'mainly concerned with enduring the psychic grief caused by the loss of one's life, which is mixed with the bodily suffering'.[14] The primary sense of 'sadness' (*tristitia, dolorosa*) that Müller identifies in Thomist courage is the feeling of grief or mourning – that induced by the thought of one's own possible death and in response to the experience of bodily suffering. Such is the intensity of this feeling that Aquinas must posit the assistance of the virtue of patience in circumstances requiring courage, if *tristitia* is not to overwhelm reason.[15] In medieval understandings, then, courage that counts on the battlefield has to do not only with love or joy but also (not unexpectedly) with the endurance of physical and mental suffering. As such, it also has to do with the imagination: that is, with a capacity – grounded in taught knowledge, but inflected by experience – for imagining or bearing the thought of one's own death.[16] (For as Derrida observes in his meditation on courage, 'that's what *bear* means . . . to bear looking death in the face in an enduring, durable way'.)[17]

The Middle English lexis of sadness, I argue, provides vernacular writers on war with the means to express this interplay of body, affect and cognition that is established in Latinate and scholastic traditions. Middle English 'sadness', moreover, since it encompasses not only grief and suffering but also firmness and constancy, rivals Thomist 'patience' as the virtue which prevents grief from overcoming the willed choice to face death. 'Saden', according to the *MED*, means to 'harden', 'solidify', or 'strengthen', but also 'to become sated' and 'to grow weary or indifferent'. The notion of 'sadness', as it catenates across a number of medieval traditions, extends from the physical properties of coldness,

---

13   Thomas Aquinas, *Summa theologiae*, gen. ed. Thomas Gilby, 60 vols. (London, 1964–81), XLII, 2, 2, q.123 a.8: 'Principalis vero actus fortitudinis est sustinere aliqua tristitia secundum apprehensionem animae . . . et iterum sustinere aliqua dolorosa secundum tactum corporis.' ['Indeed, the chief act of courage is the enduring of certain trials with the soul's full awareness of them . . . or again, the endurance of pains, involving physical contact.']: 24–5.

14   Müller, 'In War and Peace', 95–6.

15   Ibid.

16   Fradenburg, 'Pro patria mori', notably treats 'facing the thought of death' in medieval chivalry as the source of 'the absolute intensity that is interiority's version of immensity': 25–6.

17   Jacques Derrida, *The Beast and the Sovereign II*, ed. Michel Lisse, Marie-Louise Mallet, and Ginette Michaud, trans. Geoffrey Bennington (Chicago, 2011), 153.

hardness and strength, through an affective state of indifference or habituation, to a cognitive mode of imagining death. This goes beyond
a recognition of the (potentially unbearable) co-presence of joy (love
for the 'comynte', for doing the right thing) and fear (love for one's
own life) in medieval theories of chivalric sacrifice. It requires that we
also admit the complex interplay of physiology (temperature, density,
blood), affect (actual-present pleasure and pain), and cognition (bearing the thought of future-possible good, on the one hand, and future-
possible suffering and death, on the other).

Becoming Sad

The process that endows a man with the capacity to choose to remain
on the battlefield in the face of death begins in the body, and at birth. In
De regimine principum, Giles establishes a physiological model in which
the natural heat and softness of a boy's body needs to be tempered by
the cold, or be *saddened* (to take up Trevisa's Middle English term in his
translation) in order to become a knight.

Giles asserts that since the soul follows the body's complexion, physical softness makes children literally more vulnerable to the impressions
of habit-forming vice.[18] The temperature of the boy therefore affects
not just his body, but his soul.[19] The observation that 'children ben
passyng [*excessively, extremely*] hote' accounts not only for the tender-
ness of their limbs, but also their natural inclination towards hope,
magnanimity and boldness, on the one hand, and instability, lechery
and gluttony on the other.[20] The heat of the boy's body therefore needs
to be cooled in order to find a mean between these extremes of passion. The regimen designed to achieve this mean imbricates powerfully
with chivalric ethics, and in particular with the creation or failure of
courage. Thus, Giles instructs that from birth to the age of seven boys
should be 'ivsed [*habituated*] to cold', and use 'manerliche' (that is, modest, seemly) movements.[21] One reason for this is ethical: cold moderates

18   Cf. *Governance of Kings*, 220.
19   Ibid., 142.
20   Ibid., 140, 142.
21   Ibid., 237. On medieval childhood and raising boys to be knights, see Shu-
lamith Shahar, *Childhood in the Middle Ages* (London, 1990), 210–14; Nicholas
Orme, *Medieval Childhood* (New Haven CT, 2001); and Nicholas Orme, *From*

the natural heat that otherwise inclines boys to immoderate passions (such as recklessness), and to moral impressionability.[22] The second is chivalric: getting boys used to the cold is profitable for the deeds of arms, since 'colde fastneth [*makes firm, stable*] the lymes and membres and maken hem sad, so that thei ben the more able to do dedes of armes whanne thei comen to age'.[23] Modest, seemly movements and exercise likewise make 'the lemes and membres sad'.[24] Thus movement, like the cold, acts to cool the innate heat of the child: 'for whan the body is hoot by moderat meuynge superfluyte is put out therof'.[25]

From the age of seven, boys should do more exercise, but not deeds of arms nor overly strenuous work, since they are still soft and easily injured.[26] But from the age of fourteen, when 'the heer spryngeth in the schaar [*groin*]', they should take on wrestling, riding and 'som dedes liche to the dedes of armes'.[27] Deeds 'liche to the dedes of armes' take the form of imagining fighting one's enemy: the 1408 Middle English translation of *De re militari*, made for Thomas Berkeley, instructs that knights-in-training should fight 'with signes and profres of werre as thogh it were his enemy', proffering strokes as though to the head, now to the face, 'now lepinge out, now leping in to him, as his enemy were there present'.[28] Playing at fighting might teach a boy to love it, but also to become inured to it, before fighting for real.[29]

For a boy or man to remain immoderately hot and soft is to fall short not only of chivalric identity but also masculinity, producing weakness and effeminacy. Such men are defined in *De regimine principum* as

Childhood to Chivalry: The Education of the English Kings and Aristocracy 1066–1530 (London, 1984).

22 'First, for heele [*health*] of the body. Therfore the philosofer seith that vsyng to cool maketh good disposicioun in children by cause of heet that is withinne hem': *Governance of Kings*, 238.

23 Ibid.

24 Ibid. Notably, Giles explains that movement determines the kind of body, virtue determines the will and science the understanding.

25 Ibid., 244.

26 Ibid., 238.

27 Ibid., 240, 242.

28 *The Earliest English Translation of Vegetius' De re militari*, ed. from Oxford Bodleian Douce 291, ed. G. Lester (Heidelberg, 1988), 60. Cf. *Book of Fayttes of Armes*, 30–1.

29 See Walter of Milmete's endorsement of the Roman practices transmitted via *De re militari*, in *Political Thought*, ed. Nederman, 56–8.

'molles', that is, 'nesche' (soft), and 'sone ouercome'.[30] In this regard, clothing – which, since it touches skin and wraps the body, both literally forms and shapes the body and metaphorically interchanges with it – becomes an extension of the means by which bodies get used to the cold and are hardened. Thus those who wear soft clothing, Giles asserts, 'semen more wommanliche than manliche'.[31] Soft clothing in *De regimine principum*, however, is not just associated with indulgence in fleshly pleasures (rich foods, soft beds and the lechery attendant upon them),[32] but, more problematically for a knight, with fear: 'to nesch clothyng maketh a man ferful. For armure and iren ben som del [*somewhat*] hard, therfore he that vseth alwey nesche clothing dredeth to take suche thinges vppon hym and is imade ferful'.[33] It is thus in childhood that a boy's body must be saddened – made masculine, but also habituated to fear – by dressing him in coarse, rough materials, and by giving him load-bearing exercises. As Giles elaborates:

> ther is greet difference betwene hardnesse of yren and neschenesse of selkene clooth and likynge of pleye and scharpnesse of fightynge. For to speke of bataylle generalliche al men wol be good werriours; but whanne thei comen to assay of particuler dedes and tasteth the hardynesse of yre and myght of armure and how gret the trauaille is of fightyng and how sore the wondes ben that enemyes geuen, comynlich he is hard of flesch and strong of body if he draweth hym not for suche thinges out of the bataile.[34]

All men, Giles says, *want* to be good warriors, and imagine themselves as such: but to those who are accustomed to silken cloth, the hardness of iron, the weight of armour, and the travail and pain of battle will

---

30 *Governance of Kings*, 106. *The Book of Chivalry of Geoffroi de Charny*, ed. Richard W. Kaeuper and Elspeth Kennedy (Philadelphia, 1996), warns likewise against delicate living, because 'desire for such things makes it more difficult for [knights] to endure, and their hearts and bodies find it less easy to bear the lean fare in food and drink which the quest for such honor requires. A man will be reluctant to risk death who has not learned this': 111.

31 *Governance of Kings*, 235.

32 Cf. *Book of Fayttes of Armes*: ancient noblemen 'made not theyre children to be norisshed in the kyngis & prynces courtes for to lerne pryde | lechery nor to were wanton clothing', 29.

33 *Governance of Kings*, 235.

34 Ibid., 409.

likely prove too much.[35] Indeed, the man who does *not* flee is one who
is demonstrably 'hard of flesch and strong of body', one, that is, who has
been saddened.

In Christine de Pisan's *Book of Fayttes of Armes*, the same nexus of
ethics and physiology provides the framework for selecting a man suitable
to be a military leader. Such a man should be 'amesured', 'sadde in coun-
tenaunce', 'hardy: sure: & dyligent'. So too should he eschew 'curyous'
(sumptuous) clothing, and instead be 'habylled & arrayed | rychely in
harnoys [*armour and weapons*] & mountures [*mounts*] | & contiene [*con-
tain, occupy, behave*] hym fiersly'.[36] In Caxton's translation, containing
the body in armour and with the trappings of war blurs into containing
the bold, warlike conduct of the man itself. The 'lyf delycate', on the
other hand, with its soft clothing and soft beds is here, as elsewhere,
inimical to the body brave.

Getting to the right temperature and becoming habituated to a
'hard' life not only forms a strong body, but also provides the physiological basis for the passions and virtues required to act nobly in battle.
Temperature, both literally and figuratively, lies at the heart of this process: the extremes of cold and heat underlie the physiology of fear and
recklessness; their temperateness in turn helps produce the courage or
fortitude required to make the *mind*, not just the body, of a man strong
enough to count on the battlefield. Likewise, physical hardness or softness is directly linked to affective dispositions and the ability to make
reasoned choices. If an overly hot man is disposed either to effeminate
softness, or to unreliable recklessness, an excess of cold disposes a man
to fear and cowardice.[37] Thus, in explaining the characteristics of old

---

35   For the weight of medieval armour, see Andrew Ayton, 'Arms, Armour,
and Horses', in *Medieval Warfare: A History*, ed. Maurice Keen (Oxford, 1999),
186–208. Ayton records an increase in size and weight of horses from the
eleventh to the fourteenth century 'in response to the demands of mounted
shock combat and the burden of armour': 191. Of armour, he records the steady
increase in weight between the twelfth and fifteenth century: 199. In the fifteenth century, armour might weigh 50 to 60lb: 206. Cf. Jeffrey Jerome Cohen,
'The Inhuman Circuit', in *Thinking the Limits of the Body*, ed. Jeffrey Jerome
Cohen and Gail Weiss (New York, 2003), 167–86: 'Men's bodies had to adapt
to this increase in armaments through a more rigorous development of the
thighs, chest, shoulders, for the full gear of an armed knight was composed of
fifty pounds of iron': 174.

36   *Book of Fayttes of Armes*, 23.

37   *Governance of Kings*, 126.

age, *De regimine principum* observes that old men are 'iprest togedres in hemself by cold and ben as it were inmeuable so that they dar not do, nother trowe [*believe*], nother hope so that thei recche not to be excellent'.[38]

In addition to the body's temperature and density, blood also plays a part in determining the physiological disposition of a knight to fearfulness or courage. The medieval science of *complexio* holds that those with less blood are naturally more fearful, and so make bad knights.[39] Thus Giles comments, following Vegetius:

naciouns that ben nygh the sonne ben dryed with greet heet of the sonne, and ben sleigh [*cunning*], but thei hauen but litel blood and hauen therfore nother stedefastnesse nother trist in fightynge for kyndelich [*naturally*] thei dreden wondes. And for kyndeliche thei hauen litel blood, kyndelich thei dreden lost of blood. Therfore thei ben not prest [*willing*] and redy to bataille nother to strokes.[40]

Conversely, those from the colder north, with a moist complexion, may have an excess of blood, which disposes them to fearlessness, and carries the risk that they may, without training, be rash and reckless fighters.

The quantity of blood in the body therefore correlates with a predisposition to fear, to be rash, or to occupy the mean between these two. Blood itself, moreover, is central to creating the sensation of fear (just as all other affects) and its physical effect. As Giles explains, fear is produced when blood rushes inward to the heart, leaving the outer members and limbs and making them cold. This causes a loss of control over one's limbs (because the sinews cool and contract), making the man 'astonied [*stunned, numbed*] and ischronke [*shrunken*]'.[41] For Giles, the physiology of fear directly mirrors the behaviour of the coward on the battlefield: 'whanne men dreden in feeldes, anon he fleeth to castellis other to tours; and whanne me dredeth [*when one is in fear*], the heete

38 Ibid., 146.
39 On medieval anthropological theories see Robert Bartlett, 'Medieval and Modern Concepts of Race and Ethnicity', *Journal of Medieval and Early Modern Studies* 31 (2001), 39–56.
40 *Governance of Kings*, 397. Cf. *Book of Fayttes of Armes*, which repeats the wisdom, though also expresses scepticism as to its truth: 38.
41 *Governance of Kings*, 126. Elsewhere, 'drede stonyeth a man and maketh kynde vnmeuable': Ibid., 72.

that is in the ottere membris fleen anon in to othere membris'.[42] This mirroring of internal physiology and behaviour in battle is revealing: not only are the two inextricably linked, but the process of bringing reason to bear on affects (abiding instead of fleeing as the blood flees from the outer members to the heart) requires the difficult task of recalibrating physiology.

The inward movement of blood to the heart and the consequent cooling of the outer members is the body's natural, untrained response to the feel of armour, to the fear of being wounded and the prospect of death, but also, as some Middle English treatises make clear, to the sight of another man slain. It is this total battlefield experience to which a boy's body gradually needs to be accustomed – become saddened, that is, inured or grown indifferent to – if, in the running of the battle, he is not to flee but to stay and fight. Thus *Knyghthode and Bataile*, a mid-fifteenth-century Middle English paraphrase of Vegetius, advises 'hardy hem; for whos is vnexpert | Of werre, and woundis seeth, and summe slayn, | He weneth euery strok go to his hert, | And wiste he how, he wolde fle ful fayn'.[43] Without experience, the unsaddened man imagines every stroke goes 'to his hert', and so, if the opportunity were provided, he would gladly flee. Alternatively, but equally problematically, 'if a man hath a nesche herte and is wommanliche and agrised of [*abhors, is disturbed by, feels deep compassion for*] schedyng of blood, he dar not wounde his enemye'.[44] Here, too much feeling for others, too much sensibility, is also inimical to war. Courage in battle must therefore be formed not just by physical and affective 'sadness', but also by cognitive habits, willed and reasoned choices that are likewise 'sad' (*MED*, 'steadfast', 'firm, resolute') in the face not only of one's own suffering but also that of others.

<hr/>

42   Ibid., 126. This is a good example of what Fradenburg, 'Pro patria mori', discusses as a form of mapping of the external experience of battles on the knight's interior: 25–6. In medieval terms, however, this mirroring is between the physiology of affects and actions on the battlefield. If '[c]hivalric interiority' is, indeed, 'produced and shaped by mirroring and thus perfecting the warrior's prowess', medieval treatises make clear that this is a result of the ways in which the body and its care act upon and shape affect, cognition and the operation of virtue and vice.

43   *Knyghthode and Bataile: A Fifteenth Century Verse Paraphrase of Flavius Vegetius Renatus' Treatise 'De re militari'*, ed. R. Dyboski and Z. M. Arend, EETS o.s. 201 (London, 1935), 61.

44   Ibid.

As *De regimine principum* describes, then, it is 'more difficulte and more hard to abyde' the perils of war than it is other perils, for three reasons.[45] First, because the perils of war 'bien more iknowe and more ifeled than othere periles'.[46] In contrast, it is argued, the peril of sickness is hidden within; and in the case of the peril at sea, the 'touch' of water, though potentially fatal, is not immediately painful as is the 'touch of the swerd'. Notably, the description of the openly known, keenly felt nature of the peril of war echoes that used to describe the sense of touch itself. Trevisa's translation of the Latin encyclopaedia *On the Properties of Things* relates of touch (and of taste, which is understood to be a kind of touch), that 'these tweye wittis . . . beth of the beynge of the best and demeth more opunliche of thinges that he felith and knoweth'.[47] Of all the body's sensible powers, touch is the most felt, and contains the greatest capacity to transmit and inflict pain. War is so frightening because in pitching bodies against bodies it doubles the effect of touch. So too, Giles elaborates, because it is 'openliche iknowe, and also for it is most ifeled', 'we ymageneth and dredeth most sore harm and hurtynge' in the peril of war.[48]

Imagination functions here in relation to pain: the knight's exercise of courage is potentially hindered by his imagining the strokes of a sword piercing his heart, and by imagining the pain of violent blows. The Middle English verb 'imaginen' includes the common sense 'to form a mental picture of something not present', but it also means 'to plan (sth.), intend, plot; devise (a scheme)'. It is this sense that underlies Giles's second reason as to why the peril of war is the most difficult to bear: the man in battle 'ymageneth and hopeth to voyde and askape such periles' by withdrawal or flight. A man might well imagine the terrible end of a terminal disease, or the horror of his likely death by drowning if shipwrecked, but he cannot choose but to remain in these perils. In the case of the peril of war, the problem is that a man must choose to submit to and then remain in it; so too must he choose when and how to look to escape and when to risk injury in the running of the battle. Without a proper epistemological basis, this suggests, imagina-

---

45   *Governance of Kings*, 63.

46   Ibid.

47   *On the Properties of Things: John Trevisa's Translation of Bartholomaeus Anglicus 'De proprietatibus rerum'*, ed. M. C. Seymour, 3 vols. (Oxford, 1975–88), I, 119.

48   *Governance of Kings*, 64.

tion might lead to precipitous, cowardly action, not only through planning escape, but also through imagining the pain a blow will produce, rather than *knowing* the pain a blow produces and thus also the body's capacity to withstand or endure it.

The third reason Giles gives for the difficulty of bearing the peril of war is that, by it,

> we taketh most violent deeth, for deeth in bataille is by maymynge of membris and by sore strokes, wondes and keruyng of the body by the whiche we taken most violent deeth. And deth that cometh by som seeknesse othere by som othere manere, semeth not so contrarie to kynde of the body as deth of werre and in bataille by the whiche the body is hakked, iwonded and icorue.[49]

The death that results from war, then, is held to be unnatural – it is 'contrarie to [the] kynde' of the body. Its unnaturalness is derived in particular from the fact the body is maimed and dismembered. The accretion of verbs needed to describe this unnatural death – in Trevisa's Middle English translation, 'hakked, iwonded and icorue' – reflects the difficulty of adequately accounting for what is done to bodies in battle. But it also provides the vivid images needed to imagine what fighting is like; reading here becomes an exercise in saddening. We cannot fail too to notice the affective charge of this passage: the peril of war is so hard to bear, not only because of the pain the knight feels or imagines, because he hopes for escape, or because of the unnaturalness of the death of those slain in battle, but also because of the visual horror of seeing bodies in bits and pieces strewn on the battlefield. Betraying something of 'the psychic grief caused by the loss of one's life', by facing the thought of one's own death, this passage from *De regimine principum* makes clear the sadness and horror of being witness to the death of others.

The centrality of 'imagining' to Giles's account of the peril of war in *De regimine principum* shows that, more than simply shaping the body and forming affects, sadness also needs to shape the knight's cognitive processes, his reasoned responses and his willed choices, if he is to act courageously. In this context, one further sense of Middle English 'imaginen' is particularly important: 'to be far-sighted, look into the future, think ahead'. According to medieval psychological

---

49   Ibid.

theory, while affects such as fear and hope arise in the body, it is in
the soul that they are experienced and acted upon. This is, however,
not a process of repressing body and affect: as the final section of this
essay argues, reason instead needs the cognitive materials furnished
by the body, in the senses and in the imagination, for its prudent
judgements.

Actual-Present and Future-Possible

The importance given in these accounts of the body in battle to the
interrelation of physiology, affect and cognition arises fundamentally
from medieval beliefs about the body-soul relationship. In the body-soul
composite, understanding and will are held to be located in the intellective appetite (that is, in the higher faculties of soul), and the irascible
and the concupiscible in the sensitive appetite (that is, in the body
and in the lower faculties of soul).[50] Thus Trevisa's translation of *On
the Properties of Things* records that the soul has three kinds of 'vertues'
(powers)—the *racionalis*, *concupiscibilis*, and the *irascibilis*:

> In the racional is knowinge (soth), in the concupiscible is wille and
> desire of goode thinge, in the irascibil his flight of contrary & of euel.
> And so eueriche vertu itake in this maner knowith soth, othir de-
> sireth gode, othir moueth to fle harme. Also the wittis cometh of that
> vertu racional and apprehensiue. Al affectiouns and desire cometh of
> the *concupiscibilis* and *irascibilis*. Affecciouns beth foure: ioye, hope,
> drede, and sorew. The firste tweyne cometh of the *concupiscibilis*, for
> of the thing that we coueitith and desireth we haueth ioye and for
> ioye we hopith. The othir tweye, drede and sorwe cometh of the
> irascibel, for of thing that we hatith we haueth sorowe, & in sorowe
> we dredith.[51]

Those things acted on by the concupiscible we desire to rest in; those by
the irascible we desire to flee. Sharing this understanding, *De regimine
principum* elaborates that 'abiding' therefore requires, firstly, that we
know what is good (that is, have a natural love of it), secondly, that we
strive to get what is good (that is, desire it), and finally that we get it

50   Ibid., 14; see also 37, 38, 114.
51   *On the Properties of Things*, I, 95.

(that is, experience joy) and remain in it. In contrast, 'fleeing' requires that we know what is evil (that is, have a natural hatred of it), that we strive to forsake it (that is, loathe it), and, if we do not, experience sorrow or grief because of it.[52]

In common with animals, the sensitive appetite, uninformed by the intellective, models and forms our instincts – natural behaviours – essentially aimed at preserving life; thus in origin at least, these instincts are morally neutral.[53] Fear is therefore in some ways the proper response to peril: according to the 1408 Middle English translation of *De re militari*, 'it is wel nyh kindeliche [*natural*] eueri man to tremble and quake when he comith to stryue and fighte with his enemyes'.[54] The *Book of Fayttes of Armes* likewise says that it often happens that almost 'all the corages of men are troubled in hem self whan they shall goo to the bataylle'.[55] For affections (such as fear) arising in the sensitive appetite to become morally valent – that is, to become a virtue or vice – they must be acted upon by the understanding and will. Indeed, as Giles reminds his readers, a disposition to virtue or vice is an habitual choice of action, the effect of reason and the will's repeated judgement: 'A vertue is an habite of choys, and is in the myddel, as it is iseide, ii Ethicorum.'[56] The processes – physical, physiological and psychological – whereby a man stands and fights are therefore complex: natural instinct (which is morally neutral, but perhaps, in the spectrum of 'kynde', potentially positively valorised) must be recalibrated, and acted upon by reason and the will. Only a repetition of this process will result in the required consistency of courage, performed by the saddened, habituated body.

In the case of battle, this process of recalibration requires that the affects of either fear or hope, joy or sorrow, form the basis for cognitive engagement both with what is being presently experienced, and with judgement and forethought about what is to come. Thus, in the irascible, 'we may take hede of euel in twey maner wise: for it is to comynge other it is present'. With regard to evil 'comynge' either 'we

---

52 *Governance of Kings*, 114–15.

53 Ibid., 64: 'dredfol perels ben comonliche sorweful, and eche man kyndeliche fleeth and voideth thing sorweful'. It continues to point out that abating fear of things that we desire to flee is difficult; moreover, it is easier to increase 'hardynesse' that it is to abate fear.

54 *The Earliest English Translation of Vegetius' De re militari*, 134.

55 *Book of Fayttes of Armes*, 85.

56 *Governance of Kings*, 14; see also 8.

aventreth ther vppoun [*expose ourselves to risk*], and so is hardinesse, other we voyden and fleen it, and so is drede.' If evil is present either 'we arisen to take wreche [*revenge*] of that euel', which is wrath, or 'we leven [*omit*] to take wreche', which is 'mansuetudo' (clemency).[57] The apprehension of present and future danger produces and is inseparable from a feeling (recklessness, or fear, or anger). The knight can therefore act instinctively – by fleeing, by becoming reckless – or he can make instinct and affect subject to reason. In this process, love plays a central role: each man should have in his 'entent and in his mynde what is worthi to be loued'.[58] It is this centrality of love, not just to ethical action but all actions, that goes some way to accounting for how it is that a man might feel joy in the abhorrent experience of war. Love, indeed, is the foundation of all other affections: love's object (love for one's own life, or contrarily, love for the community) will therefore bear upon the kinds of affects that subsequently arise in the body and how they are acted on by the soul. Notably, 'entent' shares a semantic range with 'imaginacioun': 'a plan, scheme, device, intention'. The medieval mode of risking the body, then, is not about an unthinking love of violence, but rather, it is amongst a complex range of physiological processes, an ability to hold future-possibles in mind at the same time as the actually present. Courage to endure the fear of conflict's dangers is about an ability to hold in mind, and indeed fully to feel, that which is more worthy of love than one's own living self. To do so requires that reason be informed both by experience and by a knowledge of what might happen (that is, prudence), moderated by a temperate understanding of the relative values of each.

To feel fear and not to flee, but rather to make reason act upon fear, is to face the thought of one's own death. Medieval theories suggest that responding ethically to the thought of one's own death cannot be a purely abstract cognitive act; it must be rooted in experience. Experience in its broadest sense must in some ways have saddened the knight, inured him to suffering, made him indifferent to the hardship of the life of a soldier and the violence of conflict; but also have enabled him, in Derrida's definition of courage, to 'bear looking death in the face in an enduring, durable way'. The *Book of Fayttes of Armes* iterates insistently the need for the knight to become physically inured to suffering – to strenuous activity, inadequate comfort, and frequent pain

57   Ibid., 115.
58   Ibid., 120.

and damage: 'exersyce they must also haue | that is to enure hem self so to peyne and trauayll and to be harde.' Those suited to warfare, it continues, are those who 'ben acustomed to endure and suffre bothe hete and cold Hard rest & sharp fare for noo thyng can com vnto theym but they haue assayed and *knowen it a fore*' (my emphasis).[59] Similarly, *De regimine principum* stresses the importance of experiential knowledge: those who are expert in war, who 'tristeth in here awne experience and *knoweth* perels of batels' (my emphasis), will abide in the running of the battle. Those who are not, when they hear clashing of armour, 'fleeth anoon and *conneth not knowe* what is perilous or not perilous in batel' (my emphasis).[60] Without the proper epistemological basis of experience, a man cannot know what is perilous or not, is inevitably susceptible to the horrors of imagined pain and the hope of imagined escape, and so cannot act with true courage. Even the expert knight, when the battle is so fierce that it passes his experience, will turn back and flee: and he may not be wrong to do so.[61] As the *Book of Fayttes of Armes* suggests, if the captain of an army sees fear in the faces of those he knows to be 'enured with thexersyce of armes', then 'maken doubte of hyt | he ought to delaye the bataylle' (78).

Consideration of the future-possible is facilitated by the virtue of prudence: as William Caxton translates in *The Book of the Ordre of Chyualry* (1483–85), prudence 'is a scyence | by the whiche a man hath knowleche of the thynges that ben to come by the thynges presente'. Prudence is particularly requisite for knights, because 'no men put theyr bodyes in so many peryls as done the knyghtes | what thyng is thenne to a knyght more necessary than the vertue of prudence'.[62] It is thus not just the innate, natural ability to 'imagine', to look ahead, that enables a knight to endure pain and suffering (and to decide the wisdom of doing so), it is rather the habitual *practice* of imagining. The 1408 translation of *De re militari* outlines the way in which those selected for knighthood should be taught, 'in comyn walkyng in the felde, studyeng or thinking how he schal haue forknowynge and wys insyght of all perellis and harmes' that befall in battle.[63] The man suited for battle, then, is one that is 'sad', used 'cotidianlich' to

59 *Book of Fayttes of Armes*, 47.
60 *Governance of Kings*, 67.
61 Ibid., 66–7.
62 *The Book of the Ordre of Chyualry*, 95.
63 *The Earliest English Translation of Vegetius' De re militari*, 49.

exercising his limbs and strengthening his body, but also used to training his mind to predict what is to come, and to respond virtuously.
Saddening, hardening, the body is formed in a matrix of habituation
to, but also in the studied imagining of, the circumstance and conditions of battles.

Part of the imaginative work that lies behind battle, then, is the
cognitive and affective work around the notion of 'comyn profit' –
that 'end' of war – the striving after which nourishes a virtue that
locates the object of desire outside the self, and also around the love
held between knights. It is here that reasoned affects become more
important than sheer physical strength for success in battle. The army
that is bound together by love is more to be feared than one that
is not:

> For eche loue is a certeyne vertue of onynge [*uniting together, mak-
> ing as one*], and loue oneth more the hertes of hem that loueth
> thanne vnyte of place oneth the bodyes of hem that ben there inne.
> Wherfore if vnytee of place and gederyng of fightyng men maken
> hem the more strong and myghty, loue and vnyte of hertes maketh
> hem the more manlich and strong.[64]

The physical and mental saddening a knight must undergo if he is to
be able to bear the thought of his own death, and so risk his body in
battle, is therefore not one that is predicated on the absence of feeling, but rather on training the knight's responses to feeling – to love,
but also to sadness. It is therefore the full semantic range of the notion
of sadness that I suggest must be allowed to its use in Middle English
writings on war:[65] 'sadness' refers to the hardening of the knight's body,
to the process of inuring him to the conditions of war, to training him
resolutely to hold to future-possible good in the face of actual-present
pain; but it also leaves space for grief, for an acknowledgement of the
misery and the senselessness of war; in other words, it leaves space for
feeling. Whilst 'feeling' must be acted on by 'reason', its continued
presence – in the particular feeling of 'sadness' – holds out the possibility for the knight to act courageously while sensible to his own pain
and suffering, to mourn and grieve over it even in the very running
of battle.

---

64   *Governance of Kings*, 419.
65   *MED*, s.v. 'sadnes(se'.

Editorial Coda: 'Insensibility'

Wilfred Owen considered precisely these questions in 'Insensibility', written over the winter of 1917–18. He begins with ironic praise of the man inured to battle and death:

> Happy are men who yet before they are killed
> Can let their veins run cold.
> Whom no compassion fleers
> Or makes their feet
> Sore on the alleys cobbled with their brothers.[66]

This state of indifference becomes a sensory blankness: 'And some cease feeling | Even themselves or for themselves' (lines 12–13); the spirit is cauterised by experience. Owen's bitterness here is apparent; this 'saddening', in Walter's terms, is not the process by which courageous warriors are forged, but rather by which men are diminished and traduced, their hearts 'small-drawn', ready for death. Yet the poem does not sustain this reading of the experience of battle; indeed, the poem itself is evidence to disprove these opening stanzas. Dullness and insensibility move instead to define those who have never seen the front: 'Happy the soldier home, with not a notion [. . .] Happy the lad whose mind was never trained':

> Alive, he is not vital overmuch;
> Dying, not mortal overmuch;
> Nor sad, nor proud,
> Nor curious at all.[67]

It is the irreducible experience of war that enlivens the mind with both vitality and mortality, both sadness and pride, even as, in its excess, the relentless habituation to horror, it also threatens to dull and diminish it. In comparison with the men who have been in the trenches, 'cursed are dullards whom no cannon stuns' (line 50). It is here, then, that Owen's sense of the intensity of battle coincides with the medieval theories of martial physiology explained by Walter. In the midst of the First World War, (male) non-combatants are the agents of their own triviality; 'His

---

66   Wilfred Owen, 'Insensibility', in *The War Poems of Wilfred Owen*, ed. Jon Stallworthy (London, 1994), lines 1–5.
67   Ibid., lines 31, 34, 44–7.

days are worth forgetting' (line 35). Owen insists that those who have
not experienced battle are irretrievably un-alive; the soldier at the front
may become insensible to killing, but the soldier who has never left
home has no idea what genuine sensibility would feel like: 'By choice
they made themselves immune | To pity and [. . .] Whatever shares | The
eternal reciprocity of tears.'[68]

---

68   Ibid., lines 54–9.

'Is this War?': British Fictions of Emergency in the Hot Cold War

JAMES PURDON

'But is there a war on, sir, or what?'

The officer stared at him curiously, as though doubting the evidence of his own ears.

'A war?' he chuckled at last, as though the word had amused him. 'I'm afraid you're rather simplifying the issue, aren't you? The conception of war, you know, is rather an old-fashioned one, don't you agree? There's surely not much distinction nowadays between being at war and being at peace.'[1]

MOST WRITING ABOUT British Cold War culture has concentrated on nuclearism, pacifism, decolonisation, socialism, postmodernism, Americanisation – in short, on everything but war. One effect of the attention paid to these various narratives has been to obscure the fact that citizens of the USSR and those of Western capitalist democracies alike understood and feared the Cold War *as war*, even if later accounts have tended to lose sight of what Holger Nehring has called the 'warlike character' of their experiences.[2] If the Cold War is to have any explanatory force as a context for literary works beyond serving as a useful periodising shorthand, then we need to know in what sense, if any, the literature of the Cold War era understood itself as a war literature. 'What kind of war was this?' asks the historian Anders Stephanson. 'The two sides never went to war with each other. There is no obvious beginning, no single moment of initial aggression, no declaration of war, no crossing of a certain line, and no open military engagement. Is "war" itself then perhaps also a metaphor, not an actual war but an

---

1 Jocelyn Brooke, *The Image of a Drawn Sword* (London, 2010 [1950]), 110.
2 Holger Nehring, 'What was the Cold War?', *English Historical Review* 127 (2012), 920–49; 923.

image of something "warlike"?'[3] Similar questions were posed with ominous regularity in British writing throughout the 1950s and 1960s, recorded in novels, newsreels, pamphlets and public information films. The epigraph to this article quotes the protagonist of Jocelyn Brooke's 1950 novel *The Image of a Drawn Sword*, who voices the standard mixture of puzzlement and exasperation, but Brooke's novel was hardly unique in wondering what war might now mean. 'IS THIS WAR?' reads the headline scrawled on a mocked-up newspaper placard in one of the Civil Defence films of the 1950s, the fictitious question registering a genuine strategic and semantic uncertainty.

Both Nehring and Stephanson are right, I think, to be sceptical about readings of Cold War culture that interpret every shift or event between 1945 and 1989 as symptomatic of a Cold War 'mentality', and right to seek answers by historicising the conceptual categories and cultural narratives on which the idea of the Cold War's 'war-like character' depended. Anti-Communism, pro-Communism, nuclear fear: these, as Nehring very properly suggests, were prominent concerns between 1945 and 1989, but not self-evidently or exclusively war phenomena. The present article attempts to re-historicise one aspect of British Cold War writing by suggesting an important connection between official narratives of nuclear emergency and certain marginal (or marginalised) literary works. To this end, it concentrates on a specific cultural moment that has come to be described in its global manifestation as the 'first' Cold War, before, that is, the détente marked by the first Strategic Arms Limitation (SALT 1) summits of the late 1960s. More specifically, its focus rests on what, in terms of the British imagination, might be regarded as the 'hot' Cold War, *heat* being one of the three categories of damage (along with *blast* and *fallout*) for which the Civil Defence propaganda of the 1950s and 1960s instructed British citizens to prepare. In *The Waking Point*, a Crown Film Unit production of 1951, a Civil Defence lecturer reminds his audience:

> In the last war, fire caused a great deal of damage and very heavy casualties. In the next war, the fire situation might well be a great deal worse, because we should have to deal with the heat-flash of the atomic bomb: one of the most potent of fire-raisers. We there-

3   Anders Stephanson, 'Cold War Degree Zero', in *Uncertain Empire: American History and the Idea of the Cold War*, ed. Joel Isaac and Duncan Bell (Cambridge, 2012), 19–49; 25.

fore have to consider: the heat-flash of the atomic bomb, the small magnesium incendiary bomb, the phosphorus bomb and the oil and petrol bomb.

Such rhetoric drew on a Second World War iconography of area bombardment, firefighting, rescue work and community spirit in order to defuse nuclear anxiety through narratives of preparation and training. 'The next war' – a quietly ominous phrase – turns out to be much like the last war, only with a wider variety of armaments. One index of the degree to which outmoded military concepts continued to dominate British representations of Cold War battle is that the make-believe casualties depicted in contemporary propaganda are invariably victims not of the 'cold' damage inflicted by fallout in the form of radiation sickness, but of 'hot' damage in the form of burns and impact injuries from collapsing structures.[4]

The works that serve here as test cases – Jocelyn Brooke's *The Image of a Drawn Sword* at the beginning of the period and Anna Kavan's 1967 novel *Ice* at its end – speak of a different order of Cold War experience. My proposition is a simple one: that these authors were concerned with working towards a fuller and more complex understanding of the significance of 'war' in the age of the four-minute warning and the fallout shelter. They do so, I suggest, by allowing familiar cultural narratives to mutate into uneasy allegorical or fabular fantasies. Like other victims of nuclear mutation, they have suffered from neglect precisely because of their strange forms. In that sense, they embody the unspeakable hazard that lurks behind official narratives of Cold War strategy.

Civil Defence

The Crown Film Unit propaganda short *The Waking Point* opens on a cinema audience in a British town watching an information-film-within-in-the-film. Assessing the situation after 'six years of so-called peace', the announcer warns of 'ominous signs' foreshadowing global conflict: 'riot and terror' in Berlin, war in Korea, 'the march of Communism' and the struggle between 'two worlds – theirs and ours.' Outside the

4 On the importance of conflicting thermal metaphors within Cold War culture, see Tim Armstrong, 'Introduction: Hot and Cold Rocks', in *Nuclear Stories: Cold War Literatures*, *Cultural Politics* 4.3 (2008), 261–8.

auditorium, a Civil Defence recruiting officer tries without much luck to turn the film's message to his advantage. Joe Mercer, a rescue worker during the last war, seems a good bet. 'What about you, Joe? . . . After all, you'll know most of it backwards from last time. You're just the type we want.' Joe demurs, walking home through the countryside to the sound of air-raid sirens being tested, but the idea has taken hold. 'Wouldn't have done much good last time if everybody stuck their head in the sand, would it?' he tells his sceptical wife.

Joe has to stick his head in the sand soon enough, when his son becomes trapped in a collapsed tunnel in the local sand-pit. Wielding a spade, Joe leads the local Civil Defence brigade to effect a rescue. Afterwards he joins up, working his way capably through a montage sequence of lectures and practice rescues until one day, after a heavy training session, Joe dreams that war has come. Too late, Civil Defence posts are inundated with volunteers. Jet bombers fly low overhead, flushing civilians through the chaotic streets to overflowing shelters, before an atomic flash washes across the shot and Joe experiences a literal and figurative awakening. Drawing back the curtains to reveal an England still precariously at peace, he declares, 'It hasn't happened. There's still time.'

Britain's Civil Defence Corps had been established by an Act of Parliament during the Soviet blockade of West Berlin, and the first volunteer recruits began their training in November 1949, shortly after news of the USSR's first atomic test had been announced. Films like *The Waking Point* were designed to bolster the official government line: that while there could be no doubt that nuclear war would be catastrophic, it might nonetheless be endured if the right precautions were taken. In the words of *Atomic Attack* (1958), a later information film based on BBC reports of a simulated atomic exercise, Civil Defence promised to give recruits 'that most useful of all qualities – confidence':

> It's an organisation founded on common prudence, in the certain knowledge that without some preparation, there'd be little chance of our survival. It's no use ignoring Civil Defence until a crisis is upon us: it must take its place as a permanent feature of our daily life.

As military measures lingered on after 1945 – most prominently in the form of rationing, national service, and compulsory identity papers – the seemingly permanent militarisation of daily life became central to a number of works of early Cold War fiction, among them Brooke's *Image of a Drawn Sword*. Like Joe in *The Waking Point*, Brooke's Reynard

Langrish finds himself cast back into civilian life after the 1939–45 war, 'suspended between two worlds' that can only be articulated as a distinction between dream and waking life: 'The present nightmare seemed wholly unreal – at any moment he must surely awake from it; and the past, equally, seemed a dream from which he had awoken, but which haunted him still with its disquieting images.' (123)

Like Joe, Reynard has peacetime responsibilities: not, in his case, a wife and children, but a deaf, elderly mother and a dull job at the local bank. At the beginning of the novel, Reynard walks home from work with no less unease than Joe. Reynard's anxiety, however, is caused not by siren tests, but by a kind of psychological malaise about the prospect of home that the novel articulates variously as an 'awareness of falsity', a 'disquieting sense of "unreality"' affecting the Kentish landscape, an 'intolerable sense of confinement', and (contradictorily) a kind of personal dispersal:

> [I]t was as though his personality – or the sensory images which gave it form and solidity – were undergoing some process of disintegration, as though several parts of himself lay scattered about the perimeter of a gradually widening circle . . . It seemed to him, moreover (as it had seemed on more than one occasion lately), that unless he made a prodigious effort to draw back within himself these *disjecta membra*, he would find, too late, that the process had gone beyond his control . . . [17–18; Brooke's ellipses]

Leaving aside its nuclear-age promise of chain-reaction, Reynard's psychological predicament echoes in some ways the condition of those gentlemen-at-loose-ends whose rejuvenation was the concern of countless fantasies of imperial action, adventure and espionage that proliferated in the period before the First World War. Indeed, like those earlier adventurers – and again like his contemporary, Joe – Reynard eventually finds personal renewal after being grudgingly enlisted into a quasi-military organisation dedicated to the defence of the realm. The crucial moment comes for him on a stormy night when, seemingly by chance, a knock on his mother's cottage door brings him face to face with Roy Archer, a physically attractive, athletic young man who gradually inducts Reynard into a secretive battalion of soldiers stationed somewhere in the nearby countryside against an undisclosed but imminent crisis.

With the boundaries of his psyche crumbling, it comes as no surprise that Reynard finds 'the idea of enlisting in some form of "Territorial" organisation . . . curiously attractive' (38). To conclude the enumeration of parallels with *The Waking Point*, Reynard's discovery of personal purpose comes, like Joe's, in an apocalyptic moment ending with an inspirational flash. Out of the rain steps Roy – all belted mackintosh and blond coiffure, the very model of the modern English *Übermensch* – with the force and self-possession of an atomic blast, promising the kind of psychological border security that Reynard craves:

> Suddenly, with a clamour that made him spring to his feet, the noise of the front-door bell pealed through the house. [. . .] In the same instant he was stricken, more acutely than before, with the sense of some vast impending dissolution: it was as though, within his brain, some seismic disturbance was taking place, some revolution of natural forces which he was powerless to resist.
>
> Unsteadily, as though the very ground were heaving beneath him, he moved to the hallway, switching on the light as he did so. As he crossed the hall, the bell pealed once more, and to its clamour was added a thunderous knocking. Trembling, as if the action were fraught with some immense and world-shaking significance, he lifted the latch of the front door . . .
>
> Immediately he staggered backwards, with difficulty preventing himself from falling. At the moment of his lifting the latch, a particularly violent gust of wind had hurled itself against the house, and the door, facing its full blast, had swung open with irresistible force. So powerful was the inrush of air that a vase of dahlias on the hall table crashed to the ground, and a straw mat rose from the floor as if possessed of a daemonic life of its own. [18–19]

Once admitted to the novel, Roy's military presence never quite leaves, and the 'daemonic' aspect it brings is among the novel's strangest features. What, for instance, should be made of the defence force barracks in the novel that seems, like a latter-day Brigadoon, to disappear and reappear at random? And what implication attaches to the strange time-lapses that occur within the narrative, so that Reynard, finding himself caught half-willingly in an inescapable web of military bureaucracy, can see his erstwhile mentor Roy advance from captain to major to area-commander in the space of what feels to him like a few weeks? At the end of the novel, when he briefly escapes from the barracks in which he has been held, Reynard finds his mother's cottage cobwebbed and dusty, 'as it might appear after months or years of neglect', and his mother's corpse long-decayed (138). This temporal problem is too much a part of the narrative's unfolding to be explained away as an effect of Reynard's troubled mind, and too unrelenting to be understood as a vision of the sort experienced by Joe Mercer in *The Waking Point*.

Mark Rawlinson, in a perceptive essay on Brooke's depiction of the militarised countryside, stresses the novel's entanglement of sexuality with cold warfare, and connects these further to Brooke's profoundly personal and life-long engagement with the 'military-pastoral nexus' of the English landscape. (He also stresses Brooke's repetitiousness, his re-use of motifs from one book to another 'with a disconcerting similarity of lexis, idiom or cadence'.) Rawlinson's reading of the novel aims to situate *The Image of a Drawn Sword* within the arc of Brooke's develop-ment – or, since one of the charges levelled is that of repetitiousness, better to say his achievement – as a writer. It therefore rightly draws attention to this confluence, to the way 'the novel's plot progressively concretizes a topography which emerges initially as a correlate of psy-chic states'. What is less clear, however, is that repetitiousness on the one hand, and the novel's temporal disintegration on the other, amount to what Rawlinson calls 'an artistic failure'.[5] As we shall see in the case of Anna Kavan (another inveterate self-plagiarist), repetition can be understood as a kind of training in itself, a mode that might be consid-ered particularly appropriate to the writing of a war experienced largely as a series of official directives to practice the appropriate forms of pre-paredness for a crisis that never came. In a novel that attaches such importance to the ritual performance of preparedness, repetition – or what Tracy C. Davis, in elucidating the performative aspects of Civil Defence, calls *rehearsal* – might seem an exactly appropriate response to the imagined exigencies of nuclear exchange.[6]

Such a reading helps to make sense of the novel's seeming lapse into vaguely gothic fantasy, since this formal disintegration, with its spec-tral figures, mists and vague implications of unnatural forces at work, establishes a strong link between the psychological aspect of the novel and a wider context of nuclear anxiety. The atomic blast of Roy's ex-plosive entrance guarantees Reynard's psychological coherence and his physical well-being, but only at the cost of a radical disturbance in the

5   Mark Rawlinson, 'Wild Soldiers: Jocelyn Brooke and England's Milita-rised Landscape', in *Fiction of the 1940s: Stories of Survival*, ed. Rod Mengham and N. H. Reeve (Basingstoke, 2001), 101–23.
6   Tracy C. Davis, *States of Emergency: Cold War Nuclear Civil Defence* (Dur-ham NC, 2007), 86–7.

temporality of the novel itself. Suffering from the sudden onset of influenza, Reynard misses the training session at which he was to decide for or against formal re-enlistment. Recovering, he finds the world around him 'curiously disturbed', the moon shining 'with a sulphurous light through a brownish pall of cloud' (64). Roy has vanished, and even Reynard's mother seems to have no recollection of his remarkable visit. Stumbling into the battalion's hidden camp through a Second World War bunker, Reynard at last emerges into a different reality, hauled by a guard before a stern sergeant-major. 'A few isolated phrases impinged on Reynard's awareness: something about "compulsory registration of non-military personnel . . . units in occupied territory empowered to enlist or cause to be enlisted . . . with effect from the first of December . . . emergency regulations . . . services for an unspecified period . . . disciplinary measures . . ." but of the essential meaning of the whole passage, he could form no idea whatsoever' (91). Thereafter, time seems to move at an unsteady rate. Just over halfway through the novel, as he crawls through the bunker into the concealed military camp, Reynard himself feels that 'the passage of time [has] become subtly deranged'; Spike Mandeville – a soldier whom Joe has recently watched boxing at the village drill-hall – claims not to have visited the place 'since the battalion was at the depot – must be five years back, now' (88, 95). By the novel's bleak conclusion, Reynard has come to accept his own re-militarisation, turning away into 'the living moment' from 'the squalid debris of a world older than time' (143).

These time-shifts are not easily explained away as evidence of Reynard's mental instability, but they do make sense in light of the peculiar time-consciousness inaugurated by the threat of nuclear warfare. Time, in the rhetoric of Civil Defence from the late 1940s onwards, is the most precious of all resources. Including compounds such as 'peace-time' and 'wartime', the word 'time' tolls on more than eighty occasions throughout *The Image of a Drawn Sword*; when, in *The Waking Point*, Joe Mercer declares that 'There's still time', his palpable relief is designed to impress upon audiences the message that there isn't much. More widely, in the literature of the hot Cold War, temporal disruption is frequently the symptom of some implied catastrophe. Perhaps the most consistent attempt to develop this theme appears in the short fiction of J. G. Ballard. In Ballard's 1956 story 'Escapement', for instance, events repeat in a 'circular time trap' after a series of 'dense eruptions of gas' affects the light from the sun. ('I'm quite all right,' one character assures another. 'It's just that everything is happening very rapidly and I don't think there's much time left.') In the future society of 'Chronopolis' (1960), time has been abolished and clocks proscribed. 'The Terminal Beach' (1964) concerns a willing castaway on a nuclear atoll entering 'a zone of non-time', in a landscape frozen into uncanny stasis by nuclear experimentation: 'The series of weapons tests had fused the sand in layers, and the pseudo-geological strata condensed the brief epochs, microseconds in duration, of thermonuclear time.' And in the stories that make up *Memories of the Space Age* (1988), from 'The Cage of Sand' (1962) to 'The Man Who Walked on the Moon' (1985), a mysterious interconnection binds together space-flight, nuclear weaponry and the 'time-fugues' suffered by Ballard's post-human protagonists. In other works of the period, such as Andrew Sinclair's *The Project* (1960), or Val Guest's 1961 film *The Day the Earth Caught Fire*, time-anxiety is transferred to the reader by means of a countdown to (in the former case) a nuclear attack on Russia or (in the latter) a last-ditch attempt to counteract the catastrophic geophysical effects of US and Soviet nuclear testing by means of a further blast. As Sinclair's novel approaches its climax, the military scientist Axel triggers 'the slow descent of arabic numerals towards their final zero' after mocking a colleague's attentiveness to a mode of time-keeping that his super-weapon research is about to render obsolete:

> Heff was the last to arrive ten minutes behind time.
> 'Do you think,' Axel said, 'that you might have been punctual for once?'
> 'I'm sorry,' Heff said, 'I was mending my clock. It's gone wrong.'
> 'A very important consideration,' Axel said. 'I congratulate you that you stopped to attend to such a very important consideration.'[7]

The troping of time in early Cold War fiction offers a way of connecting *The Image of the Drawn Sword* to the newly pervasive time-anxious narratives of Civil Defence that emerged contemporaneously with Brooke's novel, and furthermore helps to explain the disorienting time-shifts endured by its protagonist. Yet rather than simply echoing the warnings of Civil Defence propaganda that 'time is of the essence', these temporal disruptions remind us of the radical transformation of time implied by the beginning of the atomic age. In his plight, Reynard precedes Sinclair's scientists and Ballard's astronauts in their discovery that human time is precisely what the technologies of future warfare threaten to abolish in the heat of a nuclear moment.

7   Andrew Sinclair, *The Project* (London, 1960), 182.

When Is a War not a War?

If Reynard Langrish suffers from a perceived lack of time, his condition
is exacerbated by a real lack of information. 'Why have I got to enlist?'
he asks shortly after his detention. 'What's the meaning of it all? Can't
you tell me the truth, for once, so that I can understand?' (*Image*, 54).
From the moment he meets Roy Archer, the necessity for preparedness
goes hand in hand with vague allusion to a state of undefined crisis:

> Several times during the course of his friend's talk Reynard had no-
> ticed the recurrence of this word 'emergency'; at first it had puzzled
> him, but he no longer felt disposed to enquire too closely into the
> terms which Roy employed. By 'emergency', he supposed, Roy meant
> merely the general situation as it had existed since the war; indeed,
> an 'emergency' did still officially exist – it had never been rescind-
> ed. . . . The 'Crisis', so it seemed to him, had become a kind of perma-
> nent mental climate: one accepted it, as one accepted the weather,
> or the bank's working hours, without questioning it, or expecting it
> to be otherwise. [39]

Finding it politic to play along, Reynard eventually comes to accept 'the
fact of the "Emergency" . . . by a kind of auto-suggestion' (114), and
the search for meaning gives way to the reluctant admission that 'the
meaning of it all' no longer interests anyone but him. The indefinite
state of temporal and psychic suspension in which Reynard feels himself
to have been living – a suspension 'between two worlds' (and perhaps
between two wars) – now finds a parallel in the suspension of the rule
of law. 'Well, Langrish,' advises the bluff officer to whom he appeals,
'my advice to you is to brace up and make the best of it: forget all this
nonsense about why you're here, and when-is-a-war-not-a-war, and just
try to be a decent soldier.' (112)

When is a war not a war? One answer Brooke's first readers could rea-
sonably have given was, 'when it's a state of emergency'. Narratives of
emergency were prominent in the British media throughout the 1950s
and 1960s, two decades during which British-held territories were almost continually embroiled in wars and other crises to which the in-
tentionally vague term 'emergency' was routinely applied. The first and
longest of these, the Malayan Emergency, lasted from 1948 to 1960. The
government of New Zealand declared a state of emergency following
dock strikes in the summer of 1950. In 1951, after the status of the Suez
Canal was called into question, a state of emergency was declared for

British forces in Egypt. In 1952, the beginning of the Mau Mau uprising led to the declaration of a state of emergency in Kenya that would last until 1960. Cyprus followed in 1955 (after the relocation there of British Middle East military headquarters from Egypt), Southern Rhodesia in 1959, South Africa in 1960, Aden in 1963, British Guiana in 1964, and Trinidad in 1965. At home, a state of emergency was declared after a strike by rail workers in June 1955, and again a decade later in response to the National Union of Seamen's strike in the summer of 1966. Between 1948 and 1967, the British Commonwealth of Nations demonstrated with exemplary clarity Walter Benjamin's insight that in modern government the state of emergency had become 'not the exception but the rule'.[8]

The intimate connection between nuclear time and the state of emergency is the subject of the last chapter of Paul Virilio's *Speed and Politics*, in which Virilio argues that the transition '*from the state of siege* of wars of space to *the state of emergency* of the war of time' is the inevitable consequence of the development of increasingly powerful weapons technologies and increasingly rapid systems for their delivery. Emergency, for Virilio, is the name given to warfare that has moved out of the realm of territory and into that of temporality:

> Contraction in time, the disappearance of the territorial space, after that of the fortified city and armor, leads to a situation in which the notions of 'before' and 'after' designate only the future and the past in a form of war that causes the 'present' to disappear in the instantaneousness of decision.[9]

This is indeed the condition in which most nuclear fictions of the 1950s and 1960s find themselves: unable to conceive of contemporary warfare in terms other than expectant emergency on the one hand and a fait accompli on the other, they displace the experience of warfare onto either monitory post-apocalyptic speculation (the genre or mode of Cold War writing that has hitherto received most widespread critical attention) or anxious fictions of emergency, of the kind discussed here. Such fictions work to make apparent the kind of 'auto-suggestion' suffered by Reynard

---

8   Walter Benjamin, 'Theses on the Philosophy of History', in *Illuminations*, ed. Hannah Arendt, trans. Harry Zohn (New York, 1968), 261.
9   Paul Virilio, *Speed and Politics*, trans. Mark Politizzotti (New York, 1986), 156–7.

Langrish in his internalisation of 'emergency': by re-envisioning Cold Warfare through the lens of fantasy – of fairy-tale, science-fiction, and gothic – they valorise literary 'make-believe' as a response to the kind of political make-believe that legitimises narratives of 'emergency' over narratives of disarmament or détente.

Rehearsing Emergency

At the end of February 1964, a new Emergency Powers Bill came before the House of Commons for its second reading. Henry Brooke, the Conservative Home Secretary, introduced the bill by saying that the thought of extending the government's ability to invoke emergency powers first came to him 'during the prolonged bad weather' of the winter – the so-called 'Big Freeze' – of 1962–63, during which England suffered from a combination of high winds, heavy snowfall, and the coldest average temperatures recorded since the 1810s. Brooke's purpose in bringing the Bill, he said, was to ensure the availability of resources to tackle any similar conditions that should occur in future. The bill's effect would be to replace the wording of the Emergency Powers Act 1920, which permitted the proclamation of a state of emergency in cases where 'any persons or body of persons' had taken action to interfere with transportation links or the provision of 'the essentials of life', with wording that would allow the declaration of an emergency where 'events of such a nature' as to interfere with such provision had 'occurred'. The bill also clarified the legality of using the armed forces in agricultural or other essential but non-military work.

On the face of it, the Emergency Powers Bill was intended to make it possible to respond to naturally occurring emergencies, such as an unusually harsh winter, in the same way as to industrial or military action. But not all of Brooke's fellow parliamentarians were persuaded that this was the whole story, perhaps because, at certain points, his speech seemed to allude to troubling possibilities. 'The more highly organised life becomes,' he explained, 'the more the country depends on a great variety of supplies which come to us from abroad, and so, if there is any interruption of those supplies, we are the more vulnerable. Oil is perhaps the most obvious case.' The bill, he said, would ensure that measures such as rationing would be enforceable in case of any such interruption. Other participants went so far as to suggest that there were other motives involved. With economic growth sluggish, the Labour MP Sydney Silverman (one of the founders of the Campaign for

Nuclear Disarmament) wondered whether the government was preparing new powers to take action in case of a 'serious collapse', and accused Brooke of doing little more than instilling 'fears, anxieties and suspicions into people's minds when, heaven knows, they have enough to be fearful of without that'.[10]

Conditions under which emergencies were declared varied from peaceful industrial action to revolutionary warfare; those whose actions were deemed to have brought about states of emergency included unions of British workers as well as revolutionary groups in former British colonies. The declaration of a state of emergency, furthermore, was understood to be the likely response to any escalation in nuclear hostilities. In *The Warden and the Householder*, a public information film of 1961, the Civil Defence warden Mr. White waxes nostalgic during an imagined atomic crisis on the subject of the 'period of grace' granted by the 'Phoney War' in 1939: 'We won't get another chance like that,' he points out. 'And another thing: the government wouldn't have called it an Emergency and got all you people blocking up windows and making refuge rooms if there wasn't a real risk of a showdown, now would they?' The practical confidence Mr. White places in his political masters nonetheless has something strange, even self-contradictory about it. For at the very moment of his warning that there will be no Phoney War this time, no 'period of grace', he continues to advise people on the preparations they should be taking for the crisis that might come. Here, the state of emergency itself represents something like a 'phoney war', but a phoney war that threatens to become permanent beyond the cinematic imagination in the form of the preventive measures which the audience is expected to learn from Mr. White the warden and employ in their own homes.

Strangely, the extreme weather of 1962–63 that so inspired Henry Brooke has not until now been suggested as a context for Anna Kavan's apocalyptic novel *Ice* (1967), in which a soldier returns to an unnamed, frozen country 'to investigate rumours of a mysterious impending emergency'.[11] Like Reynard Langrish in *The Image of a Drawn Sword*, this man too finds that the familiar landscape through which he moves has been denatured, 'the unreality of the outside world' becoming in some way 'an extension of [his] own disturbed state of mind' (52). The temperature has dropped to a bitter chill; glaciers have begun to cover

10   *Hansard*, 20 February 1964, cols. 1409–45.
11   Anna Kavan, *Ice* (London, 1967), 6.

the surface of the world, literalising the gelid metaphor that governs Cold War rhetoric. Word arrives of 'a secret act of aggression by some foreign power [. . .] a steep rise in radioactive pollution, pointing to the explosion of a nuclear device, but of an unknown type'. Meanwhile, the unidentified nation is plunged into chaos by 'the fuel shortage, the power cuts, the breakdown of transport, and the rapid diversion of supplies to the black market' (22). Almost as soon as it begins, however, this nuclear-apocalypse plot becomes caught up with the soldier's personal hunt for a mysterious girl who appears throughout the novel in various guises: as a painter's model in one chapter; in another, as a refugee in a snow-covered town looted by roving crowds. The fifteen chapters of *Ice* depict these intertwining quests for the book's two objects of desire: the mysterious, frail girl, and the nature of the emergency that has caused the onset of what appears to be a new ice age. Yet they do so by way of a strange and dreamlike repetition. At several points, the soldier finds the girl and makes good their escape together, only for the reader to find in the next chapter that the quest has begun again in a different form, or indeed in a different genre. In one fantastical chapter, the soldier fails to prevent a mob of angry townspeople from offering the girl as a human sacrifice to a dragon; in the next section, she turns up once again as the prisoner of a mysterious warden – a familiar title from the lexicon of Civil Defence. No sooner saved from the warden, she reappears once again as his captive. 'I should have to start searching for her all over again,' the soldier-narrator says with characteristic affectlessness. 'The repetition was like a curse.' (99)

On one level, it is tempting to read repetition in Brooke and in Kavan as symptomatic of a generalised paranoia or anxiety that has so often been imputed to the writing of the Cold War. But the easy capaciousness of those overlapping psychopathological categories should give us pause. At the very least, Cold War criticism has to give justifications for invoking these terms in the context of individual works of fiction, and has to demonstrate that they do indeed help to illuminate real, specific connections between individual psychology, cultural zeitgeist and literary narrative. My contention is that the formal problems of repetition, temporal disruption and generic instability that these Cold War fictions display are most intelligible when read within the historical context of their emergence. Anxiety and paranoia, in other words, like the formal features that can be understood as their textual expression, were not amorphous or self-generating elements of Cold War writing; on the contrary, they were responses by individuals more or less attuned to specific modes of address: propaganda texts, broadcasts, warnings, Civil Defence practices and other easily overlooked features of Cold War culture.

Kavan for one was very well-attuned to such modes of address. One could legitimately say that she had been waiting for the Cold War all her life. Born Helen Emily Woods, she had first published realistic fiction under her married name, Helen Ferguson; after her marriage and a subsequent relationship broke down in the 1930s, and she lost her only son during the Second World War, she took the name Kavan from one of her own characters to compose the series of experimental and idiosyncratic short stories and novels that culminated with *Ice*. Helen Ferguson's early fiction is already pervaded by a sense of repressed violence on a domestic scale, and the global expression of that theme after 1945 gives Kavan's later work a timeliness and wider relevance matched by few of her contemporaries. Without expecting biography to shoulder too much of the work of criticism, one can say that Kavan – a regular heroin-user from her mid-twenties onward – understood how habitual repetition could take on the aspect of both curse and cure.[12] Yet in Kavan's case, as in Brooke's, biography must come into it. Both writers, after all, went to great lengths to establish continuities between life and work. Brooke's avowedly autobiographical fictions clearly take place in the same Kentish landscape as *The Image of a Drawn Sword*, and in the preface to *The Goose Cathedral* (published the same year as *Image*) he described his writing as 'neither entirely fictitious nor entirely autobiographical; . . . a hybrid breed'.[13] Kavan, like Brooke, was apt to repeat herself between different works, as well as within them, to a degree that renders the separateness of work from work, and work from life, extremely problematic. *Eagle's Nest* (1957), for instance, prefigures some of the elements of *Ice*: the gothic, 'fortresslike' castle in which some of the book takes place; the unfathomable demands of a rigid bureaucratic régime; the dreamlike inconsequentiality of actions which nonetheless appear to be of the greatest significance. Similarly, the posthumously published novel *Mercury* is clearly related to *Ice* in several ways. Beginning, like *Ice*, with a man stopping for petrol in the midst of a 'real freeze-up', *Mercury* deploys many of the same motifs and scenes, though here the 'nameless disorder' that has 'invaded the world' is not traced back to any military cause.

In *Ice*, meanwhile, the language of modern warfare is everywhere.

---

12   David Callard, *The Case of Anna Kavan* (London, 1992), 31.

13   Jocelyn Brooke, *The Goose Cathedral* (London, 1950), 9.

Torches affixed to the pillars in the warden's castle resemble 'bundles
of rockets' (62). At one point the soldier and the girl follow a guide
through a deserted battlefield filled with 'the debris of shattered weapons and war supplies [. . .] mines, unexploded bombs' (113). Later on
there are rumours of 'thermo-nuclear weapons, previously supposed to
have been destroyed', and a kind of doomsday device: 'a self-detonating
cobalt bomb, armed, at a pre-set, unknown moment, to destroy all life,
while leaving inanimate objects intact' (100–01). In the catastrophe's
'fatal phase', the superpowers face off after the destruction of smaller nations: 'Both principals held stocks of nuclear weapons many times in excess of the overkill stage [. . .] some of the lesser countries also possessed
thermo-nuclear devices, though which of them was not known: and
this uncertainty, and the resulting tension, provoked escalating crises,
each of which brought nearer the final catastrophe' (122). *Ice* pulses to
the fear of 'the expected crisis' (12), 'the crisis due in the next few days'
(71), 'escalating crises' (122), until the end of the book finds its protagonist 'pretending we could escape', 'making the most of the minutes'
(157). So too, the 'impending emergency' (6) that the soldier has come
to investigate remains 'the coming emergency' (12), 'the approaching
emergency' (18), the 'emergency imminent' (22). The same kind of
deferral is apparent in the title of 'Five More Days to Countdown', a
story Kavan published in *Encounter* only a few months before her death.
Here, against a background of *les événements* of 1968, an unnamed (and
ungendered) protagonist tells a story of increasing civil unrest. Again
repeating elements of *Ice* and her other novels, Kavan begins in a mode
of relative realism before the genre of the story suffers (or achieves?) the
same collapse as the rule of law in the city it describes. 'Five More Days'
also contains Kavan's most succinct statement concerning the way in
which Cold War nuclearism has done more than simply produce new
weapons for the prosecution of warfare. The 'giant mushroom-shape
menacing us' is no 'mere bogey, to be eliminated simply by depriving
children of war-like toys', but rather the symbol of a civilisation that has
'exalted war to unprecedented heights, regarding it as the finest flower
of human endeavour and scientific progress, subordinating everything
else in life to it as a matter of course'.[14]

That neither *The Image of a Drawn Sword* nor *Ice* find satisfactory
ways to end tells us more about the difficulties and uncertainties of Cold

14   Anna Kavan, 'Five More Days to Countdown', *Encounter* (July 1968),
45–8; 45.

War writing than about the ability of their authors. Both novels take emergency as a structural device as well as a background situation precisely because emergency – a political fiction designed to preserve at all costs the status quo ante – names a condition of suspension in which the emergence of a radical or catastrophic break in the existence of the state is disallowed. What is at stake, time and again, is the meaning of warfare; the meaning of warfare in turn is newly uncertain because the meaning of 'war' has become unstable. In this respect these works are emblematic of a wider interpretative uncertainty. 'This was the meaning of Monte Bello,' concludes the voiceover of *Operation Hurricane*, the Central Office of Information's 1956 film about the development of British nuclear weaponry, as a black nuclear cloud covers the film frame. The murky bomb-cloud, it might be thought, makes the meaning of the nuclear test less rather than more apparent to the viewer. Again, in the Pathé newsreel short *Doom Town* (1955), volunteers are made up to resemble casualties in a Home Office training exercise. 'This is what nuclear warfare means,' the announcer declares. 'Yes, it's all make-believe, but it's make-believe as realistic as the Army and the Home Office can make it.' In the rhetoric of Britain's hot Cold War, the new meaning of warfare is no sooner invoked than displaced, occluded or revealed as pure simulation. Most commonly, such simulations took forms familiar from the recent world war. In *Bristol Trains to Beat A-Bomb* (1951), for instance, a Pathé announcer narrates while Civil Defence workers and army reinforcements scramble over the rubble of a bombed-out district: 'Besides engineers, medical squads and dispatch riders, [the army] provides even cooks. Hitler provided the devastated areas.'

Hitler's devastation continued to influence literary fictions as well as the training scenarios concocted by the Home Office. As imagination trembled at the apocalyptic power of atomic and thermonuclear weaponry, fiction became caught in suspension between a war endured and a war imagined. Like the romantic leads in John Wyndham's apocalyptic *The Day of the Triffids* (1951), the fiction of the hot Cold War dances 'on the brink of an unknown future, to an echo from a vanished past'.[15] And like Wyndham's couple, writers sought ways of enduring the prospect of futurelessness by looking to familiar phenomena. In *The Image of a Drawn Sword*, Civil Defence training becomes the basis for a queer fable about military preparedness and its discontents; in *Ice*, the state of emergency structures an eccentric quest that flits oneirically between

15   John Wyndham, *The Day of the Triffids* (London, 2000 [1951]), 105.

disconnected scenes and genres. But these model narratives repeatedly fail in fiction, as they did in life, to offer any kind of certainty. The peculiarity of Brooke's and Kavan's novels – what sometimes appears to the contemporary reader as a kind of generic, tonal, or formal instability – is best understood as a response to this ongoing state of suspension. Written at a time when 'make-believe' had become standard defence policy, they offer their own kind of make-believe as a literary response to a crisis of the geopolitical imagination. They speak the new language of unspecified crisis as a way of working out what war might mean, and what war writing might be, under the new conditions of permanent nuclear standoff.

II

Interpretations

Crossing the Rubicon: History, Authority and Civil War in Twelfth-Century England

CATHERINE A. M. CLARKE

CIVIL CONFLICT DEMOLISHES notions of identity and community in particularly violent and destructive ways. The project of writing civil war challenges the traditions and conventions of historiography and exceeds normal representational modes and idioms. England's twelfth-century civil war, during the reign of King Stephen (1135–54), is presented by contemporary texts as a calamity beyond the reach of conventional chronicle writing or received rhetoric. The Peterborough recension of the Anglo-Saxon Chronicle exclaims that:

> I ne can ne I ne mai tellen alle þe wunder ne alle þe pines ðat hi diden wrecce men on þis land; ꝼ ðat lastede þa xix wintre wile Stephne was king, ꝼ æure it was uuerse ꝼ uuerse.[1]

> I am neither able, nor wish to, tell all the horrors nor all the tortures that they did to the wretched men in this land; and that lasted nineteen winters while Stephen was king, and it always became worse and worse.

While the term 'the Anarchy', traditionally used to describe this period of civil conflict, is now challenged by some historians,[2] there is no doubt that the contemporary medieval texts see the reign of Stephen as a time of extreme collapse, chaos and violence that goes beyond the

---

1   *The Peterborough Chronicle: 1070–1154*, ed. Cecily Clark, 2nd edn (Oxford, 1970), 56. For a comparable claim that the events of the civil war are beyond articulation, see the *Chronicle of John of Worcester*, ed. and trans. P. McGurk, 3 vols. (Oxford, 1998), III, 270, 271 (1139, from McGurk's manuscript 'G').
2   See, for example, David Crouch, *The Reign of King Stephen 1135–1154* (Harlow, 2000), 1–7. For further discussion of the notion of 'civil war' in relation to twelfth-century England and medieval constructions of nationhood, see Catherine A. M. Clarke, 'Writing Civil War in Henry of Huntingdon's *Historia Anglorum*', *Anglo-Norman Studies* 31 (2009), 31–48; 47.

norms of medieval warfare and martial engagement. The texts react to the particular horrors of civil war with a range of rhetorical and representational strategies and responses, from literal accounts that push the direct depiction of brutality and torture to its limits, to the use of metaphor (such as tropes of madness or 'rabies', or imagery of ruptures in the earth), to formalist experiments including the use of prosimetrical structures or fractured and fragmented idioms. Twelfth-century texts also make recourse to the inherited models of classical *auctoritas* to express and interpret the experience of civil war.

This essay will survey some of the techniques used to represent civil war in a selection of twelfth-century texts, including the Chronicle of John of Worcester, the *Gesta Stephani* ('The deeds of Stephen'), William of Newburgh's *Historia rerum Anglicarum* ('The history of English affairs'), Henry of Huntingdon's *Historia Anglorum* ('History of the English') and the Peterborough continuations of the Anglo-Saxon Chronicle. After exploring a range of historiographical approaches across these sources, it will focus in particular on uses of the classical author Lucan in texts from twelfth-century England. Lucan's *Bellum civile* ('Civil war'), which covers the conflict between Caesar and Pompey in the first century BCE, has been described as the '*locus classicus* for the treatment of the subject of civil war in the Middle Ages'.[3] The influence of Lucan's poem extends widely across medieval literature,[4] yet the presence of the *Bellum civile* in medieval accounts of contemporary civil conflict poses contradictions, ambiguities and challenges. The transposition of Lucan's bleak, nihilistic version of human history into a medieval cultural context pulls beliefs and epistemologies into antagonistic confrontation. Lynn Staley has written recently of the 'providential shape' that underpins the histories of twelfth-century writers such as William of Malmesbury and Henry of Huntingdon, in which 'instances of recurrent chaos are superseded by ever more significant triumphs of order'.[5] Such an understanding of history as process and progress – even through the horrors of civil war – cannot simply assimilate Lucan's dark and absurdist vision.

---

3   George M. Logan, 'Lucan – Daniel – Shakespeare: New Light on the Relation between *The Civil Wars* and *Richard II*', *Shakespeare Studies* 9 (1976), 121–40; 125.

4   See for example Alfred Hiatt, 'Lucan', in *The Oxford History of Classical Reception in English Literature*, vol. I, *The Middle Ages*, ed. Rita Copeland (Oxford, forthcoming 2014).

5   Lynn Staley, *The Island Garden: England's Language of Nation from Gildas to Marvell* (Notre Dame, 2012), 3, 35.

This essay will interrogate the ways in which twelfth-century texts both read with and read *against* Lucan in their representations of contemporary events, examining distinctions between uses of the *Bellum civile* as a formal or rhetorical model and as a source of historical or moral exempla. Major tensions and contradictions appear for these twelfth-century authors in using the *Bellum civile* as a textual framework for their own civil war, resulting in transgressive readings, and revealing problems in placing classical *auctoritas* in apposition with contemporary events. While the primary focus of this essay, then, is on tools and techniques for writing civil war in the context of the Anarchy, and especially on the use of Lucan as a model, the discussion also speaks more broadly to questions of the reception and adaptation of textual *auctoritas* in medieval England, illuminating the sophisticated, independent and radical ways in which medieval authors could engage with the classical past.

The title of this essay alludes to Lucan's widely known narrative of Caesar crossing the river Rubicon into the territory of Rome – the symbolic act of incursion that marks the beginning of the conflict as Caesar 'moras solvit belli tumidumque per amnem | Signa tulit propere' ('loosed war from its bonds and carried his standards in haste over the swollen stream').[6] Responding to this powerful and richly suggestive episode, this essay will pay particular attention to thresholds, crossing points and acts of transgression in these twelfth-century texts. Accounts of the twelfth-century 'Anarchy' include many literal depictions of acts of trespass, incursion and transgression: striking features of a civil conflict in which lines of possession, allegiance and hostility are continually being re-drawn. But close attention to uses of Lucan in these twelfth-century sources also reveals a series of textual thresholds where authors cross between accounts of contemporary events and appropriated historical exempla and rhetorical models. At these textual limens, classical authority collides with medieval experiences and ideologies. The thresholds between different historical moments and texts emerge as productive and creative but also tense and potentially hostile. The idea of 'crossing the Rubicon' thus offers a framework for examining not only the violence and violations of England's twelfth-century civil war, but also the transgressive acts of medieval writers in their appropriation and (mis-)use of classical *auctoritas* to articulate and contain contemporary experience.

6   Lucan, *The Civil War*, trans. J. D. Duff (Cambridge, Mass., 1928), I, lines 204–5.

Direct representations of the Anarchy in twelfth-century texts push their vivid descriptions of trauma and violence to the limit.[7] The Peterborough Chronicle offers a horrific catalogue of the terrors and tortures inflicted on the population of England during this period.

Þa namen hi þa men þe hi wenden ðat ani god hefden, bathe be nihtes 7 be daies, carlmen 7 wimmen, 7 diden heom in prisun 7 pined heom efter gold 7 syluer untellendlice pining; for ne uuæren næure nan martyrs swa pined alse hie wæron. Me henged up bi the fet 7 smoked heom mid ful smoke. Me henged bi the þumbes other bi the hefed 7 hengen bryniges on her fet. Me dide cnotted strenges abuton here hæued 7 uurythen it ðat it gæde to þe hærnes. Hi diden heom in quarterne þar nadres 7 snakes 7 pades wæron inne, 7 drapen heom swa. Sume hi diden in crucethur – ðat is, in an ceste þat was scort 7 nareu 7 undep – 7 dide scærpe stanes þerinne 7 þrengde þe man þærinne ðat him bræcon alle þe limes.[8]

Then they took men who had any wealth, both by night and by day, churls and women, and put them in prison and tortured them for gold and silver with unspeakable torture; for no martyrs were ever tortured as they were. They hung them up by the feet and smoked them with foul smoke. They hung them by the thumbs or by the head and hung mailcoats on their feet. They knotted ropes around their heads and twisted it until it went into their brains. They put them into a dungeon in which there were adders and snakes and toads, and killed them in this way. Some they put into a crucet-house – that is, a certain chest that was short and narrow and shallow, and put sharp stones in there and crushed the man inside so that all his limbs were broken.

The Chronicle makes it clear that these extremes of torture and brutality transgress the limits even of the violence associated with conventional warfare, with the imagery here echoing the tropes of contemporary hagiography or devotional writing in which descriptions of intense physical

7 For a discussion of the use of the term 'trauma' in relation to the events of the twelfth-century civil war, see Catherine A. M. Clarke, 'Signs and Wonders: Writing Trauma in Twelfth-century England', Reading Medieval Studies 35 (2009), 55–77.
8 Peterborough Chronicle, 55.

suffering are used to elicit affective and pious responses. The Chronicle's representation of the violent horrors of the civil war is a staged version, however: it transforms hidden, private experience into a public spectacle and elides (or evades) the authenticity of individual experience even as it uses a familiar rhetoric of pain to shape the engagement of its monastic audience. Marla Carlson has commented, 'Because pain so powerfully elicits the spectator's engagement, aestheticized physical suffering plays a vital role in creating communities of sentiment and consolidating social memory, which in turn shapes the cultural and political realities that cause spectators to respond in different ways at different times.'[9] The Peterborough Chronicle's visceral pageantry of pain and suffering serves to direct its community's response to contemporary events and to reinforce a shared institutional memory of the twelfth-century civil war. Other twelfth-century sources also articulate the horrors of Stephen's reign as a kind of monstrous performance, betraying an attendant concern with the potential slippage of historiographical record into voyeuristic exposure. In a chapter that gives a stark account of the horrors and degradations of the civil war, the *Gesta Stephani* refers to 'hæc quidem lacrymosæ miseriæ facies, hic questuosæ tragœdiæ inhonestissimus modus, sicut ubique per Angliam publice committebantur' ('things so lamentable and wretched to look upon and such an utterly shameful tragedy of woe . . . being openly performed all over England'), while elsewhere the text interprets the Anarchy as long-held private or secret enmity 'sese publice retegens' ('revealing itself to the public gaze'), 'in lucem nunc proferens aperte declarabat' ('now brought to light and openly displayed').[10] The *Gesta Stephani* reveals, at moments, an acute unease with its own project of not merely looking upon but also rehearsing these 'shameful' events, suggesting a sensitivity to the dangers and possible excesses of direct, literal representation. Whilst the use of received tropes means that textual narratives can only gesture towards the reality of contemporary experience, these aestheticised chronicle accounts of human suffering are themselves in danger of re-staging this extravagant pageantry of violence.

It is unsurprising, then, that many twelfth-century texts make use of metaphorical language to articulate aspects of the civil war in a way which avoids (or provides an alternative discourse to) such graphic

---

9   Marla Carlson, *Performing Bodies in Pain: Medieval and Post-Modern Martyrs, Mystics and Artists* (New York, 2010), 2.
10   *Gesta Stephani*, 154, 155 and 4, 5.

literal description. One striking metaphorical system depicts civil conflict as *rabies* or madness, thus aligning it with the more widely used
metaphor of madness for internal rebellion or treason in the Middle
Ages.[11] Henry of Huntingdon is typical in his references to atrocities
caused by 'Normannorum rabiosas prodiciones' ('the mad treacheries
of the Normans') or the 'rabies' ('madness') of the war.[12] The image of
rebellious *rabies* is also found in Lucan's depiction of Caesar ('O rabies
miseranda ducis!', 'Oh, wretched madness of the leader!'), although it is
such a common motif in medieval literature that these twelfth-century
authors need not be citing the *Bellum civile* directly.[13] Another recurrent
series of metaphors relates to the idea of the land itself, using imagery
of broken, fractured earth to suggest the division and violence that rips
apart twelfth-century England. In Book X, Chapter 12 of his *Historia
Anglorum*, Henry of Huntingdon gives a survey of the events of 1140
that Diana Greenway notes is 'almost totally devoid of fact', instead
presenting an emotive picture of the 'luctus et horror' ('lamentation
and terror') of war.[14] Within this chapter, Henry includes a poem (itself
a technique for writing the experience of civil war that I will explore
in further detail later) that imagines the very earth of England torn
apart through unnatural violence. Henry exclaims here that 'Aduenit
caligo Stigis dimissa profundo, | Que regni faciem conglomerata tegit'
('Stygian gloom has come, released from the underworld, and thickly
veils the face of the realm').[15] This classicising imagery responds to
and imaginatively extends the idea of a land broken and divided, with
Henry imagining a rupture in the earth releasing terror and darkness.
The metaphor is paralleled (and perhaps inspired) by Henry's reference
in the same verses to the atrocities of a gang that 'cimiteria . . . refringit'
('breaks into graves'), another emotive act of desecration of the ground.
While the poem refers directly to particular forms of violence and violation, the horror of civil war is expressed more powerfully and unset-

11   See Daniel Power, '"La Rage méchante des traîtres prit feu": Le Discours
sur la révolte sous les rois Plantagenêt (1144–1224)', in *La Trahison au Moyen
Âge*, ed. M. Billoré and M. Soria (Rennes, 2009), 53–65.
12   Henry of Huntingdon, *Historia Anglorum*, 700, 701 and 706, 707 (in this
instance specifically associated with 'periurio et prodicione', 'faithlessness and
treachery').
13   Lucan, *The Civil War*, II, line 544.
14   Henry of Huntingdon, *Historia Anglorum*, 724, 725; for Greenway's comment see 724–5, n. 73.
15   Henry of Huntingdon, *Historia Anglorum*, 724, 725.

tlingly in this imagery of ruptured, fractured earth. The elegiac verses conclude with a final apostrophe: 'Ecce Stigis facies consimilisque lues' ('Behold! Here is a glimpse of the Styx and a comparable plague').[16] These glimpses of dark, disturbing worlds through the ruptured land-scape of England suggest the alienation and distress associated with civil war, albeit, once again, articulated through the resources of received rhetorical conventions and recognisable classical images.

Imagery of broken, ruptured earth, which exposes strange and un-settling sights within, is also prominent in William of Newburgh's *Historia rerum Anglicarum*, though there the metaphor works in a more troubling, insistent way, refusing to give clear signals (such as explicit allusion to familiar classical mythology) as to how it should be read. Embedded within William's account of the Anarchy is a series of stories purporting to offer accounts of strange discoveries from within the earth, replaying a narrative in which the fractured ground reveals strange, disturbing sights within. The stories, grouped consecutively, include the well-known account of the Green Children of Woolpit, as well as monstrous discoveries in two quarries, and finally an otherworld hidden under a hill.[17] Whilst William claims to offer a faithful record of genuine historical wonders, the placing of these episodes at the heart of his account of the horrors of the twelfth-century civil war suggests that they may be linked to the contemporary experience of this catas-trophe. The replayed narrative elements of William's wonder tales – supernatural disturbance, attempted containment or circumscription, and then failed closure – resonate with twentieth- and twenty-first-century theories of trauma and trauma writing, suggesting that this may be a further textual expression of the unspeakable horrors of civil conflict.[18] The association between civil war and unnatural events or

16   Ibid.

17   William of Newburgh, *The History of English Affairs*, Book I, ed. and trans. P. G. Walsh and M. J. Kennedy (Warminster, 1988), Chapters 27 and 28, 115–21.

18   These stories have generated highly varied critical readings. The historian Nancy Partner dismisses them as 'wonderfully pointless miracles' (*Serious Entertainments: The Writing of History in Twelfth-century England* [Chicago, 1977], 122). More recently, Jeffrey Jerome Cohen has interpreted the Green Children as a metaphorical exploration of the suppressed 'otherworlds' and alternative histories within Anglo-Norman England ('Green Children from Another World, or the Archipelago in England', in his *Cultural Diversity in the British Middle Ages: Archipelago, Island, England* [London, 2008], 75–94, though he

monstrosity is itself a well-established trope stretching back to Lucan.
At the opening of Book II of the *Bellum civile*, Lucan declares that

> . . . legesque et foedera rerum
> Praescia monstrifero vertit natura tumult
> Indixitique nefas.

> Nature, conscious of the future, reversed the laws and ordinances of
> life, and, while the hurly-burly bred monsters, proclaimed civil war.[19]

A similar, apparently deliberate, association between civil war and unnatural (or supernatural) signs and wonders is found in the Chronicle
of John of Worcester, where revisions produced during the Anarchy
(probably by John himself) systematically interpolate details of troubling portents and monstrous omens (especially celestial signs such as
comets and eclipses) to the final years of Henry I's reign, prefiguring the
catastrophe to come.[20] Again, textual metaphor gestures towards the
horror of civil war and its unwriteable reality.

The strains placed on conventional chronicle writing by the attempt
to write the extreme experience of civil war are evident across twelfth-
century texts. The insistent, replayed narratives of troubling discovery
embedded in William of Newburgh disrupt the chronological order of
his history, and the extensive revisions and retrospective interpolations
in John of Worcester's Chronicle similarly suggest an attempt to go
beyond the norms of annalistic writing and articulate the intensity of
contemporary events. Henry of Huntingdon's *Historia Anglorum*, Book
X ('De Hoc Presenti'; 'On the present time') is characterised by stylistic and formalist experiments, through which the author draws on and
adjusts existing rhetorical conventions in order to suggest the division,
fragmentation and confusion of civil war. Most strikingly, Book X of the

separates the story from the comparable wonder tales in Chapter 28). For a full
discussion of these accounts as potential 'trauma writing', see Clarke, 'Signs and
Wonders', esp. 68–73.
19   Lucan, *The Civil War*, II, lines 2–4.
20   *The Chronicle of John of Worcester*, III. xxxii–xxxiv. Once again, interpretations of the meaning of these additions vary, with C. Warren Hollister suggesting that they have the purpose of merely 'edifying, perhaps even amusing [the
chronicler's] readers' (C. Warren Hollister, *Henry I* [New Haven CT, 2001],
468). For a full discussion of the additions to the Chronicle during the reign of
Stephen, see Clarke, 'Signs and Wonders', 61–6.

Historia is prosimetrical in structure, the prose narrative account of the reign of Stephen periodically broken by verses that articulate aspects of contemporary experience through different idioms and stylistic modes. Several commentators have noted the inclusion of verse alongside the prose in this section of Henry's *Historia*, though until recently scholars dismissed this feature too readily as mere 'decoration' and rhetorical flourish.[21] Diana Greenway, the most recent editor of the *Historia Anglorum*, rightly rejects this with her insight that 'rhetorical conventions [in the *Historia*] are not merely decorative: they pervade the whole text – its conception and structure, as well as its language'.[22] The poem in Chapter 12 opens with a rhetorical question typical of the performative language that characterises the verse, as the authorial voice cries:

> Quis michi det fontem (quid enim potius?) lacrimarum,
> Vt lacrimer patrie gesta nefanda mee?

> Who is to give me a fountain of tears (what better?) that I may weep for my country's impious deeds?[23]

Throughout, the poem is riven by apostrophes ('o noua furta!', 'res miseranda!', 'proh pudor!'; 'O novel robberies!', 'lamentable deed!', 'O for shame!') as the intensity of affect and personal experience fractures the verse lines. Writing in elegiacs, and drawing on classical and biblical allusion (such as the echo of Jeremiah 1:9 here), Henry exploits the potential of verse form as an alternative, more immediate and intense expression of the pain and horror of civil war: poetry can articulate what contained, ordered historical prose cannot. The prosimetrical structure of Book X of the *Historia* presents the historian's own voice as fractured and divided, broken by the experience of civil conflict and the weight of the events it strains to narrate.

In the prose history that surrounds the poems of Book X, however, Henry also employs stylistic techniques to suggest the divided loyalties and competing claims of the civil war. In particular, his use of set-piece battle speeches presents the leaders of each of the different

---

21 See Partner, *Serious Entertainments*, 26–7.

22 Diana Greenway, 'Authority, Convention and Observation in Henry of Huntingdon's *Historia Anglorum*', *Anglo-Norman Studies* 18 (1995), 105–21; 110.

23 Henry of Huntingdon, *Historia Anglorum*, 724, 725.

warring factions as noble warriors whose words affect and persuade. In his account of the siege of Lincoln, Henry first gives us speeches from Ranulph, earl of Chester (who aims to attack Stephen's forces and take the city), and Robert of Gloucester (who also leads a faction against Stephen). Ranulph of Chester's speech employs emotive strategies to reinforce the sense of an affective bond between those on the battle-field, further suggesting the earl's willingness to sacrifice himself unself-ishly for his fellow fighters.

> 'Gratias tibi multas, dux inuictissime, uobisque procures et commili-tiones mei cum summa deuotione persoluo, qui usque ad uite pericu-lum amoris effectum michi magnanimiter exhibuistis. Cum igitur sim uobis causa periculi, dignum est ut periculo me prius ingeram, et infidissimi regis, qui datis induciis pacem fregit, aciem prius illidam.'

> 'To you, invincible duke [Robert], and to you, my noble comrades-in-arms, I render many thanks, from the bottom of my heart, for you have generously demonstrated that you will risk your lives out of love for me. So since I am the cause of your peril, it is right that I should put myself into danger first, and should be the first to strike out at the line of this treacherous king, who has broken the peace after a truce had been allowed.'[24]

Robert of Gloucester similarly speaks in terms of honour and duty, urg-ing the men to act 'de Dei iusticia' ('on God's justice') and leads his army 'erectis in celum unanimiter dextris' ('together raising your right hands to heaven').[25] But then Baldwin Fitz Gilbert of Clare, loyal to Stephen, makes a speech that is equally emotive and convincing.

> 'Virtus autem ipsius regis infinita uobis loco perstabit milium. Cum igitur sit in medio uestrum dominus uester, unctus Domini, cui fi-dem deuouistis, uotum Deo persoluite, tanto donatiuum maius a Deo accepturi, quanto fidelius et constantius pro rege uestro, fidi contra infidos, legitimi contra periuros, pugnaueritis.'

> 'The king's own boundless valour will stand fast, equal to thousands of you. Since, therefore, your lord is in your midst, the Lord's anoint-

24   Ibid., 726, 727.
25   Ibid., 730–3.

ed, to whom you have pledged your faith, discharge your vow to God, and receive from Him a reward that will be all the greater the more faithful and constant you are to your king – the faithful against the faithless, those who remain true against those who are false.'[26]

Henry presents a dilemma here for his readers: a series of affective, rousing speeches that each draw on honourable codes and religious imperatives, and make convincing claims to the audience. Even in gesture, the armies opposing and defending Stephen are evenly matched: as Robert urges his men to raise their right hand, so Baldwin commands his troops to 'extendite igitur animos uestros et dextras inexpugnabiles' ('stretch out your courage and your invincible right hands'), a familiar gesture of martial courage and determination from Lucan's *Bellum civile*.[27] The reader's sense of loyalty and sympathy is divided: the text does not supply helpful moral glosses or comments to guide interpretation, but instead conveys the bewildering fragmentation of authority in civil war.

Diana Greenway has commented on the influence of Lucan in these set-piece speeches, as well as throughout the later books of the *Historia Anglorum*.[28] Indeed, Henry's formalist experiments seem to use Lucan as a model and respond to the radical stylistic techniques of the *Bellum civile*. John Henderson has argued that Lucan's poem 'breaks rules, inflicts pain and suffering', deliberately subverting and fracturing the structural, ideological and stylistic principles of Golden Age epic.[29] Jamie Masters, another scholar whose reappraisal of Lucan has helped to shape recent critical interpretations, claims that 'the poem itself is a civil war', which uses a deliberately 'fractured voice' to express the division and alienation of civil conflict.[30] Drawing on Lucan as a rhetorical model, Book X of Henry of Huntingdon's *Historia* refuses a linear, monolithic account of recent history, and instead presents it as multiple, divided and contested. Even the historian's voice, split between prose and verse, restrained chronicle and anguished poetry, expresses this rupture.

26   Ibid., 734, 735.
27   Ibid., 736, 737. Greenway also notes 'an echo of Julius Caesar's battle speech' here (736, n.101 and 732, n. 92).
28   Ibid., xxxv.
29   John Henderson, 'Lucan/The Word at War', *Ramus* 16 (1987), 122–64; 123.
30   Jamie Masters, *Poetry and Civil War in Lucan's 'Bellum civile'* (Cambridge, 1992), 10, 90. See also Shadi Bartsch's study, *Ideology in Cold Blood. A Reading of Lucan's 'Civil War'* (Cambridge, Mass., 1997).

Lucan's influence extends beyond this subject of civil war, and is important across medieval historical writing and rhetorical traditions. From the early commentary tradition to uses in medieval Latin and also in the later medieval vernacular, Lucan's importance is comparable to that of Virgil.[31] However, whereas Virgil can be characterised as a poet of optimism, triumph and aspiration, Peter von Moos has described Lucan as 'poète de la destruction'.[32] Similarly, Edoardo D'Angelo has claimed that 'unstable times love Lucan',[33] an assertion mirrored in von Moos's reflection that

> Les périodes de crise aiguisent la sensibilité pour un poète qui, ne voyant plus d'issue à son idéal politique, compense son désespoir par sa 'fureur poétique', par des paradoxes amers, des images excessives et des pointes d'une extrême obscurité recherché.[34]

It is perhaps no coincidence, then, that Lucan appears to be a particularly prominent and important textual source in the later twelfth century. Indeed, Edoardo D'Angelo identifies 'the Lucanian *Fortleben* in the Anglo-Norman area in the second half of the twelfth century' as an important direction for future scholarship on the medieval reception of the author.[35] Surprisingly, despite the recent revival of interest from classicists, Lucan is still largely neglected as an author by medievalists, remaining 'pratiquement ignoré' in many discussions of uses of classical authority and tradition.[36]

---

31 For good overviews, see Paolo Esposito, 'Early and Medieval *Scholia* and *Commentaria* on Lucan', in *Brill's Companion to Lucan*, ed. Paolo Asso (Leiden, 2011), 453–64; Edoardo D'Angelo, 'Lucan in Medieval Latin: A Survey of the Bibliography', in *Brill's Companion to Lucan*, 465–81; G. M. Logan, *Lucan in England: The Influence of the* Pharsalia *on English Letters from the Beginnings through the Sixteenth* Century, (Cambridge, Mass., 1967); Peter von Moos, 'Lucain au Moyen Âge', in his *Entre histoire et literature: Communication et culture au Moyen Âge* (Florence, 2005), 89–202.

32 Von Moos, 'Lucain au Moyen Âge', 99.

33 D'Angelo, 'Lucan in Medieval Latin', 473.

34 Von Moos, 'Lucain au Moyen Âge', 188: 'Periods of crisis sharpen sensitivity to a poet who, no longer seeing any possibility of a political resolution, compensates for his despair with his "poetic fury", through bitter paradoxes, outrageous images, and touches of extreme, studied obscurity.'

35 D'Angelo, 'Lucan in Medieval Latin', 478.

36 Von Moos, 'Lucain au Moyen Âge', 90.

CROSSING THE RUBICON 73

Lucan's influence in the Middle Ages seems to have formed two, usually distinct, branches. Medieval authors tended either to use Lucan as a formal model, imitating rhetorical tropes and borrowing formulae, or to appropriate elements of the narrative content of the *Bellum civile* for use in historical or moral exempla.[37] This bifurcation results in a widespread separation between the narrative content of the *Bellum civile* and Lucan's rhetoric as a poet, which are used in different contexts and for different purposes by medieval writers. Moreover, conventional medieval attitudes to classical *auctoritas* create another contradiction and tension in uses of Lucan in the Middle Ages. Peter von Moos associates Lucan with 'l'absurdité', 'désespoir' and 'pessimisme', echoing the 'suicidal implosion' that Henderson sees in the *Bellum civile*, mitigated by '[n]o glimpsed remedy, alternative promise'.[38] Yet, made to serve the purposes of moral and historical exemplum, the *Bellum civile* is forced into a more ordered, rational, even providential vision of history. Edoardo D'Angelo argues convincingly, for example, that '[m]any Medieval Latin intellectuals misunderstand the sense (atheist and desperate) of Lucan's pessimism: they convert it into a useful element for eternal values and peace'.[39] In such instrumentalist readings of the *Bellum civile* the crucial connection between the text's rhetoric, form and world-view dissolves and the poem becomes instead a repository of cautionary tales, hubristic figures and historical mirrors for contemporary concerns.

Yet some medieval readings of Lucan are more complex and self-conscious than a simple 'misunderstanding' of the classical text. Rather, some medieval uses of the *Bellum civile* can wilfully misread the text, arrogating it for subversive ends and to reach conclusions deliberately antagonistic to the apparent meaning of the original classical poem. These uses of the *Bellum civile* are purposefully transgressive readings, which

---

37   See, for example, Ibid., 98. For a relevant discussion of the exemplum in the Middle Ages, and especially its use 'to prove and convince, not to obtain knowledge . . . to convey, elucidate and didactically strengthen a doctrine which is already known or even dogmatically fixed', see Peter von Moos, 'The use of *exempla* in the *Policraticus* of John of Salisbury', in *The World of John of Salisbury*, ed. Michael Wilks (Oxford, 1984), 207–62; 211.

38   Von Moos, 'Lucain au Moyen Âge', 99 and *passim*; 'Henderson, 'Lucan/ The Word at War', 124.

39   D'Angelo, 'Lucan in Medieval Latin', 472–3. D'Angelo also suggests that the use of the *Bellum civile* in the exemplum tradition forces it into the categories of either *contemptus mundi*, *tragedia* (or *satira*) or *dehortatio a civili bello*: 475.

trespass the boundary between medieval citation and classical *auctoritas*, making violent incursions into the original Lucanian text. A well-known example of this occurs in John of Salisbury's *Policraticus*, another twelfth-century English text which, as a work of political theory rather than history, is less commonly associated with the events of the reign of Stephen and the Anarchy. However, written between 1154 and 1156, immediately after the end of the civil war, John's work reflects the experience of these catastrophic years, and a recent editor of the *Policraticus* has made this connection, noting that John's 'later writings reveal a consistent horror of civil war of the sort engendered by Stephen's usurpation of the throne'.[40] Book VIII, Chapter 23 of the *Policraticus* deals with the subject of schism, moving from the example of civil war to that of ecclesiastical division and schism (a religious version of conflict 'plusquam civile' or 'worse than civil', the famous description of Caesar and Pompey's enmity in the first line of the *Bellum civile*), and making frequent use of quotation from Lucan throughout. In this chapter, John responds to Lucan's account of the conversations between Brutus and Cato in Book II of the *Bellum civile*, in which Brutus seeks counsel from his kinsman, the revered *praetor* and Stoic. At first, Brutus's position is emphatically against joining the war, and he speaks eloquently of the catastrophe of civil conflict, asking Cato:

> Pacemne tueris
> Inconcussa tenens dubio vestigia mundo?
> An placuit ducibus scelerum populique furentis
> Cladibus inmixtum civile absolvere bellum?

Are you the champion of peace, keeping your path unshaken amid a tottering world? Or have you resolved to stand with the arch-criminals and take your share in the disasters of a mad world, and so clear the civil war of guilt?[41]

Cato acknowledges that civil war is the worst wickedness ('Summum . . . nefas civilia bella fatemur')[42] but argues that it is a necessary evil to protect the Republic.

40   John of Salisbury, *Policraticus*, ed. and trans. Cary J. Nederman (Cambridge, 1990), xvii.
41   Lucan, *The Civil War*, Book II, lines 247–50.
42   Ibid., line 286.

> Sic fatur, et acres
> Irarum movit stimulos iuuenisque calorem
> Excitat in nimios belli civilis amores.

Thus Cato spoke, filling the younger man with strong incentives to battle and prompting his high spirit to excessive desire for civil war.[43]

In John of Salisbury's reading of this passage of the *Bellum civile*, however, Brutus's initial intention to abstain from the civil war is praised, at the expense of Cato, who persuades him to join Pompey's side. Discussing the evils of civil conflict and schism, John comments that 'Vtinam secuti essent qui ea uiderunt tempora consilium Bruti' ('If only those who reflected upon these events had been following the counsel of Brutus'), adding that Brutus:

> . . . manus suas ab armis continere ciuilibus, quibus quanto quisque libentius et forties immiscetur, tanto iniquior et immanior est. Ait ergo:

> > Nunc neque Pompeii Brutum nec Cesaris hostem
> > post bellum uictoris habes.[44]

> . . . resolved to hold back his hand from the civil strife, since to the extent that one willingly and forcefully becomes enmeshed in such conflict, one is in that measure the more iniquitous and the more savage. Therefore he [Brutus] asserts: Neither in Pompey nor in Caesar will Brutus | have an enemy after victory in the war.[45]

John favours Brutus's arguments for abstention and restraint rather than Cato's call to arms.[46] Brutus emerges here not as the weak, indecisive figure inferior to the great philosopher (and widely vilified as a traitor in the Middle Ages), but as the voice of wisdom and moral courage. This

---

43 Ibid., lines 323–5.

44 *Ioannis Sarresberiensis Episcopi Carnotensis 'Policratici'*, ed. C. C. J. Webb, 2 vols. (Oxford, 1909), II, 402.

45 *Politraticus*, ed. and trans. Nederman, 218 (citing Lucan, *Bellum civile*, Book II, lines 283–4).

46 See Von Moos, 'Lucain au Moyen Âge', 177, and D'Angelo, 'Lucan in Medieval Latin', 476.

bold, deliberate misreading of Lucan resonates with John's discussion of exempla and their uses in his Prologue to the *Policraticus*. John explains his purpose of drawing exempla from a range of authors to serve his purposes, asserting that

> Omnes ergo qui michi in uerbo aut opere philosophantes occurrunt, meos clientes esse arbitror et, quod maius est, michi uendico in seruitutem . . .[47]

> All whom I encounter who are philosophers in word or deed are judged to be my clients, and what is more, I arrogate them to myself in servitude.[48]

Larry Scanlon has commented on the 'overtly, even blatantly, appropriative' attitude here, as John makes explicit his desire to exploit (and manipulate) *auctoritas* in the most expedient way.[49] Indeed, John's discussion of the value of exempla at the very beginning of the Prologue gives further insight into his attitude to classical texts and their uses. He declares that 'maxime est litterarum fructus, quod omnium interstitiorum loci et temporis exclusa molestia' ('the pursuit of letters is especially fruitful because it excludes all annoyances stemming from differences of time and place').[50] As Scanlon observes, 'the textual enables space and time to be easily surmounted';[51] exempla bring past and present into contiguity. However, as ancient exempla are drafted into contemporary medieval debates, this creates a threshold between historical moments and texts which is not only productive, but also tense and potentially hostile. John of Salisbury's use of Lucan demonstrates how crossing between present experience and textual *auctoritas* is not always straightforward, but rather a process of incursion, trespass and annexation.

---

47 John of Salisbury, *Policraticus I–IV*, ed. K. S. B. Keats-Rohan, Corpus Christianorum Continuatio Mediaevalis 118 (Turnhout, 1993), 24.

48 *Policraticus*, ed. and trans. Nederman, 6.

49 Larry Scanlon, *Narrative, Authority and Power: The Medieval Exemplum and the Chaucerian Tradition* (Cambridge, 1994), 91. Of course, medieval uses of textual authority are often complex and ambivalent. See for example Ruth Morse, *Truth and Convention in the Middle Ages: Rhetoric, Representation and Reality* (Cambridge, 1991).

50 *Policraticus I–IV*, ed. Keats-Rohan, 21; *Policraticus*, ed. and trans. Nederman, 3.

51 Scanlon, *Narrative, Authority and Power*, 90.

Uses of Lucan abound across twelfth-century historical texts, sometimes in the form of direct textual quotation and sometimes in broader echoes of the *Bellum civile*. For example, the *Gesta Stephani* begins with an overview of the breakdown of social and familial bonds during the Anarchy, in which 'rupta protinus in populo ueneranda sanctæ amicitiæ fœdera; dissoluta mutuæ cognationis coniunctissima uincula' ('the sacred obligations of hallowed friendship were at once broken among the people; the closest bonds of relationship were loosened'), recalling the words about war between friends and kinsman at the opening of the *Bellum civile*.[52] Citations from Lucan occur throughout Henry of Huntingdon's *Historia Anglorum* and, slightly earlier, Lucan is also a source for William of Malmesbury.[53] Even when historians of the twelfth century look back to earlier periods of civil unrest and rebellion, Lucan is drafted into their account. John of Worcester, writing about the conspiracy against William II in 1088, laments that

Ecce factum execrabile, ecce bellum, et *plusquam ciuile*. Pugnabant enim parentes in filios, fratres in germanos, amici pridem in cognatos, ignoti in extraneos.

This was war, a cursed affair, and what was worse than a civil war! Fathers fought against sons, brothers against brothers, friends against their kinsmen, strangers against strangers.[54]

McGurk notes the echo of the *Bellum civile*, Book I, lines 1–7 here: given this clear allusion, a more appropriate translation of 'et plusquam ciuile' might be 'and worse than civil', using Lucan's own words to make the same point that war between friends and kinsman is the worst division of all.

Returning to Henry of Huntingdon's *Historia Anglorum*, the presence of Lucan is nowhere more powerful than in the poem in Book

---

52 *Gesta Stephani*, 2, 3. Lucan, *Bellum civile*, Book I, lines 1–7. The *Gesta Stephani* includes another deliberately classicising reference here, by going on to lament that those who had worn the cloak ('toga') of peace now put on war.
53 See Greenway's index of textual allusions in Henry of Huntingdon, *Historia Anglorum*, 853–4. Many of these are formulae used to introduce or conclude battle speeches. For William of Malmesbury, see J. G. Haahr, 'William of Malmesbury's Roman Models', in *The Classics in the Middle Ages*, ed. A. S. Bernardo and S. Levin (Binghampton NY, 1990), 165–73, esp. 170–2.
54 *The Chronicle of John of Worcester*, ed. McGurk, 48, 49 (McGurk's italics).

X, Chapter 33, in which the voice of England itself calls out to Duke
Henry (the future Henry II) for aid as he prepares to cross the English
Channel. The poem begins with the personified England crying out in
distress, lamenting its current wretched state in fragmented, halting,
highly affective language.

> Dux Henrice, nepos Henrici maxime magni,
> Anglia celsa ruo, nec iam ruo tota ruina.
> Dicere uix possum 'fueram', 'sum' namque recessit.
> Si michi que miseris superest uel spes superesset,
> Clamarem, 'Miserere, ueni, succurre, resiste!
> Nam sum iure tui iuris, potes, erige lapsam.'
> Sed nunc ora rigent, nunc uox, nunc uita recedunt.

Duke Henry, greatest descendant of great Henry, I am falling into
ruin – I, noble England, am falling, though not yet in complete ruin.
I can scarcely say 'I had been', for 'I am' has departed. If even the
hope that remains for the wretched remained for me, I would cry,
'Have mercy, come, help, stop! Rightfully I belong to you, so you
have the power – raise me from my fall.' But now my speech freezes,
my voice, my life are going.[55]

England then begs Duke Henry for aid, declaring that only Henry has
the power to restore her to life. Henry then replies, vowing that 'pacem
tibi sanguinem quero' ('through the bloodshed I seek peace for you') and
finally swearing 'Te potiar, si pace tamen per me potiare' ('May I gain
possession of you only if, through me, you gain peace'). The poem draws
on a range of rhetorical tropes and conventions, portraying Henry as a
messianic figure in his *adventus* to his rightful kingdom, with the feminised persona of England recalling both the biblical bride awaiting her
bridegroom as well as traditions of knightly service and rescue.[56] But the
most striking textual allusion here is to Lucan, and the image of Rome,
personified as a distressed woman, lamenting as Caesar and his troops
cross the river Rubicon.

> Clara per obscuram voltu maestissima noctem,
> Turrigeo canos effundens vertice crines,

55   Henry of Huntingdon, *Historia Anglorum*, 760, 761.
56   See the detailed analysis of this poem in Clarke, 'Writing Civil War', 40–3.

Caesariae lacera nudisque adstare lacertis
Et gemitu permixta loqui: 'Quo tenditis ultra?
Quo fertis mea signa, viri? si iure venitis,
Si cives, huc usque licet.'

Her mighty image was clearly seen in the darkness of night; her face expressed deep sorrow and, from her head, crowned with towers, the white hair streamed abroad; she stood beside him with tresses torn and arms bare, and her speech was broken by sobs: 'Whither do ye march further? and whither do ye bear my standards, ye warriors? If ye come as law-abiding citizens, here must ye stop.'[57]

Speaking in the same broken sobs as Henry's England, Rome pleads with Caesar to stop at the boundary marked by the Rubicon and not bring his army onto Roman soil. And here is the most obvious difference between the Lucanian original and Henry of Huntingdon's appropriation of it: here the weeping figure of England does not attempt to bar Duke Henry's crossing, but instead begs for him to enter and save the nation. Henry's use of Lucan here operates in deliberate counterpoint to the original classical text, with its act of crossing portrayed as one of redemption and honour rather than transgression and desecration.

Henry's poem is set amid a series of crossings (or near-crossings) in Book X of the *Historia Anglorum*. Henry's passage across the stormy Channel to England is immediately followed by another scene involving a river crossing at Malmesbury in Wiltshire. The forces of Stephen and Duke Henry pitch their camps near the town and prepare to engage, but they are separated by a river 'quod pluuiarum et niuium inundatio tanto impulsu tanta immensitate ducebat, ut ingressuris horrorem incuteret, ingressis egressum negaret' ('which torrential rain and snow had rendered so fast-moving and swollen, that it was terrifying to attempt to ford and impossible to get out of').[58] Juxtaposed with Henry of Huntingdon's reference to Lucan in the preceding poem, the image of the turbulent, stormy river again recalls the depiction of the Rubicon in the *Bellum civile* as 'vires praebebat hiemps' ('swollen by winter') and treacherous to cross.[59] However, once again, the *Historia Anglorum* sets

57   Lucan, *The Civil War*, Book I, lines 187–92.
58   Henry of Huntingdon, *Historia Anglorum*, 764, 765.
59   Lucan, *The Civil War*, Book I, line 217.

up the Lucanian analogy only to subvert it. Neither Stephen nor Henry can cross the flooded river.

> Et quia preuiderat Deus quod puero suo terram sine sanguinis effusione contraderet, cum nullus eorum flumen transgredi posset, nec rex tantas illuuiones ultra perferre sufficeret, repedauit Lundoniam opera cassatus, molestia confectus.

> God had provided that He would deliver the land to His child [Duke Henry] without bloodshed, and so, when neither of them could cross the river and the king [Stephen] could no longer endure the great floods, he returned to London, frustrated in his exertions and worn out by troubles.[60]

The military engagement is deferred – a particular advantage for Henry, whose troops at Malmesbury number far fewer than Stephen's. Indeed, Henry of Huntingdon comments that 'Deus ipse uideretur pro duce rem agere' ('God himself seemed to be fighting on the duke's side').[61] Here, the portentous river is *not* crossed: Duke Henry's advance into England is deliberately contrasted with the tyranny and self-interest of Caesar and instead represented as the action of a divinely-sanctioned hero. The next scene at a river, a little later in Book X, Chapter 34, also subverts any initial Lucanian parallel. Henry and Stephen, alone 'amne interposito, de pace perpetua inter eos constituenda' ('on either side of a stream, had talks about arranging a lasting peace between them'), which Henry of Huntingdon notes 'prelibatum est . . . pacis negocium' ('was a foretaste of the peace treaty'). While depictions of parleys across streams or rivers are not uncommon in medieval chronicles,[62] framed here by the striking invocation of Lucan in Chapter 33, the scene once more gains further resonance as an inversion of the senseless horror of the *Bellum civile*.

This is where Henry of Huntingdon, and other twelfth-century writers, diverge most strikingly from the depiction of civil war in Lucan's *Bellum civile*. Whereas Lucan's depiction of the conflict between Caesar and Pompey is based on a vision of absurdity, chaos and deep pessimism, medieval Latin authors ultimately present the twelfth-century civil war

60   Henry of Huntingdon, *Historia Anglorum*, 764, 765.
61   Ibid.
62   See Greenway's comment, 767, n. 178.

as a phase – albeit horrific and terrifying – in the fulfilment of God's plan for England and his people. Typically, Henry 'weaves the uncertainties and the brutalities of history into a whole cloth that serves as a testimony to an order that is inherent in the identity of the nation itself'; he 'hints at a broader narrative whose end is not necessarily the present chaos'.[63] Reflecting on the peace treaty between Stephen and Henry (and the departure of Eustace, Stephen's son and claimant to the throne), the *Gesta Stephani* observes that 'talibus indiciis facile daretur intelligi nostrorum actuum prouisorem Deum uelle ducem ad regni apicem uocare, sicque pertincai discoridæ finem tandem imponere' ('from these signs it could be readily understood that God, who determines all we do, wished to summon the duke to the sovereignty and this put an end to the obstinate struggle').[64] Henry of Huntingdon concludes the *Historia Anglorum* by attributing the civil war itself, as well as its resolution, to God's plan, commenting that:

> Dispositio presertim Dei, 'faciens pacem et creans malum', condignis Anglie flagellis finem destinans, dedit eis prouentum incepti, et ab eo per ipsos pacis serenitas, concordia sacramentis confirmata, resplenduit.

> More especially through God's governance, 'creator alike of peace and woe', determining the end of England's well-deserved scourging, granted them [the architects of the peace treaty] success in their undertaking and by His will the serenity of peace shone forth through them when the concord was strengthened by oaths.[65]

Not only is the peace sanctioned and determined by God, but the war itself is rationalised as the enactment of divine punishment and justice – no longer the chaotic, senseless 'Anarchy' which it may have first appeared in the chronicle texts. Even Henry of Huntingdon, whose *Historia Anglorum* is so influenced by the formalist experiments and stylistic radicalism of Lucan's *Bellum civile*, ultimately locates the twelfth-century civil war within a narrative and ideology of Christian providence. The impact of his stylistic experiments in the later books of the *Historia* thus loses its force: his eloquent expression of the

63   Staley, *The Island Garden*, 3 and 37.
64   *Gesta Stephani*, 238, 239.
65   Henry of Huntingdon, *Historia Anglorum*, 770, 771.

fragmentation and division of civil war is circumscribed (and limited) by an underlying Christian theology and doctrine. Textual form never connects so fundamentally (and so devastatingly) with world-view as it does in Lucan's dark, nihilistic *Bellum civile*. A sense of the hidden workings of providence in human history is antithetical to Lucan's vision of the chaos and absurdity of the world.

Perhaps this, then, might be interpreted as what D'Angelo has termed the medieval 'misunderstanding' of Lucan. Perhaps twelfth-century writers merely mine the *Bellum civile* for apposite quotations and rhetorical flourishes, and fail to recognise the reality of the poem's vision. Yet Henry of Huntingdon's use of Lucan in the *Historia Anglorum* seems more complex than this, more akin to the deliberately oppositional, transgressive readings in John of Salisbury's *Policraticus*. In part, the ambivalence and complexity in Henry of Huntingdon derive from his use of Lucan as both a stylistic and rhetorical model *and* as a source of historical and moral exempla – bifurcations in the medieval Lucanian tradition which, pushed to their extreme by Henry, sit uneasily together here. Henry draws on Rome's civil war as an exemplum of destructive conflict and tyranny that serves as a moralising mirror for contemporary events. Caesar crossing the Rubicon is the archetype of the over-reaching ruler, but the anti-type of Duke Henry, who emerges as a saviour rather than destroyer. Lucan is arrogated to the purposes of twelfth-century politics and morality, and the most striking, developed allusions to the *Bellum civile* subvert rather than re-play the Lucanian narrative. Yet the didactic, providential view of history in the *Historia Anglorum* meets Henry's formalist experiments which draw on the radical, provocative idioms of the *Bellum civile* to express, convincingly, the horror and despair of the direct, immediate experience of civil war.

On the one hand, Henry of Huntingdon's providential vision disarms the destructive pessimism of Lucan's *Bellum civile* and attenuates the power of the stylistic experiments in the *Historia Anglorum*. Yet the resonance of Lucan in the *Historia* is not quite so easily contained. In his allusions to the Lucanian narrative, Henry aims to circumscribe the horror of his own contemporary civil conflict through contrast with its classical antecedent (Henry is not Caesar; God directs events rather than chance and chaos), yet the presence of Lucan's powerful rhetoric of civil war threatens to destabilise the text and subvert its confident providential message. The threshold between medieval and classical text is fragile and permeable: the powerfully dark vision of Henry of Huntingdon's poems, with their Lucanian language of fragmentation and disintegration, menaces the trusting didacticism of Christian his-

tory.[66] The friction and hostility between the two texts and historical moments (and their associated world-views) is latent throughout
the Historia Anglorum and surfaces in other works such as the Gesta
Stephani. In their appropriation of Lucan, these twelfth-century histories write into themselves a tense and uneasy border, a potential site of
assault and annexation from either side. A more substantial study of
uses of Lucan in the Middle Ages could offer broader insights on how
medieval writers made use of auctoritas,[67] as well as how the chosen language of composition shapes representation and allusion: here Lucan
features predominantly in the Anglo-Latin chronicles, whereas the
vernacular Peterborough Chronicle turns to the language of contemporary devotional practices for its imaginative framework. The use of
Lucan in the twelfth-century texts selected here forms one response
to the experience of civil war, crisis and catastrophe, and an attempt
to find a meaningful, public language with which to articulate contemporary events. Reminding us of the assertiveness – even aggression
– with which medieval writers could make use of classical auctoritas,
transgressing conventional readings and subjugating sources to their
own needs and beliefs, the presence of Lucan in these twelfth-century
works (especially in Henry of Huntingdon) also shows how a powerful
source can assault and threaten a text from within. Fittingly, writing
the 'Anarchy' is itself a process of conflict, appropriation and usurpation, where thresholds between texts and historical moments reveal
the contradictions, tensions and ambivalence in the project of representing civil war.

66   Similar observations have been made in relation to the final lines of the
eleventh-century historical text the Encomium Emmae Reginae, which seeks to
use Lucan's Caesar and Pompey as an anti-type for its protagonists. However, as
scholars have noted, by invoking Lucan in its final claim that 'hic fidelis regni
sotiis' ('here there is fidelity in sharers of rule'), the suggestion of treachery and
conflict is introduced. See Encomium Emmae Reginae, ed. and trans. A. Campbell (London, 1949), repr. and intr. Simon Keynes (Cambridge, 1998).
67   Maura B. Nolan's article, 'The Art of History Writing: Lydgate's Serpent of
Division', Speculum 78 (2003), 99–127, makes an important contribution.

'The Reader myghte lamente': The sieges of Calais (1346) and Rouen (1418) in chronicle, poem and play

JOANNA BELLIS

The fields were not sown or ploughed. There were no cattle or fowl in the fields. No cock crowed in the depth of night to tell the hours. No hen called to her chicks. It was of no use for the kite to lie in wait for chickens in March of this year nor for children to hunt for eggs in secret hiding places. No lambs or calves bleated after their mothers in this region. The wolf might seek its prey elsewhere and here fill his capacious gullet with green grass instead of rams. Larks soared safely through the air and lifted their unending songs with no thought of the whistling attacks of eyas or falcon. No wayfarers went along the roads, carrying their best cheese and dairy produce to market. Throughout the parishes and villages, alas! went forth no mendicants to hear confessions and to preach in Lent but rather robbers and thieves to carry off openly whatever they could find. Houses and churches no longer presented a smiling appearance with newly repaired roofs but rather the lamentable spectacle of scattered, smoking ruins to which they had been reduced by devouring flames. The eye of man was no longer rejoiced by the accustomed sight of green pastures and fields, charmingly colored by the growing grain, but rather saddened by the looks of the nettles and thistles springing up on every side. The pleasant sound of bells was heard indeed, not as a summons to divine worship, but as a warning of hostile incursions, in order that men might seek out hiding places while the enemy were yet on the way. What more can I say? Every misery increased on every hand.[1]

---

1   Jean de Venette, *The Chronicle of Jean de Venette*, trans. Jean Birdsall, ed. Richard E. Newhall (New York, 1953), 94.

So THE CARMELITE FRIAR and chronicler Jean de Venette described how war visited the place of his birth. His chronicle records the events of 1340 to 1368, including the battle of Crécy (1346), the siege of Calais (1346) and the battle of Poitiers (1356), becoming increasingly detailed as the events become more recent.[2] It was originally mistaken for a continuation of Guillaume de Nangis's late-thirteenth-century *Chronicon*, as it follows that work in one manuscript; but it is an independent account of the 'extraordinary events and misfortunes which . . . came to pass in France' (39). 'The English destroyed, burned, and plundered many little towns and villages', he wrote, 'capturing or even killing the inhabitants'; and with controlled understatement, 'The loss by fire of the village where I was born, Venette near Compiègne, is to be lamented' (93).

From the 1340s to the 1450s, northern France experienced more or less constant warfare, in the series of conflicts that would later be collectively known as the Hundred Years War. What began as a struggle for dynastic supremacy under Edward III, prosecuting his right to his ancestral lands in Gascony and Aquitaine, escalated into a war of self-legitimation under the Lancastrian Henry V, for whom it was as much about securing his position as a legitimate successor to the Plantagenets as king of England, as it was establishing himself as king of France. The arguments that originally underpinned the justification for war hinged on the technicalities of the Salic Law: whether the succession could pass to Edward III through his mother. But by the later stages, these arguments were tired and wearing thin. To be at war with France had become an end in itself for English monarchs: a sure way of mustering domestic support, as well as a reliable means of generating income. The set-piece victories of Crécy and Poitiers, and later Agincourt, as well as the sieges of Caen and Calais, were English history in the making: the stuff of a nationalistic legend that gained immediate self-aggrandising momentum.

But such formal engagements were the least of the ways in which the effects of war were felt by the citizenry: the *chévauchées* led by the Black Prince's commanders, lightning-raids that looted and burned communities overnight with the simultaneous purposes of wreaking havoc, subduing resistance and profiteering, terrorised the population. The late-fourteenth-century chivalric biography of the Black Prince by the Chandos Herald describes how 'to disport themselves' his troops 'put everything to fire and flame. There they made many a widowed lady

---

2 Ibid., 32.

and many a poor child orphan.'[3] Still worse were the free companies and the *routiers*, bands of profiteering mercenaries; and later the anarchic *écorcheurs*, famed for stripping their victims of the clothes on their back. Craig Taylor writes that 'the French countryside was persistently ravaged by marauding soldiers, including not only English troops, but also underpaid and poorly disciplined soldiers in service to the crown or in mercenary companies';[4] Helen Cooper calls the devastation inflicted on France in the Hundred Years War 'a series of horrors'.[5]

There was no way of combating a warfare that reduced communities to poverty overnight, that made no distinction between combatant and non-combatant. Venette described it as a reign of terror that permeated the natural as well as the social order: a dystopia in which even arable and seasonal patterns became disrupted and nightmarish. 'The king of England with his army traversed Brabant, reached Thiérache, and headed for Guise, plundering, burning, and devastating French territory,' he wrote, describing the terrain that Edward III's companies, travelling light and living off their spoils, covered in 1340:[6] his descriptions of 'burning and wasting' become commonplace. He went on to describe the 'stupefied amazement' with which, from a safe distance, he himself observed the torching of the suburbs of Paris: '[N]o one had thought ever to see such a thing. And yet these events were trivial in comparison with what the future was to bring forth' (41).

What the future did bring forth (if Venette could have foreseen it) was yet another century of bloodshed in the same cause. Under Henry V, the tactic of *chévauchée* was becoming obsolete;[7] but what emerged in its place was equally terrible. Again, there was no such category as that of the 'non-combatant' in the protracted sieges that marked Henry's

3   Mildred Pope and Eleanor C. Lodge, ed., *Life of the Black Prince by the Herald of Sir John Chandos* (Oxford, 1910), lines 236–9; trans. Richard W. Kaeuper, *Chivalry and Violence in Medieval Europe* (Oxford, 1999), 181–2.
4   Craig Taylor, 'English Writings on Chivalry and Warfare during the Hundred Years War', in *Soldiers, Nobles and Gentlemen: Essays in Honour of Maurice Keen*, ed. Peter Coss and Christopher Tyerman (Woodbridge, 2009), 64–84; 75.
5   Helen Cooper, 'Speaking for the Victim', in *Writing War: Medieval Literary Responses to Warfare*, ed. Corinne Saunders, Françoise Le Saux and Neil Thomas (Cambridge, 2004), 213–31; 215–16.
6   Jean de Venette, *Chronicle*, 33.
7   Clifford S. L. Davies, 'Henry VIII and Henry V: The Wars in France', in *The End of the Middle Ages? England in the Fifteenth and Sixteenth Centuries*, ed. John L. Watts (Stroud, 1998), 235–62; 248.

slow conquest of Normandy between 1417 and 1420, when the theatre of war was more often the farmstead, the village and the city than it was the pitched battlefield. In her *Livre des faits d'armes et de chevallerie*, Christine de Pisan denounced the English for their habit of taking prisoner those whom they should have protected – 'femmes, enfants, gens impotens [et] vieillars' ('women, children, the disabled and the aged').[8] Nobody was exempt: not for nothing did Shakespeare describe 'famine, sword and fire' as the king's 'hounds', 'crouch[ing] for employment'.[9]

The Hundred Years War was a total warfare that made no distinction between soldier and civilian. As such it could not be perpetuated – especially over such a protracted period – without raising serious doubts about its justification. The question of what constituted a 'just war' was an old one: Augustine had allowed the necessity of war in the face of the 'iniquity of the opposing side', although he considered it a thing of 'horror and cruelty' to be deplored.[10] In fifteenth-century France there was vigorous debate about the rights and wrongs of warfare. After a century of defeat and ignominy, it was 'only natural that these pressures would inspire leading French intellectuals and military leaders to engage in a wide-ranging debate about warfare and chivalry'.[11] Writers such as Honoré Bonet, Christine de Pisan and Alain Chartier probingly and publically questioned the morality of war. Their 'well-documented opinion [was] that war is an evil to be engaged in only when all other avenues have been explored, and then only in order to redress a gross injustice such as a hostile invasion'.[12] Specifically, Christine de Pisan questioned the ethics of employing mercenaries, the fate of unshriven soldiers, the protection to which non-combatants should be entitled;[13] Bonet's chapters explored 'Who are the stronger in battle, the just or the sinners?', 'What Persons cannot and must not be compelled to go to war', 'Whether a child should be made prisoner and put to ransom,' and

8   Quoted in Françoise Le Saux, 'War and Knighthood in Christine de Pisan's *Livre des faits d'armes et de chevallerie*', in *Writing War*, ed. Saunders, Le Saux and Thomas, 93–105; 102.

9   William Shakespeare, *Henry V*, in *The Riverside Shakespeare*, ed. G. Blakemore Evans and J. J. M. Tobin, 2nd edn (Boston, 1997), Prologue, lines 7–8; 979.

10   Augustine, *The City of God Against the Pagans*, ed. and trans. R. W. Dyson (Cambridge, 1998), Book XIX, Chapter 7, 928–9.

11   Taylor, 'English Writings on Chivalry', 71.

12   Le Saux, 'War and Knighthood', 94.

13   Ibid., 101–3.

'Whether a blind man can be taken prisoner and put to ransom', among many other ethical questions.[14]

Edward III's war could claim none of the justifications, nor abide by many of the moral mandates, laid out by the military theorists: it was not a defensive war; it did not respect the innocent parties caught up in it; under French law it was illegal. Very few of the civilians whose livelihoods were destroyed would have followed the intricacies of the Salic Law and its counter-arguments; and neither, probably, would the English soldiers and mercenaries who were made rich men through careers of pillaging and ransoming. For all that the English kings could claim that their enemies brought divine destruction on their own heads by wilfully resisting their rightful king, this argument did little to ameliorate the fact that the war was one of aggressive territorial expansion, marked by callous and ruthless pragmatism.

There were nominally codes of war designed to protect the rights and the honour of the French civilians who were (at least technically) Edward's rightful subjects. Chivalric literature invested a great deal in establishing the proper limitations of knightly conduct – strength properly deployed and properly restrained. Richard Kaeuper pertinently asks, 'Could one not argue . . . that in the inevitable warfare of early European history chivalry functioned as a restraining force, that war . . . was less horrific because its key practitioners were knights?'[15] However, in exactly what the 'code' consisted 'was not clear in detail, sometimes not in fundamentals'.[16] For all that a chivalric ethos 'may well have made fighting less barbaric for the knights themselves', it 'brought no radical transformation in medieval warfare, as it touched the population as a whole; . . . it imposed no serious check on the looting, widespread destruction, and loss of non-combatant lives'.[17] Kaeuper concludes that the 'yawning gap between ideal and practice' meant that 'chivalry had next to nothing to do with ordinary people'.[18]

Moreover, the argument that was used to justify the *kind* of warfare waged in France, in the full reaches of its brutality, was a biblical one. Co-opting Deuteronomy, English kings asserted that if the inhabitants

---

14   Honoré Bonet, *The Tree of Battles*, ed. and trans. G. W. Coopland (Liverpool, 1949), 156, 168, 184, 185.

15   Kaeuper, *Chivalry and Violence*, 169.

16   Ibid., 4.

17   Ibid., 169, 185.

18   Ibid., 175, 185.

of a town refused to surrender upon the first offer, they brought their destruction upon their own heads:

> If they . . . open the gates to thee, all the people that are therein, shall be saved, and shall serve thee paying tribute. But if they will not make peace, and shall begin war against thee, thou shalt besiege it. And when the Lord thy God shall deliver it into thy bands, thou shalt slay all that are therein of the male sex, with the edge of the sword, excepting women and children, cattle and other things, that are in the city. And thou shalt divide all the prey to the army, and thou shalt eat the spoils of thy enemies, which the Lord thy God shall give thee.[19]

This passage allowed the English kings to cast themselves as God's own scourge and instrument, bringing divinely sanctioned punishment on a stubborn and stiff-necked people. Of course, as Clifford Davies writes, whether either king 'believed . . . that Providence was on his side, can only be a matter for speculation'.[20] Henry V energetically cultivated his reputation for piety; but he was a tactician and a pragmatist, 'prepared, at Harfleur and at Caen, to expel the poor, women and children'.[21] Because (in an ironically circular piece of logic) God's judgement was reputedly shown in the outcome of the battle,[22] victory secured impunity in a doctrine where might was evidence of right.[23] The plight of the non-combatant did not, therefore, ultimately threaten either the king's piety or the justice of his cause. However, it remained an emotive issue for the aggressors (and their writers and apologists), just as it was a matter of survival for the victims (and their champions and ventriloquists).

This essay examines the narration of two events at either end of the Hundred Years War: Edward III's siege of Calais in 1346 and Henry V's siege of Rouen in 1418, from the contemporary accounts to later retellings. The two sieges were strangely similar: both cities were strategically and symbolically crucial; both were wars of attrition that

---

19   Deuteronomy 20:11–14, Douai-Rheims Vulgate Bible: www.drbo.org.
20   Davies, 'Henry VIII and Henry V', 255.
21   Ibid., 255.
22   See Christopher Allmand, 'The *De re militari* of Vegetius in the Middle Ages and Renaissance', in *Writing War*, ed. Saunders, Le Saux and Thomas, 15–28; 25.
23   Davies, 'Henry VIII and Henry V', 261.

involved unusually cruel suffering on the part of the inhabitants and callous pragmatism on the part of the besiegers. Siege – the slow grind of incarceration and starvation – was the form of warfare that put most pressure on the *casus belli*. By charting the trajectory of these sieges' narration from their eyewitness narrators to the accounts of subsequent centuries, this discussion suggests that the dubiousness of the conflict became more, and not less, unsettling, as the events receded into history, and that civilian suffering was the locus where the tension between the grim reality and the patriotic narrative was most keenly felt.

But it also traces a more subtle trajectory: early accounts celebrated and vindicated Edward III, including his ruthlessness as a necessary part of his military prowess, whereas later writers probed in a more troubled way the ethics of his conduct towards his non-combatant French subjects. In contrast, the contemporary accounts of Henry V's siege are more alert – perhaps because the political legitimacy of the king was a more tender point – to the ethical quickstepping necessary to vindicate, let alone celebrate, their king. In contrast, by the sixteenth century Henry V had achieved the status of epic 'star of England'. The careers of the two kings in the history books travel in opposite directions, the one beginning with unproblematic acclamation and attracting increasing infamy, the other beginning with ethical squeamishness and ending in a blaze of glory. Why exactly this was rests in the complex Tudor political investment in Lancastrian history for their own propagandistic self-promotion, which this discussion will adumbrate. The fact is that whereas Edward III receded into the safely available ethical space of history, Henry V remained a potently political and living symbol: in the sixteenth-century writing of medieval history, all was not equal.

Edward III's siege of Calais in 1346 came at the peak of his first campaign, immediately following the victory at Crécy. England needed a defensible garrison on the Normandy coast, where the fleet could assemble and the army be reliably supplied, and the fortified port-town was the ideal candidate. The siege was protracted: repeated artillery attacks failed to breach the walls, and Philippe VI managed to keep the city supplied with food and fresh water. It took from September 1346 to July 1347 for Edward to break the city, by which point Venette records that its inhabitants were 'eating their horses, and mice and rats, and many were dying miserably of hunger'.[24] Five hundred of the citizens

---

24   Jean de Venette, *Chronicle*, 45.

(mainly children and the elderly) were expelled, in order that there might be more to go round for those who remained to uphold the city's defence. The king refused to allow these evicted people to pass through his lines, and so they were left to starve to death around the city walls, until the town surrendered on 1 August. 'And thus', writes Venette, 'the king of England took the town of Calais'.

Edward's treatment of his new subjects was not magnanimous:

> He expelled all the inhabitants and all the friars of the order of Saint Mary of Carmel who resided there and put others from England in their places. He populated the whole town with English. Many of the men whom he expelled, impoverished and stripped of their pos-sessions, were forced with their wives and children to beg their bread throughout the world.[25]

This expulsion of the friars would have been felt particularly strongly by Venette, a Carmelite, who 'may well have heard it from a refugee friar in his own monastery'.[26] His description is echoed in fifteenth-century English chronicles' descriptions of Henry V's habit, to 'put out alle the Frensch peple, both man, womman and chylde, & stuffe the toun with Englisch men'[27] (one of the instances where the English claim to right-ful kingship over the French looked particularly paradoxical).

One incident in particular, not recorded by Venette, would be re-membered in the surrender of Calais. The Common Version of the Middle English prose *Brut* (to 1377) relates how

> whan they sawe . . . at the last that they had no thing amonge hem for-to ete ne lyve by, ne no socour [*aid*] ne rescuyng of the Frensshemen; on the tother syde they weste [*knew*] wel that they must deie for de-faute [*starvation*], eyther yelde up [*surrender*] the toun; and anon wen-ten & tokin done [*took down*] the banerys & the armes [*heraldic flags*] of Fraunce on every side that were hanged out, & wenten on the walles of the toun, and in other divers places, as naked as they were

25   Ibid., 46.
26   Ibid., 15.
27   Friedrich W. D. Brie, ed., *The Brut, or, the Chronicles of England*, 2 vols., EETS o.s. 131, 136 (London, 1906–8), II, 377; see also 383, 385, 397. Here and in other citations from the *Brut*, the spelling of Middle English letter forms (þ, ȝ, v/u) has been modernised.

bore [*born*], saf hire chirtys and brechys [*shirts and undergarments*], &
heldyn hire swerdus naked, & the poynt downward, in hire handez,
& putten ropys & halterys [*nooses*] abowte hire neckys, and yolden
up the keyes of the toun and of the Castell to Kyng Edward, with
grete fere and drede of hert.[28]

This arresting image of the citizens presenting themselves to Edward
wearing nooses recurs with increasing potency in the accounts of the
siege. In this *Brut* version, a continuation of the chronicle that was
written within or shortly after Edward III's lifetime, the citizens do it
of their own volition and are met with clemency: '[W]hen the King
saw this, as a mercyable king and lord, resceyved hym al to his grace.'[29]
Contemporary poetry celebrated Edward's success even more robustly:
a fourteenth-century ballad, probably by Laurence Minot, describes the
incident in triumphal terms:

Lystens now and ye may lere,	[*learn*]
als men the suth may understand,	[*truth*]
the knightes that in Calais were	
come to sir Edward sare wepeand –	[*weeping bitterly*]
In kirtell one and swerd in hand –	[*only their jacket/tunic*]
and cried sir Edward, thine are.	[*we are yours*]
Do now, lord, bi law of land	
thi will with us for evermare.	
The nobill burgase and the best	[*citizens*]
come unto him to have thaire hire;	[*reward*]
the comun puple war ful prest	[*ready*]
rapes to bring obout thaire swire.[30]	[*ropes; necks*]

28   Ibid., 301. The version is cited according the categorisation of the *Brut* and
its continuations by Lister M. Matheson, *The Prose Brut: The Development of a
Middle English Chronicle* (Tempe, Ariz., 1998), 87–97.
29   Brie, *Brut*, 301.
30   'How Edward als the romance sais held his sege bifor Calais', in Richard H.
Osberg, ed., *The Poems of Laurence Minot, 1333–1352* (Kalamazoo, 1997), lines
57–69, www.lib.rochester.edu/camelot/teams/minot.htm. See A. S. G. Edwards,
'The Authorship of the Poems of Laurence Minot: A Reconsideration', *Flori-
legium* 23.1 (2006), 145–53; David Matthews, 'Laurence Minot, Edward III, and
Nationalism', *Viator* 38 (2007), 269–88.

The poem treats Edward's subjection of the city with crowing pride, casting him as the 'boar' that political prophecies declared would harry France:

For all thaire boste thai er to blame,	[*In spite of*]
ful stalworthly thare have thai strevyn;	[*stoutly; fought*]
a bare es cumen to mak tham tame:	[*boar*]
kayes of the toun to him er gifen.[31]	[*given*]

This characterisation of Edward's actions – generous at best, jingoistic at worst – is typical of the fourteenth-century narrators.

However, in 1577 Holinshed's *Chronicles* painted a very different picture:

In the ende they were contented to yeelde, and the king graunted to receyve them and the towne on these conditions: that six of the chiefe burgesses of the town should come forth bare handed, bare-footed, and bare legged, & in their shirtes, with halters about their neckes, with the keyes of the towne and Castell in their handes, to sub[mi]t themselues symply to the kings will, and the re[si]due he was contented to take to mercie. This determinate resolution of king Edward being intimated to the commons of the towne assembled in the market place by the sound of the common [bel]l, afore the captaine, caused many a weeping . . . amongest them: but in the ende when it was perceyved that no other grace would be obteined .vi. of the most wealthiest burgesses of all the towne agreed to hazard their lives for the safegard of [the] residue, and so according to the prescript order devysed by the King, they wente forth of the Gates, and were presented by the Lorde Walter de Manny to the King, before whome they kneeled down, offred to him the keyes of the town, and besought him to haue mercie upon them: but the king regarding them with a fell countenance, commaunded streight that theyr heades shoulde be striken off. And although manye of the noble men did make greate intreatance for them, yet woulde no grace bee shewed, untill the Queene being great with childe, came and kneeled downe before the King hir husbande, and with lamentable cheare and weeping eyes, entreated so much for them, that finally the kings

---

31 'How Edward . . .', in *Poems of Laurence Minot*, lines 85–8.

displeasure was aswaged, and hys rygour turned to mercie.[32]

In this version, Edward is irascible and peremptory. It is his mandate that the citizens present themselves stripped and halter-necked; he has to be coaxed into kindness, in a familiar trope, by his pregnant wife. In contrast, the burghers are heroic in their self-sacrifice 'for the safegard of [the] residue'. *The Brut* was the direct ancestor for Holinshed's *Chronicles*, via Caxton's *The Chronicles of England* (1480), and alongside other sources for the events such as Froissart, so the transformation of this event was a deliberate departure from the medieval source.

Throughout the fifteenth century Edward III had been remembered as a heroically successful king. A number of *Brut* manuscripts contain a eulogy known as *The Character of Edward III*, which describes the king as 'of passyng goodnesse, and ful gracious amonge all the worthymen of the world; for he passyd and shone by vertue & grace geven to him fro God, above all his predecessours'. In particular it praises him as 'tretable' (*amenable*), 'soft, meke', and remarks that 'full lyghtly he bare & suffred wronges and harmes'.[33] But strangely, in the sixteenth-century chronicles, Edward's characterisation darkened: he became vengeful, vindictive, slow to show mercy, swift to remember wrongs.

This more sinister representation was magnified by the play *Edward III*, written collaboratively c.1590–94: the first history play in which Shakespeare had a hand.[34] It is a diptych, the first half depicting the king's attempted seduction of the Countess of Salisbury (he is rebuffed by her resolute chastity), and the second the invasion of France (dramatising in quick succession the battles of Sluys and Crécy and the siege of Calais). The play is rendered ambiguous by the first half, which portrays Edward as a slave to his lust and his rage in his attempt to corrupt the countess. Without this precursor, the second half could be read more straightforwardly as a patriotic romp, in the manner of *The Famous Victories of King Henry V*. Edward's reformation (like Prince Hal's) pre-

---

32   *Holinshed's Chronicles of England, Scotland and Ireland,* cited from *The Holinshed Project*, 1577 text: www.english.ox.ac.uk/holinshed/. All citations from this text henceforth from this online edition. The characters u/v and long s have been regularised according to modern usage.

33   Brie, *Brut*, 333.

34   Giorgio Melchiori, ed., *King Edward III* (Cambridge, 1998). For discussion of authorship and date, see 3–17. Numerous collaborators have been suggested for this text, among them George Peele, Christopher Marlowe, Robert Greene, Thomas Kyd, Robert Wilson, and William Shakespeare.

sents his military victories as the reward of the proper channelling of his passions; but it is difficult to forget the impression Acts 1 and 2 have made of the king's uncontrolled and self-gratifying nature.

The anger he feels for the 'stubborn' burghers of Calais is an instance of this. He declares, 'Since they refuse our proffered league', 'famine shall combat' 'this accursed town' (4.2.1, 5–6). Confronted with 'wretched patterns of despair and woe', the earl of Derby asks 'What are you, living men or gliding ghosts?' (4.2.12–13). They reply,

> . . . men that breathe a life
> Far worse than is the quiet sleep of death.
> We are distressèd poor inhabitants
> That long have been diseasèd, sick, and lame;
> And now, because we are not fit to serve,
> The captain of the town hath thrust us forth,
> That so expense of victuals may be saved. [4.2.15–21]

These are the poor unfortunates expelled from Calais. Initially, the play's presentation is generous: where the historical Edward did nothing to relieve their plight, this Edward commands 'that victuals be appointed them' and to 'give to everyone five crowns apiece' (4.2.31–2). His kindness hardens, however, towards the burghers. When surrender is announced, the king is indignant at how they 'Dispose, elect, and govern as they list!' (4.2.68). He retorts that 'since they did refuse | Our princely clemency at first proclaimed, | They shall not have it now' (4.2.69–71). He declares that he will 'accept of nought but fire and sword' (4.2.72) unless the six wealthiest merchants in the town

> Come naked, all but for their linen shirts,
> With each a halter hanged about his neck,
> And prostrate yield themselves upon their knees,
> To be afflicted, hanged, or what I please. [4.2.75–8]

This imaginative foray into what tortures Edward might 'please' to inflict upon his new subjects is revisited when the citizens duly present themselves in their smocks and nooses,

> . . . with willingness to bear
> What torturing death of punishment you please,
> So that the trembling multitude be saved. [5.1.16–18]

It is explored still further as the king declares

> Your bodies shall be dragged about these walls
> And, after, feel the stroke of quartering steel.
> This is your doom. [5.1.36–8]

As in Holinshed's *Chronicles* (one of the play's sources), the pleas of Queen Philippa are needed not only to make her husband show mercy, but to see reason, as she points out the illogic of rewarding his new subjects' hard-won allegiance with lingering execution:

> As thou intendest to be king of France,
> So let her people live to call thee king. [5.1.43–4]

Why was it that the narration of this siege, and the ramifications it had for the reputation of Edward III, changed so significantly in the narrative tradition? The town of Calais had a particular significance for the English monarchy in the sixteenth century: Mary Tudor's loss of this last bastion of English suzerainty in France to the Duke of Guise in 1558 was a source of national outrage, so much so that the queen was (apocryphally) said to have stated that were her body to be opened after her death, the word *Calais* would be found engraved on her heart.[35] David Grummitt calls it 'a tremendous blow to the national pride and morale of mid-Tudor England'.[36] Elizabeth bitterly felt her sister's loss, wishing that she might 'have this our Calais returned to us', and calling it 'a matter of continual grief to this realm'.[37] The staging of *Edward III* in the early 1590s was therefore profoundly retrospective: Edward's capture of Calais was the relief-image of Mary's loss of it; just as Edward, a robust, masculine, war-mongering king, with no fewer than five healthy sons, was the opposite of the Tudor queens' heirless, warless, anxious reigns. The authors of *Edward III* were indulging in historical nostalgia; but they were also, with the safe distance of two centuries, asking probing ethical questions about the king's motives and character.[38]

---

35 Cited in David Grummitt, *The Calais Garrison: War and Military Service in England, 1436–1558* (Woodbridge, 2008), 165.
36 Ibid., 3.
37 Cited in Richard Rex, *The Tudors* (Stroud, 2003), 196.
38 Interest in the siege of Calais did not wane after the sixteenth century. It is the subject of two French plays, Pierre-Laurent Buirette de Belloy's *Le Siège de*

Perhaps this was because war itself was a newly contentious theme in the sixteenth century. Augustine and Aquinas had allowed that it could be just, if undesirable; but Erasmus 'challenged the conscience of Europe' in his open letter *Against War* (1515), addressed to Pope Leo X and all Christian princes.[39] He rejected the *bellum iustum* doctrine as 'contrary to the spirit of Christ's teaching', replacing it with his adage *dulce bellum inexpertis* ('war is sweet to them that know it not').[40] He argued that 'nothing is either more wicked, or more wretched'.[41] War was 'a violation of uncorrupted Christian man's true nature, whose model must be Christ's own life', and as such it was 'always unjust': after all, 'Christ and the Apostles . . . took no part in armed strife'.[42] He condemned with particular vitriol the argument that had underpinned the Hundred Years War, that kings must 'fight for their right':

The strife is not, whether this city or that should be obeisant to a good prince, and not in bondage of a tyrant; but whether Ferdinand or Sigismund hath the better title to it, whether that city ought to pay tribute to Philip or King Louis. This is that noble right, for the which all the world is vexed and troubled with wars and manslaughter.[43]

Erasmus had raised the stakes; and at the Field of the Cloth of Gold

Calais (1765), and Philippe-Jacques Laroche's *Eustache de Saint Pierre, ou le siège de Calais* (1822). Luigi Marchionni's *L'Assedio di Calais* (c.1825) was based on Laroche's play, and in turn formed the basis of Gaetano Donizetti's 1836 opera of the same name. In 1913 Georg Kaiser (1878–1945) dramatised the siege in *Die Bürger von Calais*. This play, first performed in 1917, explores the motivations of the citizens who volunteered themselves. Fortuitously, Queen Philippa's child is born during the night, and in honour of his birth Edward decides to spare the citizens before they have given themselves up. The six burghers are also famously depicted in Auguste Rodin's 1889 sculpture *Les Bourgeois de Calais*.

39   Alastair Fowler, 'Spenser and War', in *War Literature and the Arts in Sixteenth-century Europe*, ed. J. R. Mulryne and Margaret Shewring (Basingstoke, 1989), 147–64; 152.

40   James Hutton, *Themes of Peace in Renaissance Poetry*, ed. Rita Guerlac (Ithaca NY, 1984), 52; Desiderius Erasmus, *Erasmus Against War*, ed. J. W. Mackail (Boston, 1907), 3.

41   *Erasmus Against War*, 4.

42   Robert P. Adams, *The Better Part of Valor: More, Erasmus, Colet, and Vives, on Humanism, War, and Peace, 1496–1535* (Seattle, 1962), 95.

43   *Erasmus Against War*, 51.

in 1520, the kings of England and France met to outlaw war for ever. When sixteenth-century writers re-examined the famous conflicts of their medieval past, it was with a new – or at least, a newly contested – philosophy of war.

Henry V's siege of Rouen in 1418 was as important a moment in securing the crown of France as the siege of Calais had been in gaining the first foothold. Rouen was the duchy's capital: sitting eighty miles north-west of Paris on the Seine, its export trade in the luxurious work of its goldsmiths and weavers made it very wealthy. It was heavily fortified and had been stockpiling food and weapons for several months. So confident was the city in its impregnability and the certainty of its rescue that it offered asylum to twelve thousand refugees fleeing Henry's conquest of Normandy. As at Calais seventy-two years earlier, the siege was a waiting game: it began in August 1418 and did not end until late January 1419. Hand-to-hand combat was frequent, especially in the early months, when the defenders made aggressive sorties from the gates. However, as the winter drew in, conditions within the walls became desperate. The English gained control of the river traffic, and the food reserves ran out. Soon, as at Calais, they were eating horses, dogs, cats and rats. In another pertinent echo, thousands of the citizens who had become too weak, sick, or who were too old or young to assist in the defence of the garrison were expelled, including many of those to whom Rouen had initially offered asylum. These *bouches inutiles* (as they became known) were not permitted by the besiegers to pass through their lines, and so, as at Calais, they remained in the ditch surrounding the city walls, where they slowly died of starvation, sickness and exposure, and were left unburied. Realising that the promised help from the Duke of Burgundy was not forthcoming, the city surrendered on 19 January 1419.

The siege of Rouen, too, was chronicled by an eyewitness. Unlike Jean de Venette, John Page was an Englishman, and possibly a soldier.[44]

---

44 The identity of John Page is a matter for speculation. Eight people of that name appear in the muster rolls around the right time: see the 'Soldier in Medieval England' database (www.icmacentre.ac.uk/soldier/database/index.php). Several other John Pages are listed in the Close and Patent Rolls for the reigns of Henry V and VI, although none of them belonged to the king's household. One recent critic asserted that 'we can be almost certain that he was not a combatant': Tamar S. Drukker, 'An Eye-witness Account or Literary Historicism? John Page's *Siege of Rouen*', *Leeds Studies in English* 36 (2005), 251–73; 257. Page's most recent editor thought the likely candidate was the prior of Barnwell Priory 1435–41: Herbert Huscher, ed., *John Page's 'Siege of Rouen': Kritische*

Rather than recording the event as a helpless onlooker, Page did so as an aggressor. Where Venette attacked Edward III unreservedly, Page defended the justice of his king's cause and the mercy of his conduct. Such a course was not easy to plot, since Henry was no less blameworthy than Edward; in fact, his revival of his usurped predecessor's claim was wearing rather thin. Davies comments on

> the disparity between the historic claim to the French throne by Edward III in the right of his mother, and the realities of the English dynastic situation since 1399, when such legitimist principles were blatantly disregarded. Whatever may be argued about the succession to the English throne, the rightful claimant to France on the Edwardian principle was Edmund Mortimer.[45]

If Edward's war had been about throwing his weight around in France in order to regain his ancestral holdings in Aquitaine and Gascony, Henry's war was as much about claiming Plantagenet rights for the Lancastrians as it was about claiming rights in France for the English.

Moreover, his behaviour towards his French subjects was as dubious as Edward's. He too is said to have washed his hands of the starving innocents:

> He sayde, 'Felowys, hoo put them them there,
> To the dyche of that cytte?
> I putte them not there, and that wote ye.'[46]

Nonetheless, Page praised his 'fayre grace' and 'goodenys' in feeding

---

Textausgabe (Leipzig, 1927), 71, 123–4. Given his high degree of information and interest in the treaty negotiations, it is quite possible that he was there in a clerical capacity rather than a military one, but the evidence is insufficient to confirm either hypothesis. For a fuller consideration of the candidates for authorship, see the introduction to John Page, *The Siege of Rouen*, ed. Joanna Bellis (Heidelberg, forthcoming with Middle English Texts).

45   Davies, 'Henry VIII and Henry V', 256. Edmund Mortimer, earl of March, was heir-presumptive to Richard II. As the grandson of Lionel of Antwerp, the second son of Edward III, his claim under strict primogeniture was stronger than that of the Lancastrians, descended from John of Gaunt, only the third son of Edward III.

46   Huscher, ed., *John Page's 'Siege of Rouen'*, 178, lines 838–40.

them – once, on Christmas Day;[47] he stopped short of detailing another of the king's notable acts of mercy, which we only know about from other sources: allowing any babies born in the ditch to be baptised, carried up to the city walls in baskets, before being returned to the ditch in the same way.

Page could hardly do otherwise than defend his king's actions. If we believe his account of himself, he lay 'with my lege';[48] and wrote his narrative while the campaign was ongoing:

> Thys procesce made Joh[a]n Page
> Alle in raffe and not in ryme   [rough, alliterative verse]
> By-cause of space he hadde no time.
> But whenne thys werre ys at a-n ende,
> And he haue lyffe, he wylle hit a-mende.[49]   [If]

His loyalty led him to follow suit in the familiar argument, that those who resisted their rightful king's rule were responsible for the consequences. However, as he contemplated the appalling plight of the civilians ('sum crokyd in the kneys, | And were as lene as any treys') and the devastation wrought on human relationships ('chyldryn sokyng on the pappe | With-yn a dede woman lappe'),[50] he was moved to a more ambivalent meditation:

> There ne was noo man so strange
> That sawe that but hys herte wolde change.
> And he consy-deryd that syght,
> He wolde be pensyffe and not lyght.
> There myght men lerne alle there lyve
> What was a-gayne ryght for to stryve.[51]

Even in this reassertion of the civilians' culpability in striving against Henry's 'ryght', Page cannot suppress his horror. His attempt to hold in tension his patriotism and his compassion is contradictory; and in one sense his text could be said to have failed. It is not, as he promised, a

---

47   Ibid., 162, lines 558–60.
48   Ibid., 136, line 22.
49   Ibid., 202, lines 1305–10.
50   Ibid., 186, lines 999–1000, 1003–4.
51   Ibid., 187, lines 1015–20.

glorious account of the most 'solemne sege' ever 'sette'.[52] It is more than that: an appalled and profoundly honest response to a sight that made his 'herte . . . change'.

The *Brut* chronicle (ten manuscripts of which incorporate Page's poem into their narrative) records, more briefly, the suffering of the Rouennais:

> And this sege endured xx^{ti} wokez [*weeks*], and ever thai of the toun hopyd for to have be rescued; but ther come non. So at the laste, thei kept so longe the toun that there deied mony thowsandez withynne the toune for defaute [*lack*] of mete, of men, wymmen and chyldryn; for thay had ete al her hors, doggis and cattez, that were yn the toun. And ofte tymez the men of armez droff out the pore pepyl at the gatis of the tounez, for spendyng of vitayle [*food*]; and anon our Englischmen droff ham yn-to the toun agayne. So at the laste, the capteynez of the toun, seyng the myschif that thay were nought rescued, and also the scarcite of vitayle, & that the peple so deied for defaute of mete, every day mony thowsandez, and also saue yonge childryn lye & sowke her modir pappis [*breasts*] that weryn ded, than anon they sent unto the King, besechinge him of his grete mercy & grace, and brought the keyes of the toun unto the Kinge.[53]

This is a later continuation (the Common Version to 1419) than that quoted earlier (to 1377), and the fifteenth-century chronicler passes no comment on the conduct of the king, other than that he 'entred yn-to the toun, & restyd hym yn the Castell tylle the toun were sette yn rewle and gouernawnce' (391). The king's actions – even at such a cost – need no vindication.

This was not the case, however, a century later. In Holinshed's *Chronicles* (1577 version), the image of these innocent civilians is not allowed to speak for itself:

> If I should reherse (according to the report of diverse writers) howe deerly dogges, rattes, mise, and cattes were solde within the towne, and how greedily they were by the poore people eaten and devoured, and how the people dayly dyed for fault of foode, and yong Infantes laye sucking in the streetes on theyr mother breastes, lying

52 Ibid., 135, line 15.
53 Brie, *Brut*, II, 390–1.

deade, sterven for hunger, the Reader myghte lamente their extreme
miseries.

The chronicle acknowledges the potency of the account, and the danger that its emotional power might destabilise confidence in the character and the cause of Henry V. It is at pains to record, after '[a] great
number of poore sillie creatures were put out at the gates', how 'king
Henrie moved with pitie, on Christmasse day in the honor of Christes
Nativitie, refreshed all the poore people with vittaile, to their greate
comfort, and his high prayse' – which earns him the marginal comment:
'A vertuous charitable prince.' In Page's account, the request of the ne-
gotiators to know whether Henry would relieve the suffering of the people in the ditch earned them the stiff retort quoted above: 'Felowys, hoo
put them there?'

In Holinshed's *Chronicles*, the interpretation of this exchange is
much more tightly controlled:

> One of them . . . shewing himselfe more rashe than wise, more erro-
> gant than learned, fyrst tooke upon him to shewe wherein the glorie
> of victorie consisted, advising the king not to shewe his manhoode
> in furnishing a multitude of poore simple and innocent people, but
> rather suffer such miserable wretches as laye betwixt the walles of
> the Citie, and the trenches of his siege, to passe through the campe,
> that they might get theyr lyving in other places, and then if hee
> durst manfully assaulte the Citie, and by force subdue it, he should
> win both worldly fame, and merite great meede at the handes of al-
> mightie God, for having compassion of the poore needie and indi-
> gent people.
>
> When this Oratour had sayde, the King . . . after hee had well
> considered the craftie cautele [*scheming*] of hys enimyes,with a fierce
> countenaunce, and bolde spirite hee reproved them, both for theyr
> subtill dealing wyth hym, and theyr malaperte presumption, in that
> they shoulde seeme to goe aboute to teache him what belonged to
> the dutie of a Conquerour.

Where Page allowed the compassion of the burghers and haughtiness of
Henry to stand, the *Chronicles* glossed the one as 'malaperte presumption' and the other as appropriate reproof. It became, surprisingly, more
important for this chronicler a century and a half after the event to keep
a tight rein on its interpretative possibilities, than it was for the eyewitness. The author(s) of Holinshed's *Chronicles* was much more interven-

tionist in his material: he has Henry explain exactly why he cannot be held responsible for the death of the *bouches inutiles* – why instead he should be congratulated as their preserver:

> And as for the poore people lying in the Dyches, if they dyed through famyne, the faulte was theyrs, that lyke cruell Tyraun[t]is hadde put them oute of the Towne, to the intente hee shoulde slea them, and yet had hee saved theyr lyves, so that if any lacke of charitie was, it rested in them, and not in hym.

In an even more remarkable protestation, Henry goes on to explain why the warfare he waged against them was intrinsically merciful:

> hee declared that the Goddesse of battayle called **Bellona**, had three Handmaydens, ever of necessitie attending upon hir, as bloud, fyre, and famyne. And whereas it laye in hys choyce to use them all three, yea, two, or one of them at his pleasure, hee hadde yet appoynted onely the meekest Mayde of those three Damoselles to punishe them of that Citye, tyll they were brought to reason.

This spin-doctoring indicates how anxious Holinshed's *Chronicles* were that their '[r]eader myghte lamente', rather than exult in, the famous victories of Henry V. After all, for the sixteenth century, that is what they were: if the siege of Calais had an emotive resonance for the Tudors, the siege of Rouen had much more so. Henry V was the 'ever-living man of memory' on the Elizabethan stage.[54] Henry VIII's invasion of France was a near-exact reprise of Henry V's, a century before him.[55] Moreover, Rouen itself was symbolic for the English: not only was it the burial-place of the heart of Richard Lionheart and of John Talbot (of Shakespearean fame), and the site of the trial and execution of the 'witch of Orléans', but it was once more the theatre of English military ambitions when it was (abortively) besieged by Elizabeth's favourite, the earl of Essex, in 1591. The trajectory of the narration of Rouen stands in clear contrast to that of Calais: Henry V simply could not be portrayed as a callous warmonger, as Edward III could be. Plays and chronicles probed the motivation and darker passions of Edward where contemporary accounts had swept them under the carpet; but

54 Shakespeare, *Henry VI Part I*, in *The Riverside Shakespeare* , IV.iii.51; 654.
55 See Davies, 'Henry VIII and Henry V'.

the deep-seated ambivalence and compassion that Page felt is done away with in sixteenth-century tributes to Henry V.

This is apparent in another chronicle, Edward Hall's *Union of the Two Noble and Illustre Families of Lancaster and York*, printed in 1542 and again in 1548 and 1550. Hall's work was more overtly propagandist than that of his successor: he began with Henry IV and ended with the death of Henry VIII. His trajectory charted the Lancastrian claim from the Wars of the Roses to the triumphal ascendancy of the united red-and-white rose. His running critique was also more intrusive, stipulating exactly what his readers' appraisal of Henry should be:

> The kyng like a grave prince consideryng that a thyng gotten without effusion of Christen bloud is both honorable and profitable, and sawe that the haute corages of the braggyng Frenchmen wer now by his hard besiegyng sore abated and almost tamed, thought it convenient to heare their lowly peticion and humble request.[56]

In this portrait, the English king sits morally above his stubborn French subjects, besieging them as God might test his servants: to humble their pride, to bring down the mighty from their seat. Far from calling into question the justice of Henry's cause, Hall exalts it to the highest cause: the usurping Lancastrian becomes the divine vicar on earth, not just in England. In Hall's version, Henry responds to 'the crafty cautell and fraudulent invencion of the French messengers' with an even more exaggerated oration:

> Thynke you O fantasticall Frenchmen that I am so ignorant and so brutall that I cannot perceive your double dealyng and crafty conveighaunce; Judge you me so simple that I know not wherin the glory of a conqueror consisteth. Esteme you me so ignoraunt that I perceive not what craftes and warlike pollicies by strong enemies are to be subdued and brought to subiection; yes, yes, I am not so loiterynge a truand as to forgette so good a lesson.[57]

Why these Tudor chroniclers invested so much effort in erasing all ambiguities and vindicating Henry, however clumsily, when they had so

---

56   Edward Halle, *The Union of the Two Noble Families of Lancaster and York* (1550) (Menston, 1970), xxviijv–xxixr.

57   Ibid., xxixr–v.

thoughtfully examined the actions and character of Edward, ultimately cannot be determined. Part of the answer must lie in the extent to which the Tudors, even more than the Lancastrians, needed dynastic legitimation. Even Henry V's propaganda campaign could not compare to that of the Tudors. Perhaps the fact that the dynasty owed its tenuous claim to royal blood, as well as its patronym, to Owen Tudor – obscure Welsh squire and second husband of Catherine of Valois – made defending the French claim even more imperative, and the memory of Henry V even more vital, once France had been lost beyond recovery.

The final word should go to the most ambiguous portrayer of Henry V. If *Edward III* had dramatised the king's lust and rapacity as the foil to his dynamism and military glory, Shakespeare's Hal in both parts of *Henry IV* and in *Henry V* just as vividly showed calculating shrewdness and cold self-preservation to be the partners of charming charisma and dazzling success. However, for all that debate has surrounded Henry's killing of the prisoners at Agincourt, his vivid threat of rape and infanticide to the unyielding mayor of Harfleur, and his washing his hands of the eternal damnation of the soldiers killed unshriven on his battlefields, Shakespeare stopped short of portraying Rouen as he and his collaborators had portrayed Calais in *Edward III*. The 'wretched patterns of despair and woe' to whom Edward had shown mercy have no counterpart in *Henry V*. Instead, the five years between Agincourt and the Treaty of Troyes disappear into the silent gap between acts four and five, in what Richard Hillman has called a 'drastically foreshortened . . . panegyric'. What fell in those years was, of course, 'the laborious step-by-step conquest of Normandy, including the single most difficult and protracted military project in which Henry engaged: the siege of Rouen'.[58] Even Holinshed's *Chronicles*, despite their rhetorical commentary, had not shrunk from acknowledging 'the enormity of the suffering of the Rouennais';[59] but Shakespeare deleted it from his history altogether.

While the ultimate motivation for the different directions in which the narratives of Calais and Rouen travelled remains mysterious, their political dynamism has implications for our understanding of the ongoing importance of representation, the legacy of war. The Hundred Years War certainly cast a long shadow, and the surprisingly long-lived

---

58   Richard Hillman, *Shakespeare, Marlowe and the Politics of France* (Basingstoke, 2002), 193–4.
59   Ibid., 195.

potency of its horrors has much to say about the way in which English dynasts were still, a hundred years on, justifying and excusing themselves in the light of it. Ultimately, we might conclude that it is the intensity of suffering that endows these accounts with their power; that that power is enduring beyond the political relevance of the events in question; and that it remains perhaps frighteningly available for appropriation.

Shakespeare's Casus Belly

or, Cormorant War, and the Wasting of Men on Shakespeare's Stage; or, Eating Wars and Digesting Plays; or, The Art of Chucking Men Into Pits; or, Shakespeare, Tacitism, and Why Plato Don't Matter

ANDREW ZURCHER

If this be magic, let it be an art
Lawful as eating.[1]

IN APRIL 1581, Arthur Lord Grey of Wilton, then Lord Deputy of Ireland, wrote to Sir Francis Walsingham to report on the state of his administration in Dublin. Grey's main concern in the spring of 1581 was the restive Irish lords and septs around the Pale, and especially the dangerous Feagh McHugh O'Byrne, lord of Ballinecor in the Wicklow mountains. Grey reported to Walsingham that two of his captains in the Irish service, Sir William Stanley and Captain William Russell, had recently raided Feagh McHugh's stronghold, and burned it, 'kyll[ing] certayne of hys kerne & churles, withowte the loss or hurtt of any of owres'.[2] In addition to this good 'service', as it was known in the official dispatches of the period, Grey commended the business of another of his captains, Humphey MacWorth, who 'hathe within this moonethe space putt too swoorde & executed very neere a hundrethe of the best of the Omoores, so as the rest of the sept hathe putt in pledge for theyr peacyble & good beehauior'. The contrast with Stanley and Russell's service is clear; they had killed some kerns and churls, but MacWorth executed a

---

1 Leontes in *The Winter's Tale*, 5.3.110–11.
2 Arthur Lord Grey de Wilton, Lord Deputy of Ireland to Sir Francis Walsingham, 6 April 1581, National Archives (NA) SP 63/82/6. All further references to this letter come from the same source.

great number of the 'best' of one of the most dangerous septs bordering
on the Pale. 'This man certaynely dezerues greate estimation not onely
for valure but goouernment,' wrote Grey, 'enter hym therfore I praye
yow into yowr Cataloge of well deseruers.' Of the rest, Grey could only
report that 'the oother garrisoones heere abowtes arr daylie nybbling vp
theyr churles & straggling knaues which beeyng of no great accounte I
lyke not mootche too aduertiss of'. The change in tone, deriving mainly
from Grey's light use of the alimentary metaphor, is striking. War is the
making of some men; others, it eats; but that, Grey seems to say, is hardly
news.

At the opening of Shakespeare's *Much Ado About Nothing*, Claudio
is being entered into Messina's catalogue of well-deservers; meanwhile,
it is by letter and messenger that Beatrice hopes to learn the fortunes of
Benedick, who has been nibbling up men:

BEATRICE   He set up his bills here in Messina, and challenged Cupid
    at the flight, and my uncle's fool, reading the challenge, subscribed
    for Cupid and challenged him at the bird-bolt. I pray you, how many
    hath he killed and eaten in these wars? But how many hath he killed?
    For indeed I promised to eat all of his killing.
LEONATO   Faith, niece, you tax Signor Benedick too much. But he'll
    be meet with you, I doubt it not.
MESSENGER   He hath done good service, lady, in these wars.
BEATRICE   You had musty victual, and he hath holp to eat it. He is a
    very valiant trencherman, he hath an excellent stomach.[3]

Beatrice's riposte to the Messenger's earnest commendation of
Benedick's service turns on two little pieces of wordplay, between
'trench' (a military fortification) and 'trencher' (a carving knife or
board from which food is eaten), and between two conventional uses of
'service' – the table service of a servant, who might be given the leftover
('musty') victuals, and the military service of a knight. Having implied
that Benedick could not have been valiant or successful in the late wars,
Beatrice insists that any men he *did* manage to kill must have been, like
'musty victual', hardly worth the fighting and therefore left to his dis-

---

3   William Shakespeare, *Much Ado About Nothing*, 1.1.37–50, in *The Oxford
Shakespeare: The Complete Works*, ed. Stanley Wells and Gary Taylor, 2nd edn
(Oxford, 2005). All further references to Shakespeare's works, unless noted other-
wise, will be drawn from the same edition, with references given parenthetically.

eased, his servile, and his voracious appetite. In her witty degradation of
Benedick, Beatrice returns to the same anthropophagous disparagement
as Lord Grey, drawing the same distinctions between the desert of a valiant gentleman, and the un-noteworthy exploits of a common feeder.
What is perhaps most striking about this parallel, though, is that while
Grey's resort to an alimentary metaphor may seem sharply cruel, characteristic of the callous brutality of English colonial power in one of
its most shameful periods, in Shakespeare's hands the metaphor is not
only unremarkable but commonplace. Indeed, it would seem odd if
Shakespeare were to write about war *without* comparing it to eating.
The association between feasting and fighting runs rife in his plays: to
name only a few, the Henriad, *Julius Caesar* and *Antony and Cleopatra*,
Troilus and Cressida, and *Coriolanus* all turn conspicuously on a close
correlation between combat and consumption. And it is in *Hamlet,
Prince of Denmark* that Fortinbras has 'sharked up a list of landless
resolutes | For food and diet to some enterprise | That hath a stomach
in't' (1.1.97–9) – while Claudius, that degenerate proponent of ap-
peasement, 'takes his rouse, | Keeps wassail', and 'drains his draughts
of Rhenish down' (1.4.9–11). The stomach is both the primary organ
of digestion, and the seat of manly valour.

Much has been written on Shakespeare's representation of war on the
early modern stage,[4] and much on his recourse to the language of the
body, which can in figures such as Falstaff, Thersites and Coriolanus reach
an almost manic register. For readers approaching his works with diverse
emphases, this latter sort of material has had varying kinds of import:
humoral-psychological,[5] material-Rabelaisian-festal-comical,[6] counter-

4   One of the best general studies of war in Shakespeare's works as a whole is
still Paul A. Jorgensen's *Shakespeare's Military World* (Berkeley, 1956). For more
focused critical and historical accounts, see Theodor Meron, *Bloody Constraint:
War and Chivalry in Shakespeare* (Oxford, 2000); and his earlier *Henry's Wars
and Shakespeare's Laws: Perspectives on the Law of War in the Later Middle Ages*
(Oxford, 1993). See also Charles Edelman, *Shakespeare's Military Language: A
Dictionary* (London, 2000).
5   See, for example, David Hillman, 'The Gastric Epic: *Troilus and Cressida*',
Shakespeare Quarterly 48 (1997), 295–313.
6   See, for example, Valerie Traub, 'Prince Hal's Falstaff: Positioning Psycho-
analysis and the Female Reproductive Body', *Shakespeare Quarterly* 40 (1989),
456–74.

ideological,[7] stoical-misogynistic,[8] counter-Reformation-corporeal[9] and so on. With a few important exceptions,[10] critical discussion of Shakespeare's writing about digestion and the body tends to focus on single characters or single works; critics generally shy away from theorising a close connection between combat and consumption, despite (or perhaps simply because of) Shakespeare's insistently recurrent correlation of the two – a connection that would immediately suggest an impracticably broad range of like-minded plays. Despite the risk of this impracticality, the purpose of this essay is to interrogate this like-mindedness, the general tendency across a range of Shakespeare's plays to collocate feasting and fighting, and to explore its contemporary cultural contexts – above all, a distinctively Tacitean take on the theory and practice of warfare characteristic of a small community of English writers and fighters in the late years of Elizabeth's reign. In the course of excavating the roots and significance of Shakespeare's rhetorical and conceptual pairing of eating and warfare, I will ultimately return to another aspect of Beatrice's critical deconstruction of Benedick at the opening of *Much Ado About Nothing* – that he is entirely in bad faith. Claudio, having done the feats of a lion in the figure of a lamb, has far outstripped his promise (1.1.12–17); Benedick the jilt, by contrast, has reneged on the promise he seems to have made to 'my uncle's fool' – that is, to Beatrice herself, 'bolting' or running from the 'bird' (a girl, or perhaps by metathetic confusion a bride). His perfidious impotence Beatrice parodies in her own promise to eat all the men of his killing, a promise she will not have to keep. As Beatrice makes clear, war is exactly like eating, but only up to a point: no one ever *actually* eats anyone else; cannibalism is a hyperbolic tall tale, the kind of story Othello might use to woo Desdemona. The braggardise of war is that, too, of the theatre; by

7   See, for example, Hugh Grady, 'Subjectivity Between the Carnival and the Aesthetic', *Modern Language Review* 96 (2001), 609–23; Grady says that 'what Falstaff embodies is the ability of aspects of the self to resist or surpass the specific, fixed social roles of Althusserian interpellation': 613.
8   Coppelia Kahn, *Roman Shakespeare: Wars, Wounds, and Women* (London, 1997).
9   Kristen Poole, 'Saints Alive! Falstaff, Martin Marprelate, and the Staging of Protestantism', *Shakespeare Quarterly* 46 (1995), 47–75.
10   See, for example, David Hillman, *Shakespeare's Entrails: Belief, Scepticism and the Interior of the Body* (Basingstoke, 2007), and David Goldstein's *Eating and Ethics in Shakespeare's England* (Cambridge, 2013), which surveys Shakespeare's writing about food and consumption across a range of plays.

concentrating on the strong contemporary correlation between feasting and fighting, particularly in the various written constructions of the long-running Elizabethan wars in Ireland, and in Shakespeare's immediate literary and philosophical context, we can see some of the appeal of this correlation for a writer busy with the articulation of his own medium's representational and ideological limitations.

Wasting and Consuming All: Feasting and Fighting in Elizabeth's Irish Wars

The close conflation of feasting and fighting, of war and eating, was a constant motif in writing about the Elizabethan wars in Ireland. Eating did not just serve English soldiers and governors in Ireland as a metaphor. The production, control and consumption of food were critical to the causes, conditions and conduct of the war in Ireland during the Tudor period. For example, one of the most regularly recurring preoccupations of sixteenth-century political and military writers on the English government of Ireland was the Irish practice of 'coigny and livery'. An Irish custom deriving from the Brehon law, coigny (from Irish *coinnemh*, 'billeting') was the right of Irish lords to impose their kern and horseboys on husbandmen and farmers – later restricted by statute to their own tenants – who were required to feed them.[11] Edmund Campion, in his 1571 treatise, *The Historie of Ireland*, calls it 'the very nurse and teat of all Irish enormities',[12] which:

11   The first of several statutes enacted by the great Council of Ireland before Richard, duke of York, in Dublin in 1450, required that 'no Marchour, nor other man shall keepe more horsemen or footemen, then they shall answere for, and maintaine vpon their owne charges and their tenants', and prohibited 'Coynee, Cuddies or night suppers'. Coigny and livery survived as an exaction permitted to lords upon their own tenants; this act was designed specifically to curtail the exploitation of coigny and livery by Irish and rebel English lords who used such billeting and night supping as a cover for military reconnaissance and ambush. See *The Statutes of Ireland* (Dublin, 1621), 13–14.

12   The mammary metaphor was striking enough to impress itself on Richard Beacon, who writes twice in *Solon His Follie*, a dialogue on Irish government, of coigny and livery as 'that Nurse and teate which sometimes gave sucke and nutriment vnto all disobedience, rebellions, enormities, vices and iniquities of that Realme': *Solon His Follie, or A Politique Discourse, Touching the Reformation of Common-weales Conquered, Declined or Corrupted* (Oxford, 1594), sig. ¶3v.

. . . extort[s] from the poore tennants everlasting Sesse, allowance
of meate and money, their bodies and goods in service, so that their
horses and their Galloglashes lye still upon the Farmers, eate them
out, begger the Countrey, foster a sort of idle vagabonds, ready to
rebell if their Lord commaund them, ever nusseled in stealth and
robberyes.[13]

By the associated custom of livery, the same tenants were responsible for
the supply and feeding of the soldiers' horses. John Dymmok writes in
his *Treatice of Ireland* (c.1599):

Lyvery is horsemeat, exacted for the horses of those which take
coyny, or otherwyse send them to the pore tenants to be fedd. The
tenant must finde the horses and boyes and geve them as much corne
and sheaffe otes wheat and barley as they will have, and yf there be
two or thre boyes to a horse as sometymes there be, the pore tenant
must be content therewith and yet besydes rewarde the boyes with
mony.[14]

By this prerogative exaction (or 'spending', as it was called), Irish lords
were able to build and maintain considerable personal forces of retainers.[15] The ability to feed their men – by imposing them upon their tenants and (illegally) upon other farmers – enabled the Irish to mount
successful ongoing challenges to English garrisons and urban defences.

In his well-known and influential dialogue, *A View of the Present
State of Ireland* (c.1596), Edmund Spenser writes similarly of the importance of feeding and victualling to the orderly government of the
Irish countryside. Unlike Campion and Dymmok, Spenser in one place
laments the suppression of the ancient customs of coigny and livery,

13   Edmund Campion, *The Historie of Ireland* (1571), in *Two Histories of Ireland*
(Dublin, 1633), 102.
14   John Dymmok, *A Treatice of Ireland*, ed. Richard Butler (Dublin, 1842),
8–9.
15   'Spendings' were the basis of the informal co-dependency of Irish tenants
and their lords; as Edmund Spenser writes in *A View of the Present State of Ireland*, Irish tenants 'weare never wonte and yeat are loathe to yealde anye Cer-
taine rente but onlye suche spendinges, for theire Comon sayinge is *Spende me
and defende me*'. See *A View of the Present State of Ireland*, ed. Rudolf Gottfried,
in *A Variorum Edition of the Works of Edmund Spenser*, ed. Edwin Greenlaw et al.,
11 vols. (Baltimore, 1936–53), X, 79, lines 1064–6.

because in a land without common inns, a travelling gentleman can find no place to eat, or to stable his horse, unless he should impose upon his tenants, which by statute incurs the danger or penalty of treason. As his experienced interlocutor, Irenius, observes, 'he is endaungered to the statute of treasone when soeuer he shall happen to fall out with his Tenante or that his saide hoste liste to Complaine of greevance As oftentimes I haue sene them verye malicyouslye doe thorowe the leaste provocacion'.[16] Limits on rights over eating and stabling, then, could adversely affect English governors and landholders, as well as Irish lords and rebels. Elsewhere in his dialogue, though, Irenius is adamant that the practice of keeping dangerous and dissolute horseboys should be suppressed, and the tradition of hosting according to the old coigny custom reformed:

> And now nexte after the Irishe kerne me semes the Irishe horsboyes woulde Come well in order the vse of which thoughe necessitye (as times now be) doe enforce yeat in the thoroughe reformacion of that realme they shoulde be Cutt of for the Cause whye they muste nowe be permitted is the wante of Conveniente Innes for lodginge of traueilours on horsbacke and of hostelers to tende theire horses by the waye, But when thinges shalbe reduced to a better passe this nedeth speciallye to be reformed for out of the frye of these rakehellye horsboyes growinge vp in knaverye and villanye are theare kerne continuallye Supplied and mainteyned, for havinge bene once broughte vpp an Idle horsboye he will neuer after fall to labour but is onely made fitt for the halter.[17]

Spenser imagines a social and economic transformation of the 'waste' Irish landscape,[18] in which private loyalties and ancient exactions would give place to a network of trading inns. Spenser's goal is the extirpation of a class of idle adventurers available for military employment; the means proposed is the reformation of customs and social practices governing the provision of food.

The threats posed by both toleration and suppression of coigny

16   Ibid., 78, lines 1030–4.
17   Ibid., 127, lines 2345–56.
18   One of Spenser's most frequently used words in A View, both of the food 'wasted and spoiled' by Irish and English soldiers and, more importantly, of the landscape itself – empty, uninhabited, wild, devastated.

and livery affected those parts of Ireland where settled husbandry predominated, that is, particularly the Irish Pale and those regions bordering it (the 'marches' of the Henrician statute), as well as the settled estates governed by prominent Old English families such as the Butlers in Wexford and Tipperary, or the Roches in Cork. In these areas the Norman invaders of the thirteenth century had bequeathed a quasi-feudal tenurial system similar to that predominant in England. In other regions of Ireland, and particularly in the north and west, the 'mere' or pure Irish septs dominated; these large and extended family groups tended to rely more heavily on transhumance, known to the New English governors of Elizabeth's reign as 'boolying' (from Irish *buailidh*, the diminutive of *buaile*, 'cattle-fold') or 'creaghting' (from Irish *caeraigheacht*, from *caera*, 'sheep'). The driving of their creaght or booly from one place to another allowed the Irish to protect their food supply in time of war; meantime, raids on other septs, or on fortified bawns and towns, during which the Irish would seize or 'take' a 'prey', allowed them to add to their creaght. This manner of transhumance particularly exercises Irenius in Spenser's *View of the present state of Ireland*:

But by this Custome of Bolloyinge theare growe in the meane time manye greate enormityes vnto that Comon wealthe for firste if theare be any outlawes or loose people (as they are never without some) which live vppon stealthes and spoile, they are evermore succored and finde reliefe onelye in those Bollies beinge vppon the waste places, wheres els they shoulde be driven shortelye to sterve or to Come downe to the townes to steale reliefe wheare by one meanes or other they woulde sone be Caughte: besides suche stealthes of Cattell as they make they bringe Comonlye to those *Bollyes* wheare they are receaued readilye and the Thiefe Harbored from daunger of Lawe or suche officers as mighte lighte vppon him. Moreouer the people that live thus in these Bollies growe theareby the more Barbarous and live more licentiouslye then they Could in townes vsinge what meanes they liste and practisinge what mischiefs and villanies they will either againste the gouernement theare generallye by theire Combinacions or againste private men whom they maligne by stealinge theire goodes or murderinge themselves; for theare they thinke themselues haulfe exemted from lawe and obedience and hav-inge once tasted fredome doe like a steare that hathe bene longe out of his yoke grudge and repine ever after to Come vnder rule againe.[19]

Irenius' proposed solution in Spenser's dialogue is to discourage tran-shumance – that is, to control and manage the Irish food supply – in order to discourage the 'enormities' that spring from its flexibility and disorder. Settled farms, certain rents and mutual obligations between landlords and tenants will all act to prevent nomadic and allegedly un-civilised people from resisting the legal and military oversight of their English colonial administrators. This was essentially the logic that led to the formation of the Munster and Ulster plantations, the first created after the seizure of the earl of Desmond's lands upon his capture and death in 1583, and the second created following the English defeat of the earls of Tyrone and Tyrconnel at Kinsale in 1603, ending the Nine Years' War. The English governors sought to reduce the wild north and west – by planting it with Protestant gentlemen and tenant farmers – to an agrarian structure antipathetic to transhumance and the extended, disorganised septs that thrived by it.

Not only did English writers like Spenser theorise the further subjec-tion of the Irish through the management of their food supply; they actively promoted the deliberate degradation of Irish food security in an attempt to defeat guerrilla rebellions. 'Scorched earth' was not a new strategy in the sixteenth century, and nor would its appeal wane for other combatants, in other theatres, in other ages; but there are few parallels for the simple brutality of the famine that Spenser witnessed in Munster after the Desmond rebellion, which had arisen from the com-bined stresses of war, disease, and bad weather. As Spenser infamously describes it in A view of the present state of Ireland:

> [E]re one yeare and a haulfe they weare broughte to soe wonderfull wretchednes as that anie stonie harte would haue rewed the same. Out of euerie Corner of the woods and glinnes they Came Crepinge forthe vppon theire handes for theire Leggs Coulde not beare them, they loked like Anotomies of deathe, they spake like ghostes Cryinge out of theire graues, they did eate the dead Carrions, happie wheare they Coulde finde them, Yea and one another sone after, in so muche as the verye carkasses they spared not to scrape out of theire graves. And if they founde a plotte of water Cresses or Shamarocks theare they flocked as to a feaste for the time, yeat not able longe to

19   Spenser, A View, 98, lines 1532–50.

Continve thearewithall, that in shorte space theare weare non all-
moste lefte and a moste populous and plentifull Countrye sodenlye
lefte voide of man or beaste.[20]

Spenser's account, as sympathetic as it appears to the suffering of the
miserable victims of the 1580s Munster famine, is part of his overall
claim that famine, or the threat of famine, *works* as a strategy for the
pacification of intransigent populations. Indeed, this vision of mass starvation is the culmination – albeit only for those hardy, obstinate rebels
who will not accept English rule – of the policies that Irenius has advo-
cated throughout the dialogue, namely 'beinge kepte from manuraunce
and theire Cattle from Comminge abroade by this harde restrainte'.[21]
Get your hands on the food supply, and squeeze, and the war is as good
as over.

A detail in Spenser's account of the Munster famine brings this discussion of the political and military discourse of Elizabeth's Irish wars
back to the 'nibbling up' with which it began. What finally dehuman-
ises the Irish victims of the famine, in Spenser's account, is their willingness to scrape the very carcasses out of their graves and – though he
leaves this to the reader's imagination – eat them. The cannibalism to
which the desperate Irish were allegedly driven transforms them from
rich and healthy husbandmen, through their degraded and emaciated
transitional state, to abject *objects* rather than *subjects* of consumption.
In Spenser's account, there are no survivors, only meals for the dead.[22]
This transformation takes place in Spenser's dialogue alongside a number of other rhetorical strategies that reconceptualise the refractory or
intransigent Irish rebels not as legitimate subjects or even persons, but

20 Ibid., 158, lines 3257–68.
21 Ibid., lines 3251–2.
22 The same rhetorical transformation characterises Thomas Churchyard's
famous account of Sir Humphrey Gilbert's 'pacification' of Munster in 1569.
Churchyard relates how Gilbert cut off the heads of any of the Irish he had
killed during the day, and laid them on each side of the way to his tent at night,
so that 'none could come into his Tente for any cause, but commonly he muste
passe through a lane of heddes, whiche he vsed *ad terrorem*'. When challenged
over the cruelty of this strategy, Gilbert allegedly replied first, that he only
practised that toward the Irish which they themselves did to the English; and
secondly (citing the example of Diogenes the Cynic), that 'the dedde felte no
paines by cuttyng of their heddes': Thomas Churchyard, *A Generall Rehearsall of
Warres, called Churchyardes Choise* (London, 1579), sig. Q3v–Q4r.

instead as diseased limbs or unwanted growths, which the careful physician or responsible gardener will remove. So, when Eudoxus asks Irenius how the reformation of Ireland is to be begun, Irenius answers:

> Even by the sworde. for all those evills muste firste be Cutt awaie by a stronge hande before anie good Cane be planted, like as the Corrupte braunches and vnholdsome boughes are firste to be pruned and the foule mosse clensed and scraped awaye before the tree cane bringe forthe anye good fruite.[23]

The reconceptualisation of the population of Ireland as a political body, or as a tree, incorporates particular human lives, in all of their material fragility, into an abstract corporate identity, the orderly management of which entails their 'cutting off', or violent death.[24] In effect, Spenser's rhetorical re-imagination of the rebellious Irish converts them through metaphor from subjects into expendable matter, so degraded that their ready 'consumption' or 'waste' is not a crime but good policy, not an ethical but a logical judgement. Indeed, Spenser's rhetoric prepares the ground for his ideologically polemical defence of Lord Grey, erewhile his master, who had been sharply criticised at court for 'a blodye man [who] regarded not the lief of [the queen's] subiectes no more then dogges but had wasted and Consumed all'.[25]

Between 1573 and 1574 two signal events took place in the colonial wars then simmering throughout the north of Ireland, which drew on a long history of associations between war and eating in Irish affairs. These two events, both part of the history of the first earl of Essex's attempt to establish an English plantation or colony in Ulster, reduce to emblematic clarity the two most important intersections between

---

23   Spenser, A View, 148, lines 2956–60.
24   Spenser was not alone in the use of these two metaphors; Sir William Herbert, in his Croftus, sive de Hibernia Liber of 1594 had similarly combined arboreal and physiological metaphors, writing that the colonial government of Ireland would 'grow like a tree' and, against the evils that should beset it, he must 'prescribe some precautions so that they may not sprout again and grow up because of a relapse in the patient'. See Herbert, Croftus, sive de Hibernia Liber, ed. and trans. Arthur Keaveney and John A. Madden (Dublin, 1992), 97. Herbert was a neighbour of Spenser's on the Munster plantation, and it seems likely this discourse was prevalent among the English gentlemen active in the plantation government in the years preceding the outbreak of the Nine Years' War.
25   Spenser, A View, 159, lines 3306–08.

conflict and consumption. The Ards is a much-contested peninsula east
of Belfast around Strangford Lough, in 1573 largely under the control
of the Anglicised Irish lord, Sir Brian McPhelim O'Neill. Following
the death of Shane O'Neill – the youngest son of the undisputed chief
of the O'Neills, Conn O'Neill, first earl of Tyrone – Brian McPhelim
sought to consolidate control over the east of Ulster, and particularly
over the Ards, and to this end he submitted himself to the queen's authority, standing her ally against the pretensions of Turlough Luineach
O'Neill, who had emerged after Shane's death as the pre-eminent chief
in Ulster. When Brian McPhelim learned that Elizabeth's secretary Sir
Thomas Smith had been granted lands in this region for the planting of
a colony, he began to build a confederation with other Ulster families
– particularly the 'degenerate' Anglo-Norman Savages – to repel the
English project. O'Neill wasted the Ards in October of 1572, fought
with Thomas Smith (the secretary's son) in the early months of 1573,
and burned the English fort at Carrickfergus in May 1573. In October of
that year, following a disastrous summer in which young Thomas Smith
was all but abandoned by the Lord Deputy, Sir William Fitzwilliam,
and failed to receive promised reinforcements from his father, he was
murdered by his own men and – according to one contemporary witness
– his body boiled, hacked to pieces, and fed to dogs.

News of Smith's death reached London from the earl of Essex, who
reported that he 'was slayne in the Ardes [. . .] by the revoltinge of certain Irishmen of his owne howshold, to whome he overmuche trusted'.[26]
The story is told in Thomas Churchyard's history of the Irish wars of
this period, A Generall Rehearsall of Warres, called Churchyardes Choise.
According to Churchyard, Captain John Malby attacked the forces of
Neall Bryan Artho in an attempt to revenge Smith's death, and thirty-
five men were 'licked vp and slaine', including one important enemy:

> Emong those menne that was slaine, was one Con Mackmeloeg, who
> before caused maister Smithe to be eaten vp with Dogges, after he
> had been boiled, and this same Con Mackmeloeg beyng slaine, was
> lefte emong wolues v. daies, and was had into a house, where his
> freendes howled, and cried ouer his dedde bodie so long, that by
> mischaunce a great deale of pouder caught fire, and sett the house
> in a flame: the Dogges in the toune smellyng this ded bodie came
> in, and tooke it out of the house, and so tore it in peeces, and fedde

vppon his carraine fleshe openly. Whiche was a thyng to bee muche marueiled at, and thought to bee sent from God, for a terrour to all tyrauntes hereafter.[27]

The consumption of the body by scavenging dogs is a recurring element in Churchyard's rehearsal of the Irish wars; here it echoes his account of Gilbert's pacification of Munster, which concludes with an allusion to Diogenes of Sinope, the Cynic philosopher, who willed his body to be thrown on the dunghill and eaten by dogs, because after death the degradation of his flesh was nothing to him. Churchyard's repetition of 'terrour' – like the phrase 'ad terrorem' in his account of Gilbert – insists on the moral and political work that this degradation is intended to accomplish, an effect only achievable if the audience of the emblem (for example, the reader of Churchyard's Generall Rehearsall) fears this degradation a very great deal. But two elements of this account of Smith's death, and the revenge for that death, stand out: first, the hypocrisy of the English, who willed and brought to pass the same corporal degradation on their enemies that they had called barbarous in their enemies; and second, the divine authority that Churchyard confers on the transition from a customary and dignifying mourning ritual (although here bestialised by the verb 'howl') to the wartime banquet of scavengers.

The young Smith was dead, but the Ards project was financially too big to fail, and Elizabeth entrusted its ongoing prosecution to Walter Devereux, the first earl of Essex. Essex was already in Ulster when young Thomas Smith was murdered; he made financial arrangements with Sir Thomas Smith to acquire certain lands, castles and plantation rights, and set about a more ruthless, and more effective, confrontation with the chief lords of the area, in particular Brian McPhelim. By this point, under pressure from his erstwhile English handlers, McPhelim was alleged to have joined forces with Turlough Luineach, now in the ascendancy in Ulster after his marriage to Agnes Campbell, the Lady of Kintyre, widow of James McDonnell, Lord of the Islands. Turlough Luineach refused any rapprochement with the Pale government, and was considered by the English government a rebel; McPhelim's association with him constituted a treasonous act, and within the year after Smith's death Essex had gathered sufficient (apparent) evidence of his traitorous designs and actions to justify a brutal offensive against him.[28]

---

27 Churchyard, A Generall Rehearsall, sig. F3v.
28 See NA SP 63/48/57/1, Essex's summary of Brian McPhelim's treasonous

Essex maintained that Brian McPhelim had intended to entrap one of the queen's soldiers, Captain Nicholas Malby, by inviting him to a banquet at which he would be surprised and murdered; instead, Essex performed the same ruse on McPhelim, and reported to the Privy Council in November 1574 that he had surprised McPhelim, his wife and his brother at a feast, and had put to the sword two hundred of his chief retainers, including fifty of his finest horsemen. Essex removed McPhelim, his wife and his brother to prison in Dublin, where they were eventually tried for treason and executed. Here we see the same motifs as before: a barbarous practice plotted by the Irish against the English, then turned with manifest hypocrisy on the perpetrators, crowned by a feast at which men are not fed, but eaten. The ill-fated history of the Ards plantation provides in the events of 1573–74 a distilled emblem of the customary, legal and social-anthropological assumptions that tied warring to eating throughout the course of Elizabeth's Irish wars. These events also illustrate in acute relief the hypocrisy and violence of an increasingly open-handed Machiavellian policy in English government – a pigment that, as we will see, deeply dyes Shakespeare's representation of war on the English stage.

Epic Dog Food

Many of the historical sources in which the Elizabethan Irish colonial project was recorded – including political and military treatises such as Spenser's *View* – were composed in succeeding decades, and reflect a slightly later turn in English historiography and political theory towards Tacitism. Cornelius Tacitus' *Annales* and his *Life of Agricola* offered his Renaissance imitators a pithy, aphoristic account of the reigns of two of the most brutal of Rome's emperors, Claudius and Nero: a blueprint both for would-be tyrants and for the men who desired to prosper – or at least survive – under their government. The influence of Tacitus' historiography on Elizabethan political theory and practice has traditionally been traced to a small group of Oxford intellectuals in the early 1580s, and through their influence to Robert Devereux, second earl of Essex.[29] At the centre of this group was Henry Cuffe, later one of Essex's

actions and designs, submitted to the Council in Westminster to justify his apprehension and summary execution in Dublin.
29   The group in Oxford included Henry Cuffe, Jean Hotman and Thomas

secretaries, who despite the fact that he did not participate in Essex's 'revolt' in August 1601, was held to be a major instigator of the earl's rebellion and was accordingly executed.[30] But in fact the importance of Tacitean historiography to English intellectual life goes back much further, for Tacitus' histories had exerted a major influence on Francesco Guicciardini, whose *Historie of . . . the Warres of Italie* (written 1537–40, first published 1561) was translated into English by the Secretary of State in Ireland, Geoffrey Fenton, in 1579.[31] Fenton knew Spenser well; both men married into the family of Sir Richard Boyle, later first earl of Cork, having worked closely in the Dublin administration between 1580 and 1582. Tacitus and Guicciardini are also frequently cited in – and their names appear regularly in the margins of – Sir William Herbert's *Croftus, sive de Hibernia Liber* of 1594, along with that pre-eminent expositor and synthesist of Tacitean political philosophy, Justus Lipsius.[32] Writers on Irish affairs during this period, then, were eager to demonstrate their knowledge of and commitment to Tacitean political and military precepts, especially as the 1590s wore on. This emphasis in their work was almost certainly a response to the rising star of the earl of Essex, whose anticipated influence in Ireland and Irish affairs was overwhelming during this period, and whose Tacitean credentials were strong. Sir Henry Savile's 1591 translation of Tacitus' *Annales*, with the *Life of Agricola*, included a prefatory letter to the reader by one 'A.B.',

Savile; their correspondence with William Camden, in London, and their later influence on Savile's brother Sir Henry Savile, on Francis Bacon and on the playwright John Hayward, created a vigorous group of Tacitean enthusiasts around Essex in the 1590s. See F. J. Levy, *Tudor Historical Thought* (San Marino, Calif., 1967), 251.

30   On Cuffe's Tacitism, see Alan Stewart, 'Instigating Treason: The Life and Death of Henry Cuffe, Secretary', in *Literature, Politics and Law in Renaissance England*, ed. Erica Sheen and Lorna Hutson (Basingstoke, 2005), 50–70.

31   On Guicciardini's reception and transmission of Tacitean 'politic history', see Alexandra Gajda, 'Tacitus and Political Thought in early modern Europe, c.1530–1640', in *The Cambridge Companion to Tacitus*, ed. A. J. Woodman (Cambridge, 2010), 253–68; and T. J. Luce and A. J. Woodman, *Tacitus and the Tacitean Tradition* (Princeton, 1993).

32   The Dutch humanist scholar Justus Lipsius edited and published the first complete text of Tacitus' works in Antwerp in 1574; his *Politicorum sive civilis doctrinae libri sex*, based heavily on Tacitus' writings, appeared in 1589, and was translated into English by William Jones as *Six bookes of politickes or ciuil doctrine* (London, 1594).

praising Tacitus, now widely thought to have been written by Essex himself.[33]

From Tacitus Spenser and his contemporaries derived several of their most distinctive rhetorical strategies in the analysis of the military and political landscape of early modern Ireland. For example, the representation of the state as the body of a diseased patient, as I have noted, is a recurrent feature of A View of the Present State of Ireland, one that enables Spenser to present and justify sometimes extreme, violent remedies. The first aphorism in Guicciardini's Avvertimenti, translated by Robert Dallington as the Aphorismes, Civil and Militarie (1613), delivers the Tacitean precept:

> In naturall bodies, the longer they subsist in perfect health, the more dangerous is the disease when it cometh, and the longer in curing; as hauing none of those humours spent, which by distemper giue foment and force to the approaching maladie. So it is in bodies politicke: when warre once seizeth vpon a countrey, rich in the plenties of a long peace, and full with the surfets of a continuall ease; it neuer leaues purging those superfluities, till all be wasted and consumed.[34]

From Tacitus, too, derived many of the aphorisms collected in Robert Hitchcock's 1590 translation of Francesco Sansovino's 1578 Concetti politici, the Quintessence of Wit.[35] This compendium of shrewd observations includes a well-known maxim on the justification of war – that 'that warre is iust that is necessarye, and those armes and weapons are godly and happye, in the which there resteth no other hope then in the said weapons and armes'.[36] The equation of justice with necessity, a hallmark of the Tacitean political theory that dominated the earl

33 Cornelius Tacitus, The Ende of Nero and Beginning of Galba (Oxford and London, 1591). On Essex's alleged involvement, see Levy, Tudor Historical Thought, 251.

34 Francesco Guicciardini, Aphorismes Civill and Militarie, trans. Robert Dallington (London, 1613), 1.

35 Sansovino's compendium of aphorisms contained a large amount of material derived directly and indirectly from Tacitus; see Vincent Luciani, 'Ralegh's Cabinet Council and Guicciardini's Aphorisms', Studies in Philology 46 (1949), 20–30, esp. 20–1. After translating Sansovino, Hitchcock completed and published his friend William Garrard's The Arte of Warre (London, 1591), including a dedication from the author to the earl of Essex.

36 Robert Hitchcock, The Quintessence of Wit (London, 1590), f. 5r.

of Essex's circle during the 1590s, led to the close collocation of the rhetoric of feasting and fighting in the work of historians and theorists who adopted the Tacitean perspective – such as the long passages in Guicciardini's *Historie . . . of the Warres of Italie* in which he narrates the various outrages committed on the states of northern Italy, and particularly upon Milan, during the French and Spanish campaigns of the early sixteenth century.[37] To save the body's health, food could be taken; to save the life of the state, war might be waged. As Leontes implies at the end of *The Winter's Tale*, there is nothing so fundamentally lawful – because fundamentally necessary – as eating.

The Tacitean political theory of Guicciardini, Lipsius, Sansovino and their English translators formed one route by which – through the influence of the Essex circle – the discourse of eating and war found its way into treatises on Ireland, and contemporary English writing on war and politics. But the Essex circle also had another reason for linking war to eating: a cultivation of heroic chivalry deriving from the epic tradition epitomised by Homer's *Iliad*.[38] The contamination of the early modern discourse of war by the alimentary metaphor had its roots in the literature of classical antiquity; brought up in English humanist grammar schools, soldier-poets, civil servants and gentlemen naturally adopted the rhetorical *habitus*, along with many of the ideological assumptions, of the Greek and Latin historians and epic poets whom as children they had studied. The *Iliad* frequently conflates eating and fighting to produce vivid descriptions of battle. The most conventional examples appear in Homer's epic similes, in which various heroes are regularly compared to lions or dogs hunting and

37 Typical of the French armies' disorders, for example, was the near famine of spring 1527, in which the duke of Bourbon's forces began to 'eate and deuour the contrie, and in that wretched insolencie they ranne into all places robbing both man and beast the better to furnish them of meanes to pay for their vittells' (Guicciardini, *Historie*, trans. Fenton, 1047). Guicciardini's constant references to the armies' appetite for and supply of food, money, and pillage reduces the history of the wars to a catalogue of carnal urges.

38 The intersection of Tacitean politic history and Homeric honour in the Essex circle was first described by Mervyn James in his famous essay on the Essex revolt in *Society, Politics and Culture: Studies in Early Modern England* (Cambridge, 1986), 416–65; 437. George Chapman dedicated to Essex his earliest English translations of the *Iliad* in 1598, calling Essex himself an English Achilles.

devouring their quarry. A typical example is this from the third book of the poem, where Menelaus believes he has cornered Paris:

> But when Menelaus, dear to Ares, was ware of him as he came forth before the throng with long strides, then even as a lion is glad when he lighteth on a great carcase [μεγάλῳ ἐπὶ σώματι], having found a horned stag or a wild goat when he is hungry; for greedily doth he devour it [μάλα γάρ τε κατεσθίει], even though swift dogs and lusty youths set upon him: even so was Menelaus glad when his eyes beheld godlike Alexander; for he thought that he had gotten him vengeance on the sinner.[39]

Most striking in this example is the way Homer's formulation of the simile stresses not the hunt – a natural parallel for the heat and violence of battle – but the feeding that follows it. The lion is not here a hunter, but a scavenger, a predator that falls fortuitously upon a dead carcase – for σῶμα, Homer's word here for the kill, always refers in both the *Iliad* and the *Odyssey* to the *dead* body of man or beast, that is, a corpse. Moreover, the ingestion of the stag or goat, in the simile, lies parallel not to a violent encounter between the two heroes, but to Menelaus' joy at finding his enemy before him; he feasts with his eyes. Finally, Homer here uses the verb κατεσθιεῖν, 'to devour', a verb to which he turns again when describing Achilles' attack on the Trojans after the death of Patroclus: 'he smote and smote [. . .] for greedily doth he devour [κατεσθίει] whatsoever one he catcheth' (*Iliad*, XXI, 20–4). Greek and Trojan heroes are like animals; when they get really cross, they *are* animals, and they feed on their victims. Homer repeats similes of this type, with light variations, in his description of Sarpedon's attack on the Achaeans (*Iliad*, XII, 290–308) and in his account of Hector's victory over Patroclus (*Iliad*, XVI, 823–8).

The *Iliad* conflates eating with fighting in two other ways, two recurrent patterns that have important echoes in English renaissance literature and particularly in the works of Shakespeare. First, feasting and banqueting are regularly invoked as the negative corollary to fighting; a Greek warrior can enjoy his heroic reputation in peacetime and, in a sense, 'spend' his greatness in the receipt of lavish honours and resources, but only on condition that he be ready, in time of war,

---

39   Homer, *Iliad*, trans. A. T. Murray (Cambridge, Mass., 1924), 3.21–9. Further references will be given parenthetically by book and line number.

to dedicate or even consecrate his life to the fortunes of the war. For this reason, Homer frequently gives his generals hortatory speeches in which they exclaim on the past pleasures of eating and drinking. So Agamemnon encourages Menestheus and Odysseus in Book IV of the poem, saying,

> O son of Peteos, the king nurtured of Zeus, and thou that excellest in evil wiles, thou of crafty mind, why stand ye apart cowering, and wait for others? For you twain were it seemly that ye take your stand amid the foremost, and confront blazing battle; for ye are the first to hear my bidding to the feast, whenso we Achaeans make ready a banquet for the elders. Then are ye glad to eat roast meat and drink cups of honey-sweet wine as long as ye will. But now would ye gladly behold it, aye if ten serried battalions of the Achaeans were to fight in front of you with the pitiless bronze. [IV, 339–48]

So too Sarpedon addresses Glaucus in Book XII of the *Iliad*, reminding him that they are 'held in honour above all with seats, and messes, and full cups in Lycia' (XII, 310–11). In these passages fighting in battle becomes a double for the consumption of food and drink in peacetime banquets; the honour accrued on the plain can be enjoyed in the hall, even as the honour enjoyed in the hall must be purchased on the plain. But this is no zero-sum transaction, for both feasting and fighting tend to produce dignity, and the Greek hero finds himself as ennobled and particularised in scenes of festal celebration as he does on the banks of Scamander. Here, as in the epic similes that recur throughout the *Iliad* and the *Odyssey*, as in Virgil's imitation of Homer in the *Aeneid*, the poet's recourse to imagery of food and consumption serves to dignify the feeder.

Sixteenth-century English literary writers on war ably emulated this convention. For Protestant English soldiers such as Thomas Churchyard and Barnaby Rich, peace was the mother not only of plenty, but of vice and luxury, while war like a refining fire purged all excess. Churchyard, commending Rich's 1578 *Allarme to England*, writes that 'peace prowlls a bowtt for pence, and warrs the mock wyll spend | that gredy gayn hords vp in hoells, god knoes to lyttell end'. The correlative relation establishes the price of honour as the destruction of vicious pleasures:

> [P]eace fills the land wyth pomp, thatt gyvs a pruey wownd
> feeds folly fatt, maeks vertue lean, and floeds off vyce a bownd,
> Daem lust her pleasuer taeks, in peace and banketts sweett

and warrs doth quenche owr hott desyers, and dawntts the dallyng
   spreete
in warrs we honor wyn, on peace reprootch doth groe
and warrs contentts owr noblest frynds, and peace doth pleas owr
   foe.[40]

Rich's prose emphasises even more strongly how the luxury and degen-
eracy of peacetime ought to be resisted by Protestant, epic aspirants:
'[P]eace is the most greatest and the most detestable enormitie that of
al others may happen, and amongst Christians most to be abhorred: for
peace is the nourisher of vices, the roote of euils, the proppe of pride,
and to be short, it is the mother of al mischiefes.' If we hadn't registered
the lurking evil of Hebrews 12:6, eventually Rich displays it altogether
openly: 'what greater argument may there be of the displeasure of God,
then where he sendeth amongst them such peace and quietnes? for as
the scriptures witnesse, Whom he loueth, them he chastiseth.'[41]

    It is quite otherwise in Homer's other, most conspicuous use of this
trope. More or less the entirety of the *Iliad* is built around the anger of
Achilles, which concludes in the total humiliation he imposes on his
great rival, Hector. The culmination and emblem of Achilles' unassuage-
able wrath comes after Hector's death, in his refusal to release Hector's
body to his family and city for honourable burial. The threat to Hector's
dignity and heroic particularity here is severe: should Achilles succeed
in degrading his corpse, refusing him honourable burial, Hector's heroic
identity, like his unanointed *sarkos*, will disintegrate; along with it, the
honour of his house and city will suffer and decay. Agamemnon encourages the Greek warriors during the battle of Book IV, promising them
that they will defeat their Trojan adversaries and 'their tender flesh of a
surety shall vultures devour' (IV, 237). Similarly, Odysseus gloats over
the body of Socus in Book XI, saying, 'Ah poor wretch, thy father and
queenly mother shall not close thine eyes in death, but the birds that
eat raw flesh shall rend thee, beating their wings thick and fast about
thee; whereas to me, if I die, the goodly Achaeans shall give burial' (XI,
452–5). Passages such as these establish the importance of the transition in the *Iliad* from the dignity of banqueting to the indignity of be-

---

40 'Thomas Churchyard Gentleman, in Commendation of this Worke', in
Barnabe Rich, *Allarme to England foreshewing what Perilles are Procured, Where
the People Liue without Regarde of Martiall Lawe* (London, 1578), sig *1v.
41   Rich, *Allarme to England*, sig. B4v–C1r.

ing fed upon. Homer's consistent representation of the indispensability of the burial rite for the conservation of family honour – an enduring feature of representations of Greek antiquity, as in Sophocles' *Antigone* – is more than a simple observation of archaic social practices; the link between the suspension of the rite and the eating of the body by scavengers is emphatic, more akin to a motif of ring composition. By the time Hector is preparing to sally out against Achilles in Book XXII, the wording of Hecuba's plea seems inevitable. Of Achilles she tells her son: 'Cruel is he; for if so be he slay thee, never shall I lay thee on a bier and bewail thee, dear plant, born of mine own self, nay, nor shall thy bounteous wife; but far away from us by the ships of the Argives shall swift dogs devour thee' (XXII, 86–9). Hector's subsequent plea, at his death, that Achilles should treat his body honourably, the Greek hero meets with scorn and a turn to cannibalism familiar from Spenser's account of the sixteenth-century Irish wars:

> 'Implore me not, dog, by knees or parents. Would that in any wise wrath and fury might bid me carve thy flesh and myself eat it raw, because of what thou hast wrought, as surely as there lives no man that shall ward off the dogs from thy head; nay, not though they should bring hither and weigh out ransom ten-fold, aye, twenty-fold, and should promise yet more; nay, not though Priam, son of Dardanus, should bid pay thy weight in gold; not even so shall thy queenly mother lay thee on a bier and make lament for thee, the son herself did bear, but dogs and birds shall devour thee utterly.' [XXII, 345–54]

No price will meet Achilles' determination to degrade Hector's body, which is more valuable to him to waste than it is to ransom. For the Greek hero in his revenge, his own dignity and immortal fame must survive through the degradation of his enemy; he must eat, and Hector must be eaten. That the poem ultimately evades the full implementation of this dyadic logic – the gods miraculously preserve Hector's body intact, despite Achilles' depraved antics, just as the poem preserves Hector's fame – provokes a question about the relationship of the first two words of the poem, μῆνιν ἄειδε, 'sing the wrath': can Achilles' passionate imperative, the consumption, degradation and total annihilation of Hector, ever be made consistent with the poem's aesthetic balance, the need to preserve Hector in order to preserve Achilles? Achilles, the paradigmatic universal wolf, does not care that the destruction of Hector will also annihilate him, and in that sense his passionate grief for Patroclus, and his self-destructive appetite for revenge, are antipathetic to the poem's

own immortalising mytho-historiographical project. At the centre of
this tension between passion and the aesthetic frame that represents it,
dogs and vultures feed; but, as Plato recognised and with great ardency
contested, Homer arrogates to the gods of his own poetic representation
the power to preserve Hector's body intact – that is, to salvage mimetic
by material integrity.

Cormorant War: Eating Men in Shakespeare's Plays

With these two contexts in mind – the historical and the literary – I
want to turn briefly to three observations about eating, war and material
degradation in Shakespeare's plays, before drawing some conclusions.
The first concerns Falstaff and trimming fat. Shakespeare is probably
closest to the Irish military context, and its discursive practices, in the
second tetralogy. These plays were written during the course of the
Nine Years' War in Ireland (1594–1603), a period of tense and violent
upheaval in Ireland, and especially in Ulster, during which the Privy
Council regularly expected a Spanish invasion, through Ireland, that
only materialised belatedly, and weakly. With this in mind, it is not
surprising to find that the rebellious career of Henry Bolingbroke, in
Richard II, begins with the seizure of his patrimony at his father John
of Gaunt's death; this expropriation of the Lancastrian family's wealth
Richard attributes directly to the 'charge' of his 'great affairs' in the
'Irish wars' (2.1.156–63). It was standard practice for Tudor monarchs
to waste the estates of loyal but dangerously influential noblemen by
sending them to serve in Ireland; Lord Grey, like Croft and Sidney before him, considered his appointment a form of exile, and bitterly re-
monstrated with Sir Francis Walsingham over the queen's parsimony in
forcing him to bear the expense of office out of his own funds. By the
time Shakespeare reached *Henry V*, in 1599, Bolingbroke's rebellious
return from exile in *Richard II* looked transparently like a model for
Essex's planned triumphant return from Ireland. The political overtones
became so insistent that Shakespeare made an explicit identification
between the Lancastrian military heroes of the tetralogy and their new
incarnation in Essex: the civil wars narrated in this tetralogy conclude
– in the choric speech at the start of Act 5 of *Henry V* – with a proleptic
celebration of the earl of Essex's campaign against Tyrone in the Nine
Years' War, the return, 'from Ireland coming', of 'the General of our
gracious Empress' (5.0.29–35). The book-ending of the second tetralogy with references to Elizabeth's Irish wars only seems belatedly or in

retrospect to indicate the flourishing but ultimately abortive career of the earl of Essex. But there is no question that Shakespeare exploited his historical material to illustrate a political philosophy, rooted in the theatrical set-pieces of *1 Henry IV*, and developed in the openly Machiavellian politics of *2 Henry IV* and *Henry V*, very popular among the Essex circle.

Falstaff's participation in *2 Henry IV* thus offers Shakespeare the opportunity to engage in withering social satire, observations on the social effects of the ongoing wars in Ireland. Given Falstaff's corpulent material presence on stage, and the constant jibes and allusions made by all his companions, including Hal, that draw attention to his consumption of sack, butter and meat – the 'fat-guts' (2.2.31), that 'tun of man' (2.5.453), 'that trunk of humours, that bolting-hutch of beastliness, that swollen parcel of dropsies, that huge bombard of sack, that stuffed cloak-bag of guts, that roasted Manningtree ox with the pudding in his belly' (2.5.454–8) – he steps forward quite naturally as the focus for a sustained materialist deconstruction of Hal's theatrical and spectacular pretensions to chivalric nobility. This should be uncontentious and indeed fairly obvious; but I want to go slightly beyond the conventional account of Falstaff's role in the history plays – as a comic subplot, a distraction from the high chronicle material, his body a vehicle for imagining the popular history of England during the Wars of the Roses – to suggest that, while he is funny, while he is popular, while his voice energises and balances the Machiavellian rise to power of the usurping Bolingbroke's scheming son, it is his body, that which stands bloated and rippling before the audience, that gives the greatest lie to Hal's military and political rise. While Hal and Hotspur negotiate like pampered princelings over their 'titles' on the field at Shrewsbury (in 5.4), it is Falstaff's apparently dead corpse, lying a few paces away, which is the – nearly literal – elephant on the stage.

Falstaff is criticised in both the first and second parts of *Henry IV* for assembling inadequate bands of footmen, first for the battle at Shrewsbury, and in Part 2 for the battle intended at Shipton Moor. In *1 Henry IV*, Falstaff confesses to the poor quality of his men, saying that he originally conscripted only fat householders, knowing that they would bribe their way out of service, and now is left with nothing but beggars and diseased men:

[N]ow my whole charge consists of ensigns, corporals, lieutenants, gentlemen of companies – slaves as ragged as Lazarus in the painted cloth, where the glutton's dogs licked his sores – and such as indeed

were never soldiers, but discarded unjust servingmen, younger sons to
younger brothers, revolted tapsters, and ostlers trade-fallen, the can-
kers of a calm world and a long peace, ten times more dishonorable-
ragged than an old feazed ensign: and such have I to fill up the rooms
of them as have bought out their services, that you would think that
I had a hundred and fifty tattered prodigals lately come from swine-
keeping, from eating draff and husks. A mad fellow met me on the
way and told me I had unloaded all the gibbets and pressed the dead
bodies. No eye hath seen such scarecrows. [4.2.23–38]

Falstaff's band, in short, consists of men so diseased and reduced, so
starved and wasted, that they might be taken either for corpses, or for
the mere figures of men. The correlation of the fat glutton with the
spare soldiers draws attention to the unstable identity of the starving
poor – are they lean, or fat? Immediately after Falstaff's speech, Hal
enters, and has a predictable exchange with his gross earthly father:

PRINCE   I did never see such pitiful rascals.
FALSTAFF   Tut, tut, good enough to toss, food for powder, food for
     powder. They'll fill a pit as well as better. Tush, man, mortal men,
     mortal men. [4.2.64–7]

Falstaff's corpulent body in *1 Henry IV* acts as a visual emblem for the
gross material anxiety provoked by Hal's political and military agenda.
Hal's future has been and will be purchased by blood – Richard's,
Hotspur's, but also the blood of numberless – because insignificant and
thus illegible – soldiers. Their humanity must be degraded – stripped,
starved, gouged, cut off – and finally *fed to* the wars. By the time they
have become 'food for powder', they are things to fill a pit withal.
Shakespeare simply riffs on the theme in the second part. The men whom
Falstaff reviews for his band, with the help of Shallow and Silence, bear
names attesting to their material function in the consumption of the
wars: Bullcalf, Mouldy, Wart, Feeble and Shadow. Bullcalf the stocky
husbandman, and Mouldy the allegorical 'man of earth', purchase their
exception from Falstaff's impress. The insubstantial Feeble and Shadow
remain, along with Wart, a superfluous callosity that, according to the
chirurgical manuals of the early modern period, was generally 'cut off'.[42]

42   Peter Low numbers warts among things 'superfluous' that the chirurgeon
should 'take away': Low, *The Whole Course of Chirurgerie* (London, 1597), sig.

Left with Wart, Feeble and Shadow, Falstaff is criticised by his fellows for selecting only the leanest and unlikeliest men. His self-serving argument recapitulates his performance in Part 1: 'Care I for the limb, the thews, the stature, bulk, and big assemblance of a man? [. . .] O, give me the spare men, and spare me the great ones' (3.2.254–66). The pun on 'spare' – meaning 'lean', but also 'superfluous' – sets us right back in the paradox of material anxiety so typical of the discourse of war in this period: Falstaff might as well have said, give me the starving fat. War is a banquet, and the meagre poor must be served.

My second point is about vermiculation, and the king making his progress through the guts of a beggar. If the Henriad is closest to the discursive practices of the Elizabethan Irish wars, two plays from the turn of the seventeenth century are without doubt closest to the epic, and particularly the Homeric tradition. *Hamlet* features in its second act a long alleged quotation from Marlowe's *Dido Queen of Carthage*, in fact more of a parody; Marlowe's original is in turn based on Virgil's *Aeneid*, which takes its material from Homer.[43] The inset passage, concerning Pyrrhus' revenge on Priam for the death of Achilles, echoes the epic heroic frame in which it appears, the revenge of Fortinbras on Denmark for the death of his father Fortinbras. *Troilus and Cressida*, like *Hamlet*, deals directly with the epic Homeric source, though it mingles it with Chaucer's romance narrative of the love of Troilus and Criseyde. Both of these plays are suffused with a disgusted fascination with the human body. Hamlet is fixated on his father's tettered corpse, his mother's degenerate sexuality, and his uncle's ambering eyes and weak hams. The language of *Troilus and Cressida*, like that of many of Shakespeare's plays, is preoccupied with venereal and other diseases, but also with blood, bile, phlegm; with the vilia, the sinews and muscles; and with wounds, tumours and fluent sores. The entire structure of *Hamlet*, as I have already remarked, is built around the opposition of Claudius' drunken carousing and Hamlet's fatness, on the one hand, and Fortinbras' lean and hungry epic action, on the other – a dyad with which Shakespeare had also recently structured the menace of Cassius' conspiracy against Caesar (*Julius Caesar*, 1.2.193–6). Shakespeare takes pains to link this

---

B2v. Thomas Vicary, in *The English-Mans Treasure* (London, 1641), also calls warts 'superfluous' (2), and instructs the chirurgeon 'with a paire of Sizers [to] cut off the heads of the Warts' (199).

43   The passage in *Hamlet* (2.2.453–521) echoes the long narration of Aeneas' escape from Troy in *Dido Queen of Carthage* (2.1.106–299, esp. 221–64).

opposition in *Hamlet* directly to its Homeric original, not only in the Player's Pyrrhus speech, but at moments like this one from the 'eggshell' soliloquy. As Hamlet contemplates Fortinbras' army, ostensibly on its way to fight a pointless campaign in Poland, he compares himself unfavourably to his rival:

HAMLET   How all occasions do inform against me
   And spur my dull revenge! What is a man
   If the chief good and market of his time
   Be but to sleep and feed? – a beast, no more.
   Sure, he that made us with such large discourse,
   Looking before and after, gave us not
   That capability and god-like reason
   To fust in us unused. [Q2, 4.4.*23–30]

Hamlet exclaims against the bestial in humanity, against the appetites and limitations that separate us from the divine. It is curious that at this moment Shakespeare should cop a phrase from Homer. 'Looking before and after' is a distinctively Homeric phrase, the direct English translation of ὅρα πρόσσω καὶ ὀπίσσω [*hora prossō kai opissō*]; this phrase occurs three times in Homer's *Iliad*, and most saliently in Book XVIII of the poem, where the Trojan leaders Hector and Polydamas both offer their counsel about how to respond to Achilles' return to the Greek army. The original passage in the *Iliad* stresses that Polydamas and Hector are to be considered equals, even two members of a pair, for they were born on the same night; 'howbeit in speech was one far the best, the other with the spear' (*Iliad*, XVIII, 252). Polydamas counsels the Trojans against open engagement with an enemy as dangerous as Achilles; Hector, ever honourable, urges them back out into the field. The parallel with *Hamlet* is striking, especially considering Shakespeare's repetition of the phrase 'looking before and after' – a phrase that exists in nothing like this formula in the standard sixteenth-century French translation of the *Iliad*, or in the version that, around the turn of the century, George Chapman was composing.[44] As Hamlet stands watch-

---

44   Cf. *Les XXIIII. livres de l'Iliade d'Homere, prince des poëtes Grecs*, traduicts par M. Hugues Salel et Amadis Iamyn (Paris, 1580), f. 308v:
Le bon Polydamas à parler commença
Au milieu du conseil selon ce qu'il pensa
Car seul il entendoit les choses ia passees

ing his martial double lead an army to certain, heroic death in Poland (as he speculates), his self-castigation, complete with Homeric echoes, is complete: Fortinbras' wasty-wasting men go to fill up a hole in the ground, while Hamlet sits safely immured at home, worrying about how to live for ever.

Hamlet's preoccupation with the material body in Act 5 of the play is well known, and especially his anxiety over the reduction of the great Macedonian general Alexander to a lump of clay that might stop a bunghole. But in his musings on vermiculation, when describing the decomposing body of Polonius, he comes close to the lexis of feeding that also flares, suddenly and jarringly, in the 'baked and impasted' streets of Troy through which Pyrrhus runs after his murder of Priam (2.2.462). Hamlet's quip to Claudius after Polonius' murder, that the king will find the 'unseen good old man', now dead, 'at supper', leads him to qualify his statement in a suggestive way: 'not where he eats, but where a is eaten' (4.1.11, 4.3.18–20). The man who would feed in quiet here becomes fed upon; this phrase constellates the various points of anxiety throughout the play over dead men and women not afforded decent burial: old Hamlet, who has burst his cerements; the men led by Fortinbras, who fight for a piece of ground in Poland that is *not* tomb and continent enough to hide the slain; Ophelia, who nearly cannot be buried in hallowed ground, and whose body is displaced from its grave by the antics of her blowhard brother and the prolix prince; and, finally, Hamlet himself, the full fate of whose body the play does not disclose. Behind them all, perhaps, lurks the fate of the Polonius figure in the original Amlethi narrative, by Saxo Grammaticus, preserved by François Belleforest in his *Histoires Tragiques*: cut into pieces, cast into the privy and fed to the hogs.

The degradation to which Hamlet submits Polonius in *Hamlet* is abstracted in *Troilus and Cressida* into a quasi-allegorical function, again intimately tied to Homer's construction of the *Iliad*, and embodied in the figure of Thersites. In a world freed from the distinctions of rank, warns Ulysses in the play's second scene, appetite will, like a 'universal wolf', consume all things, and at last turn its jaws upon itself. In both the love plot between Troilus and Cressida, and the war between the Trojans and Greeks, just such a loss of distinction transpires. The

Et les autres voyoit qui n'estoient commencees.
Chapman probably hadn't got this far with his translation by 1604; but in any case, his language is nothing like.

war is supposed to demonstrate the comparative value of Achilles and Ajax, and to that end Nestor and Ulysses devise a scheme, and sell it to Agamemnon at the start of the play: the Greeks will seem to pre-fer Ajax, suspecting that Achilles, goaded to competition, will prove himself the better man. In fact neither Ajax nor Achilles learns any-thing of the kind: Ajax never fights with Hector, and Achilles sets his Myrmidons upon the disadvantaged Hector in an ignominious ambush. The agent of this cynical (that is, 'dog-like') deconstruction of the epic ideal is the 'dog', the 'cur' Thersites, whom Agamemnon notes at the beginning of the play for his 'mastic jaws'. The slow 'digestion' of the 'cormorant war' is meant to reduce, sift and bolt the various excellences of the Greek and Trojan heroes, distinguishing them from one another as Pandarus fails to do in the second scene of the play. This is what the word 'digestion' seems to promise: not a blending or mingling, but a separation or division of the ingested nourishment into its constituent elements. Instead, the play confounds and diminishes them all. In both *Hamlet* and *Troilus and Cressida*, heroes are served to the mastic jaws of scavengers.

The critical term of *Troilus and Cressida*, 'distinction', also struc-tures the thought of one of Shakespeare's latest plays, *Coriolanus*. As in *Troilus and Cressida* (1.1.13–26), one of the central images of this play is the winnowing of wheat, ready for baking and consuming. Menenius Agrippa, whose fable of the belly in the opening scene of the play calms the mutinous, starving plebeians, says of Caius Martius:

MENENIUS   Consider this: he has been bred i' th' wars
    Since a could draw a sword, and is ill-schooled
    In bolted language. Meal and bran together
    He throws without distinction. Give me leave,
    I'll go to him and undertake to bring him
    Where he shall answer by a lawful form,
    In peace, to his utmost peril. [3.1.322–8]

This metaphor only extends the use of 'chaff' and 'bran' elsewhere in the play (e.g. 1.1.146, 5.1.26–31). Martius is incapable of distinction; as he shows in scene after scene, he cannot moderate his behaviour decorously, appealing to distinct audiences. His lack of decorum leads the tribunes to call, in the same scene, for a flattening of the social and political order, a revolution that Coriolanus himself says will 'bring the roof to the foundation, | And bury all which yet distinctly ranges | In heaps and piles of ruin' (3.1.203–6). This play has no end of war, but unlike the plays of the *Henriad*, *Hamlet* and *Troilus and Cressida*, it has no eating – for not only do the plebeians starve, but Martius himself does not eat, cannot sift or digest. The principle of digestion – the process of sifting that places like with like – remains anathema to a soldier and a Roman who resists the very concept and operation of similitude. He is not only unlikeable, but absolutely singular, *un*like any other. Indeed, when Coriolanus is banished, and goes to take his leave of his mother and friends, Volumnia encourages him to 'determine on some course | More than a wild exposure to each chance | That stands i'th' way before thee' (4.1.36–8); Coriolanus' response is chilling, telling them only that they shall hear of him, 'and never of me aught | But what is like me formerly' (4.1.53–4). Coriolanus names himself. What is he like? Himself. How best can his triumphs be honoured? As Menenius says, 'with honours like himself' (2.2.48). His mother's final triumph over him, at the end of the play, she effects by a simple comparison, a rehearsal of likeness, between Martius and his son, which he is unable to deny – 'this child', she says, is 'like him by chance'. The audience is reminded here of the earlier, at the time apparently inconsequential, moment in Act 1, scene 3, when Volumnia and Virgilia listened to Valeria recounting how young Martius had tortured and killed a butterfly (1.3.59–68). Again and again he pursued its erratic and unpredictable movement, its flight unlike anything in the world – unlike anything except the boy, that is, who could follow it with such precision that he caught it every time. That boy, the master of chance, in 'one on's father's moods', shows that likeness *must* prevail over chance, or Coriolanus cannot be like himself – the hunter of the lion Aufidius, for example. As he dies, it is no wonder that the play makes reference to his son's exploits with the butterfly, in one of Shakespeare's typically occult verbal allusions:

CORIOLANUS   Cut me to pieces, Volsces. Men and lads,
    Stain all your edges on me. 'Boy'! false hound,
    If you have writ your annals true, 'tis there,
    That, like an eagle in a dove-cote, I
    Flutter'd your Volscians in Corioles.
    Alone I did it. 'Boy'! [5.6.112–17]

This is the only time in all his plays that Shakespeare uses the word 'flutter'; whatever it is that this eagle does to these doves – the best the *OED* can suggest is 'throw into confusion, agitation' – when it flutters them it is certainly not eating them. The resistance to eating in

Coriolanus offers its protagonist, until the final scenes, the possibility that he might escape the material degradation, the public performance of attrition, wasting and dismemberment to which every other warring figure in Shakespeare is eventually subject. But sifting and sorting – digestion – catch up with Coriolanus in the end.

In closing, I want to suggest that consumption and material degradation, in Shakespeare's plays about war, tend to consort in his language and scene construction with another kind of degradation, *mimesis* itself. There are intimations in various of Shakespeare's plays, where the language of ingestion and digestion emerges, that he recognised a parallel between those two universal wolves, war and the theatre, and intimations too of a complicity between his theatrical practice and the ideological operations that made the material degradation of war both possible and fashionable. As Beatrice pointed out, Benedick's claims to kill and eat, to imitate Achilles, were always in bad faith. His mimesis was only the figure of a hero. In every one of the plays I have considered here, the protagonist fears something worse than the material degradation of the battlefield, and that is the mimetic degradation of the playhouse. Hamlet writes his own play to avoid misrepresentation, though Fortinbras causes his corpse to be borne to the stage (5.2.349–52); Ulysses, Nestor and Agamemnon plot against Achilles because of his theatrical parodies of their rank and status (1.3.142–84); Falstaff and Hal debunk Hotspur's pretensions to heroic valour in their elaborate skits and set-pieces (*1 Henry IV*, 2.5); even Coriolanus cannot bear the public performance, the civic theatre of his bid to become consul.[45] The reduction of the material, embodied identity to the persona, the name, the mask, represents the final stage in the deconstruction of heroic in-

45 Coriolanus' anxiety about the theatre, acting or playing, the scene, and its 'monstering', surfaces at several points during the play, most obviously when, after having sought the 'voices' of the plebeians and suffered the tribunes' condemnation, he reproaches Volumnia: 'Why did you wish me milder? Would you have me | False to my nature? Rather say I play | The man I am.' (3.2.13–15) It is important that, when his wife and mother approach him outside Rome's walls in the final act, he imagines their petition as an emasculating theatrical spectacle, saying to Virgilia, 'Like a dull actor now | I have forgot my part, and I am out | Even to a full disgrace' (5.3.39–41), and to Volumnia, 'The gods look down, and this unnatural scene | They laugh at' (5.3.185–6). Cominius once said of Coriolanus (at 2.2.96) that as a child gone to war, Martius proved a man even 'when he might act the woman in the scene'; as the play closes, he finally does just that.

tegrity. Beside Falstaff's corpulent bulk, as he exits the stage in *2 Henry IV*, walk Wart and Feeble, but also Shadow – the player.

I want to suggest, then, that Shakespeare's recurrent coordination of material and mimetic degradation acts to align his theatrical representations with the ideological operations of a text such as Spenser's *View*. Shakespeare's representation of war developed in the shadow cast by English anti-theatrical polemic such as Stephen Gosson's *Schoole of Abuse* (1579), which had first posited a binary relationship between play-going effeminacy and manly militarism, an opposition between the buskin and the buckler;[46] Shakespeare's figuration of the theatre's ideological operation may not so much resist Gosson's attack, as embrace with Tacitean shrewdness the theatre's social function, in a much stronger sympathy with war's cormorant mouth than even Gosson had allowed. Perhaps the most articulate contemporary witness of this Tacitean potential is Thomas Nashe, who in his satirical romp *Piers Penilesse His Supplication to the Diuell* (1592) delivers a backhanded defence of the theatre in just these terms:

> That State or Kingdome that is in league with all the world, and hath no forraine sword to vexe it, is not halfe so strong or confirmed to endure, as that which liues euery houre in feare of inuasion. There is a certaine waste of the people for whome there is no vse, but warre: and these men must haue some employment still to cut them off. *Nam si foras hostem non habent, domi inuenient.* If they haue no seruice abroad, they will make mutinies at home. Or if the affayres of the State be such, as cannot exhale all these corrupt excrements, it is very expedient they haue some light toyes to busie their heads withall, cast before them as bones to gnaw vpon, which may keepe them from hauing leisure to intermeddle with higher matters.
>
> To this effect, the pollicie of Playes is very necessary, howsoeuer some shallow-braind censurers (not the deepest serchers into the secrets of gouernment) mightily oppugne them.[47]

If the term 'pollicie' is not enough to tip us off, Nashe makes explicit the connection to Tacitean political theory when he argues that plays consume rebellious and martial energies; 'read *Lipsius* or any prophane or

46   Stephen Gosson, *The Schoole of Abuse* (London, 1579).
47   Thomas Nashe, *Piers Penilesse His Supplication to the Diuell*, in *The Works of Thomas Nashe*, ed. Ronald B. McKerrow, 5 vols. (Oxford, 1966), I, 211–12.

Christian Polititian, and you shall finde him of this opinion.'[48] Indeed, Nashe might well have been thinking not of Lipsius, but of Tacitus' *Life of Agricola*, which recalls the 'Polititian' Agricola's use of luxury and vice to subdue the ancient Britons:

> For whereas the Britans were rude and dispersed, and therefore prone vpon euery occasion to warre, to induce them by pleasures to quietnesse and rest, he exhorted them in priuate and helpt them in common to builde temples, and houses, and places of publicke resort, commending the forward and checking the slow, imposing thereby a kinde of necessitie vpon them, whilest ech man contended to gaine the Lieutenants goodwill [. . .] After that our attire grewe to be in account, and the Gowne much vsed among them: and so by little and little they proceeded to those prouocations of vices, to sumptuous galleries, and bathes, and exquisite banquettings; which things the ignorant termed ciuilitie, being indeede a point of their bondage.[49]

Much has been made by critics, over the centuries, of Shakespeare's invention of the human, his creation of modern subjectivity, his early witness of a new kind of selfhood and consciousness.[50] For Shakespeare's historical subjects, as Cleopatra knows, the real self was in the grave; Shakespeare's plays draw forth the names from their tombs, and make them act. And how easy it is to kill a name, to 'cut off' that which has already been degraded! Shakespeare may have invented the human; but the human of his invention always threatens to shrink up, into that pale, wasted shadow of vigour once scorned by Plato's *Republic* – precisely because, *pace* Plato, it has been stripped of its living sinew and bulk. This is politic theatre, dog theatre: a theatre that eats the human.

48   Nashe, *Piers Penilesse*, 215.
49   Cornelius Tacitus, *The Life of Iulius Agricola*, in *The Ende of Nero and Beginning of Galba*, trans. Sir Henry Savile, 2nd edn (London, 1598), 192–3.
50   The obvious example is Harold Bloom's *Shakespeare: The Invention of the Human* (New York, 1998); other, often more rigorously historical, studies of Shakespeare and early modern 'subjectivity' or 'interiority' include Joel Fineman, *Shakespeare's Perjured Eye* (Berkeley, 1986) and John Lee, *Shakespeare's 'Hamlet' and the Controversies of Self* (Oxford, 2000).

Unnavigable Kinship in a Time of Conflict: Loyalist Calligraphies, Sovereign Power and the 'Muckle Honor' of Elizabeth Murray Inman

CAROL WATTS

[A] dark wall of rule supports the structure of every letter, record, transcript: every proof of authority and power. I know records are compiled by winners, and scholarship is in collusion with Civil Government. I know this and go searching for some trace of love's infolding through all the paper in all the libraries I come to.[1]

The Contest is not between Ministers and the Colonies, but between Parliament and the Colonies; and whichever of them conquers will be Sovereign Power.[2]

EXPLORING THE RECORDS of loyalist refugees during the American revolutionary war, I have wanted to understand their diverse forms of attachment to sovereign power, its insistence in lives often torn apart by conflict. It was a revolution experienced by many as a civil war, in which colonial Americans and their British kin discovered themselves internally divided, a felt set of betrayals and desires separating one from another, 'Bone of our Bone' in John Adams' words.[3] This was a war, as Dror Wahrman puts it, 'irreducible to any reliable map of "us" and "them" based on a stable criterion of difference',[4] and it rebounded in

---

1   Susan Howe, *The Birth-mark: Unsettling the Wilderness in American Literary History* (Middletown CT, 1993), 4.
2   John Mein to James Murray, London, 11 January 1775, *James Murray Robbins Family Papers*, MHS: MS N-801. Henceforth listed as letter date followed by MHS: JMR.
3   John Adams, letter dated 24 April 1773, referring to the 'vile Serpent' Thomas Hutchinson, quoted in Howe, *The Birth-mark*, 75.
4   Dror Wahrman, 'The English Problem of Identity in the American Revolution', *American Historical Review* 106 (2001), 1236–62: 1238.

America on every aspect of daily living, bonds and everyday certainties
suddenly opened to urgent question. What did it mean to be 'loyal', and
to whom, at the very point when the terms of sovereignty were being
transformed and divided into winners and losers? In what sense was
loyalism irreducible to the 'command expressions' that would come to
name it as history?[5] In what ways might accounts of change and transformation always already associated with radical positions – and revolutionary history – at times make the everyday practice of subjecthood
surfacing in these written documents unthinkable? If the study of loyalism is in part about the charting of a complex reaction-formation, it is
also concerned with forms of continual action, decision and brokerage
across the duration of individual lives, set running by events in multiple
and unintended ways.

　　The field of historical work on loyalism has expanded in recent years
with new research building on substantive phases of scholarship, producing a richly variegated and interstitial account of the movements
of those subjects who stayed loyal to the Crown, or found themselves
outside the terms of belonging determined by the emerging republic.[6]
With this research, often based on the contingencies of local biogra-
phies, loyalism emerges as a complex set of affective attachments. It existed as an ideological and principled commitment to Tory beliefs about
Church and state. It was also articulated within fluid forms of expedi-
ency that led for some to uncertain freedom (not least those thousands
of slaves who joined the British lines)[7] or imperial remaking across the
globe, for others to trials of reintegration on both sides of the Atlantic.

5　Howe, The Birth-mark, 3.
6　See Jerry Bannister and Liam Riordan, eds., The Loyal Atlantic: Remaking
the British Atlantic in the Revolutionary Era, 2nd edn (Toronto, 2012), for a sense
of the field and scope of loyalist studies, including Robert M. Calhoon's 'After-
word: Loyalist Cosmopolitanism', 277–85; Ruma Chopra, Unnatural Rebellion:
Loyalists in New York City during the Revolution (Charlottesville VA, 2011); Alan
Gilbert, Black Patriots and Loyalists: Fighting for Emancipation in the War of Independence (Chicago, 2012); Maya Jasanoff, Liberty's Exiles: The Loss of America
and the Remaking of the British Empire (London, 2011); Cassandra Pybus, Epic
Journeys of Freedom: Runaway Slaves of the American Revolution and Their Global
Quest for Liberty (Boston, Mass., 2006); Judith van Buskirk, Generous Enemies:
Patriots and Loyalists in Revolutionary New York (Philadelphia, 2002).
7　Thus setting in train the largest slave rebellion in American history, as
Gary B. Nash explores in The Forgotten Fifth: African Americans in the Age of
Revolution (Cambridge, Mass., 2006).

It could appear at once as a physical wiring of a self as seemingly fundamental as a drive or instinct, and as an external category conferred
because of economic or kinship affiliations and interests. Loyalism sur-
faced differently among men and women according to local histories,
regional ties, religious emphases, forms of subjection and class privilege.
If it is a term that brings together heterogeneous and sometimes con-
flicted identities, there are nonetheless experiences in common, forms
of wounded attachment[8] and solidarity, which might gave it shared
meaning. As Keith Mason has explored, the 'distinctive trajectory of
harassment, persecution, and, for many, exile' brought with it

> a series of social deaths and rebirths, a repeating circuit of dislocation
> and dismemberment, marked nevertheless by an unceasing desire to
> reconstitute the self through family, friends and community.[9]

Reading the records and the silences of archives as material symptoms
of such a culture during a period of armed insurrection and war is to ask
questions about the everyday experience of change at a time of the leak-
age of social and political power, and its violent realignment.

There seems something often curiously phantasmatic in the way
loyalists began to imagine their relation to an authority they could no
longer be certain of during this period of emergency. Love and violence
are imbricated here. Interpellation in such circumstances cuts to the
quick, demands allegiances and a signing up to tests. Rendered in scraps
of handwritten letters, deep in the archives, are scenes that suggest the
forces and desires at work in attachment to competing forms of authority. It is through these inscriptions, the imprint of particular hands, and
those of women in particular located outside the terms of political society, that I have begun to read the lineaments of attachment to sovereign power that was at this time splitting, undergoing a fundamental
reimagining. This involves a conceptual labour, which concerns the
thinking of sovereignty and subjectivation in a time of war. But it is
also a potential discovery of what is unspoken in these histories, caught

8   In the sense that woundedness or pain becomes the basis for social identity.
See Wendy Brown' s concept of wounded attachment in her *States of Injury:
Power and Freedom in Late Modernity* (Princeton, 1995).
9   Keith Mason, 'The American Loyalist Problem of Identity in the Revolutionary Atlantic World', in Bannister and Riordan, eds., *The Loyal Atlantic*,
39–74: 41.

in the very material gesture of the making of script, before it becomes writing as such – the way chance and the body come together in 'quick particularities of calligraphic expression', in Susan Howe's words.[10]

My work here pursues an experimental form of enquiry that moves towards and around such calligraphic moments. It is a beginning of a larger project, and provisional as such. Rather than exploring the debates among historians, I find an entry into the period of the revolutionary war as it is illuminated by the poetics of Susan Howe, her textual and material practice in the archive and engagement with the nature of its 'Sovreign Woods'.[11] In order to think the question of sovereign power and to grasp the intensity of political change in the early years of the revolution I will turn briefly to Antonio Negri's account of the moment when 'freedom assumes the form of a frontier' in the Boston of 1775–76.[12] The speed at which British-American loyalists became potentially stateless as a consequence – and thus, to use the words of Hannah Arendt, risked losing their 'political status in the struggle of [their] time'[13] – is also accompanied by their apparent rapid disappearance or evacuation from historical accounts of the progress and futurity of the state (whether republican or imperial) which such accounts work to legitimate. Part of the struggle in loyalist private records, I want to suggest, was to encounter and refuse the shock of their own sudden anachronism, against the tide of the times; yet in such dislocation was also a potential, for some even a freedom, loosed from traditional ties, to inhabit such a fundamental realignment – and their own social misrecognition – to new ends.

Two instances of loyalist script, both by Bostonians, allow me to test this ground and its relation to authority further. One is a spidery phrase – 'like a Thunder Clape' – from the letterbook of Henry Caner, in the record of a letter written in 1778.[14] Caner, then a highly connected

---

10   Howe, *The Birth-mark*, 4.

11   'And now We roam in Sovreign Woods': the line is from Emily Dickinson's poem 'My Life had stood – a Loaded Gun –', which is central to Howe's engagement with sovereignty in *The Birth-mark*, and in her *My Emily Dickinson* (Berkeley CA, 1985), 34.

12   Antonio Negri, *Insurgencies: Constituent Power and the Modern State*, trans. Maurizia Boscagli (Minneapolis and London, 1999), 146.

13   Hannah Arendt, *The Origins of Totalitarianism* (New York, 1973), 301.

14   Henry Caner to Deacon Thomas Foster, London, 10 January 1778, *Henry Caner Letterbook*, Bristol University Library. Henceforth listed as letter date followed by HCL. Thanks to Bristol University Special Collections for permission

Anglican clergyman in his seventies, had long worked and reported for the Society for the Propagation of the Gospel. He was Minister of King's Chapel in Boston from 1747 to his last service in 1776, and had held out hopes for the establishing of a bishopric in America. An evacuee who would end his days in Cardiff and Bristol, he was at this point still unsure about returning to his previous life, recording intermittent news of the 'insults and violence' meted out by 'misguided Zealots'.[15] He was, as he declared to the British government in hope of increasing his allowance, 'obnoxious to the Rebels'.[16] The second instance is a letter in the cursive hand of Elizabeth Murray Inman, which becomes notably gigantic as she writes. She was by this time a wealthy independent shopkeeper and Scottish emigrant, whose family connections and commercial links with Britain underlined her loyalist standing. She chose to remain, and writes late at night with her house under occupation by the patriot army in 1775. Before approaching these examples of loyalist record, the imprint of particular hands, however, it is necessary to take something of a route through 'Sovreign Woods'.

Pathfinding

At first glance Susan Howe's engagement with the archive might seem an unlikely route to the world of the Boston loyalists, since her distinctive account of New England history works through its buried antinomianism, the radical voices from the margins that were themselves put on trial and exiled by puritan law. Seventeenth-century New England figures such as Anne Hutchinson, whose belief in a doctrine of grace gave her unmediated relation to a revelation of God's authority and a means of resistance, are part of the same ground, Howe argues, that later produces the poet Emily Dickinson, and her roaming in a wilderness of 'Sovreign Woods'. It is a puritan inheritance, with its sense of the sinful freight of king-killing, that might seem a long way from the

to use my digital image of the original letterbook.
15   Henry Caner to Rev. Mr. [Wingders?], London, 10 January 1778, HCL.
16   Henry Caner, application for the augmentation of existing allowance, transmitted to the Treasury in March 1777. See Richard C. Simmons, A Brief Introduction to the Microfilm Edition of The Letterbook of the Rev. Henry Caner 1728–1778 (Wakefield: Microform Academic Publishers and British Association for American Studies, n.d.), 9.

conservative investment in paternal authority of many Boston loyalists, who would have regarded such radical enthusiasm as something
to curb. But in her textual paralleling of fragments from the time of
Anne Hutchinson with the later period of her great-great-great grandson Thomas Hutchinson, Governor of the Massachusetts Bay colony,
Howe suggests continuities nonetheless:

> Together with his preoriginal representation, Anne, Thomas
> Hutchinson was fated to serve as scapegoat for a new political op-
> position. Both were despised by founding fathers. John Winthrop
> loathed Anne. John Adams loathed Thomas. Thomas was also ban-
> ished from the colony though he was banished for his conservatism.
> 'My temper', Governor Hutchinson once wrote, 'does not incline to
> enthusiasm'. Much to his regret, he died in England.[17]

'So you are working on traitors,' someone said to me on a first visit to
the Massachusetts Historical Society archives, built, as it turns out, on
the land confiscated from the Reverend Henry Caner. Howe's observation comes in a chapter of *The Birth-mark* entitled 'Incloser'. The enclo-
sure she names is as much about the action of thought and its 'apparatus
of capture' as the history of those who arrived in America to escape
the logics of exclusion and repression in England, only to find them
recapitulated. The dynamic at work in Howe's writing concerns patterns of exclusionary constitution, the way communities violently make
themselves through scapegoating and its trials; but also a particular and
founding tension between freedom and law – marked by instances of
civil war – which can determine who speaks from the archive, who is
discovered wandering in sovereign wilds.

At the same time Howe's poetics offers a method that might promise
to move by other means, suspending thought which falls into the binaries she risks in that tension between antinomianism and (political)
law. In an interview Howe talks about a 'tychic encounter' in her work,

---

17   Howe, *The Birth-mark*, 74. Howe also notes that Thomas Hutchinson was
the author of the significant early colonial history, *The History of the Colony and
Province of Massachusetts Bay* (1765), which includes an account of Anne's trial.
He would continue writing a history of the revolutionary period in exile. For an
interesting account of Hutchinson's loyalist historiography see Eileen Cheng,
'On the Margins: The Mediating Function of Footnotes in Thomas Hutchin-
son's *History of Massachusetts-Bay*', *Early American Studies: An Interdisciplinary
Journal* 11 (2013), 98–116.

picking up on a concept of chance she derives from Charles Sanders Peirce, and its related categories, such as synechism:

> *Synechism* is the tendency to regard everything as continuous in the way no 'scholarly interpretation can be'. It suggests the linkage of like and like-in-chance contiguities and alignments. That idea is in my writing generally. He was willing to carry the doctrine so far as to maintain that continuity governs the domain of experience, every part of it.[18]

Tracking her textual movement through historical fields, the layers of voices sounded and stuttering in archive fever, seems to involve the chance of aleatory connections and yet the apprehension of a certain necessity in such 'alignments'. How then to move through loyalist materials this way, thinking continuities alongside radical diremption; including tychic elements, haptic encounters with the shape or sound of a hand, that might cause thought to 'stray'?[19] Where the designations of a naming might themselves be an occupation of the archive, what *occupies*, as an army does, subject to the ordeals of 'print border warfare'?[20] Or where such an occupation could also be seen as a haunting, a return, in which names arrive in the fantasy of 'a pure past that returns to itself unattackable in the framework', and waiting to be spoken.[21] My essay tries out a particular movement enacted in the title of Howe's collection *Thorow*, a pathfinding, in which 'God and grammar' spell things out, but where the thickets revealed in the material soundings of language sometimes suggest there is 'no thorow passage navigable that way'.[22] What is the intensity that is being named as (un)navigable in this writing? What or whom is recognised? In the stuff of the archive, what is the demand and what kind of listening does it call out?

18 Susan Howe, interviewed by Maureen N. McLane, 'Susan Howe, The Art of Poetry No. 97', *Paris Review* 203 (2012): www.theparisreview.org/interviews/6189/the-art-of-poetry-no-97-susan-howe.

19 See Richard Shiff on the pragmatic uses of the 'tychic' in his interview with Katy Siegel in *Brooklyn Rail*, 6 May 2008: www.brooklynrail.org/2008/05/art/richard-shiff-with-katy-siegel.

20 Susan Howe, 'Personal Narrative', in *Souls of the Labadie Tract* (New York, 2007), 17.

21 Susan Howe, 'Preface: Frame Structures', in *Frame Structures: Early Poems 1974–1979* (New York, 1996), 26.

22 Susan Howe, *Thorow*, in *Singularities* (Middletown, Conn., 1990), 40, 41.

This Time of Conflict: Sovereign Power

The fragments I've chosen come from a time of intense change, around the period of the Declaration of Independence, several years before the declaring of peace in 1783. To think of the nature of sovereign power here is to consider a field of forces, in which nothing is yet settled, the culturing of opposition in process, rather than the stable division between Sovereign Powers which appeared in my epigraph, as the loyalist John Mein saw it in 1775. Mein reported that many in England regarded the contest simply as a 'declared Rebellion' soon to be put down: 'outlawries, Confiscation and Executions are looked upon to be the certain Consequences'.[23] In this revolt of 1775–76, for Antonio Negri, is the moment of the founding of American constituent power, a temporality of democratic revolution marked by Tom Paine's phrase in *Common Sense* (1776), 'the *time hath found us*':[24]

> [W]hat is certain is that for the first time in modern history we are witnessing such a complex process, so massified, and at the sametime so compressed in such a short time, so powerful and rapid, so effective and unconcluded in its action.[25]

Alongside this vision of compression and speed, comes a sense of passage, as protest and resistance turn into a 'moment of innovation', a rupture which refuses continuity with previous modes of colonial legitimacy, British rule: 'a political climate in which the ideological prescriptions and the material pulsions push rapidly toward irreversible results and radically innovative determinations'. With this innovation in which 'everything is shaken from its depths', comes 'a process of the constitution of new subjectivity', integral to a fundamental transforming of a cultural imaginary that 'sets out to transform man, his imaginative capability, his will to power':

23   John Mein to James Murray, London 11 January 1775, MHS: JMR. Mein was a Scot who started the *Boston Chronicle*, the loyalist newspaper, and founded the first circulating library in Boston. His newspaper war, after being blacklisted under the non-importation measures, resulted in a near lynching during which he shot a soldier. He escaped to London, where he was imprisoned for debt, before returning again to Boston.
24   Thomas Paine, *Political Writings*, ed. Bruce Kuklick (Cambridge, 1989), 30.
25   Negri, *Insurgencies*, trans. Boscagli, 146.

What constituent strength offers to the citizens, to the new citizens, is a progressive power, a formative progressivity. The founding act is extremely radical: it destroys memory, creates new organizations and orders, constructs functional myths: constituent power reveals itself as ontological facticity.[26]

The figuring of Wilderness – Dickinson's 'Sovreign Woods' – is for Negri, as for Howe, testimony to what he calls the 'savage dimension of American freedom' and its immense spatial dynamics: 'a "first" nature of which freedom, that is the American "second" nature, can be shaped' (143). But it is subject even as it takes constitutional and juridical form to capture and containment, for Negri as differently for Howe; in which the appropriation of space in the name of freedom becomes an internal form of empire, founded on slavery and expropriation. Negri keeps hold of that vision of progressivity and its continuing potential as 'the scandal of freedom' in America (190), while noting that the gradual capturing of that constituent potential in the 'strenuous centralization of the constitution' entails that eventually 'nothing is left of the sociality and the universality of the political expressed by the revolutionary movement' (175). To consider the shifting forces of 1775–76 is to address the moment when 'freedom assumes the form of the frontier', in Negri's account, and also I would add its predication on the imaginative capability of a male citizen-subject. For her part, Howe's writing positions this constitutive tension between freedom and law in America in a longer arc, and it is women in particular, as I will want to begin to explore, who testify to its 'scandal', its *unsettling*.

To think loyalist attachment to forms of sovereignty in the light of an account of democratic constituent power might entail, as certain historians have argued, that loyalism is thereby viewed from one side only – as it illuminates or is illuminated by the revolutionary narratives of the time – rather than through the diverse and heterogeneous freedoms, accommodations and interests corralled under its name. But it seems at once important to think the place of loyalism conceptually within these 'material pulsions' in more everyday and dialectical ways, perhaps as one key site where that antagonism of freedom and law is internalised, or violently worked through: in bodies, lives, property. How to register, for example, that lived attachment to the imperial state, law, tradition, the status quo, and then its literal *evacuating* as a continual

26   Ibid., 147, 146, 147–8.

action within this conflict, a becoming-refugee that is also caught con-
stitutively in a becoming-citizen or becoming-subject? And to see that
action as working internally, within the subjective imaginary, as well
as in the determinations – the 'ontological facticity' – of that moment,
and its typologies; before the cashing out into who stays, and who goes,
into seeming winners and losers.

In her chapter 'Imperialism' in *The Origins of Totalitarianism*, Hannah
Arendt considers what it means for a person to lose status in 'the struggle of his time':

> The human being who has lost his place in a community, his politi-
> cal status in the struggle of his time, and the legal personality which
> makes his action and part of his destiny a consistent whole, is left
> with those qualities which usually can become articulate only in the
> sphere of private life and must remain unqualified, mere existence in
> all matters of public concern.[27]

If loyalist 'evacuations' are to be thought of in these terms, the fact that
they become knowable largely through a registry of private struggles
and biographical materials is given a larger frame. Their experience of
statelessness at this time is sudden and unexpected, could feel absolute
or partial, a civil death or a temporary condition. Some expulsions were
permanent, like that of Elizabeth Murray Inman's brother James, who
had been burnt in effigy and forced to leave, like many loyalist Boston
refugees, for Halifax, Nova Scotia, where he would die. '[W]e Refugees',
he wrote, 'must make the best shift we can.'[28] Others, who found their
way to Britain, may have invested in the hope that their statelessness
was no statelessness at all, since surely all were to be thought of as subjects of the British imperial state, no less than those residing in the heart
of the metropolis, and might come to the mother country to breathe its
famously 'free air'.

The more than five thousand loyalists who submitted claims for repa-
ration to the Loyalist Claims Commission after the end of the war had
to make a case for losses that had been suffered 'in consequence of . . .

---

27   Arendt, *Origins of Totalitarianism*, 301. While statelessness is the issue here,
Arendt's account of revolution (both political and social) would need address-
ing in this context, and in relation to the discussion of constituent/constitu-
tional power.
28   James Murray to John Innes Clark, Halifax, 6 January 1779, MHS: JMR.

loyalty', and were met with equivocation, as Maya Jasanoff has detailed, since the peace treaty had stated in Article V that there were 'real British subjects', and therefore others across the empire who might be deemed less so. As she explains, there was no right to recompense as many believed, but a form of paternalist responsibility that the British state was prepared to shoulder, if not for all. For those who could not claim a 'legal personality' in Arendt's terms – such as the women who had no means of corroborating their losses, or the black loyalists whose declarations that they were 'free born and that they had property' were dismissed as 'two things that are not very probable', as the Commission reported – indeed, not to be credited in 'one syllable'.[29] That space of private injury, and of lives confronted with their own 'mere existence', would remain 'unqualified' in the debits and credits of British public concern.

The case of the loyalists, then, opens up an active field of attachment and loss, caught between evacuations from one form of transforming sovereign power and imaginary and anxious identification with, and loyalty to, another. A curious state of suspension perhaps, the ramifications of which would last long beyond the end of the war, but which I want to catch now in two instances of script, the first from 1778.

Like a Thunder Clape: Shock and Kinship

Henry Caner's letterbook is scrupulous. Decisions are annotated, letters 'not sent being founded on Misinformation'.[30] Criticism of the weak agents of the Crown he saw as responsible for the deepening crisis in Boston of 1773–74 arrives by way of Latin quotations, as if invoking a cryptic authority shared only with those who had the same educated memory for classical precedent. The management and power of record mattered. Caner reported to the bishop of London, among others, throughout the conflict in Boston, conveying a sense of the speed and intensity of change, its impellingness: '[A] republican Spirit can never rest, the same levelling principles which induce them to withdraw from strong wholesome Establishment of the Church operate with equal force in throwing off the restraint of Civil Government.'[31] Gradually

---

29   Jasanoff, *Liberty's Exiles*, 132, 122–3 134–5.
30   Henry Caner, annotation to letter intended for the Right Reverend Richard [Terrick], Lord Bishop of London, Boston, September 29 1773, HCL.
31   Caner to bishop of London, Boston, 22 July 1775, HCL.

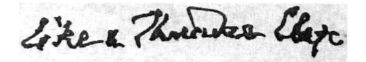

Fig. 1: 'Like a Thunder Clape': Henry Caner to Deacon Thomas Foster, London, 10 January 1778. Henry Caner Letterbook, Bristol University Library. With thanks to Bristol University Special Collections for permission to reproduce the author's digital image of the original letterbook.

the conflict bites: trade is ruined, people driven out and beaten (1774), food becomes scarce and famine a possibility as Boston is surrounded, epidemics erupt and his health suffers (1775). 'If the Town falls, I am an old man, and am content to fall with it,' he wrote to John Breynton in 1775,[32] but as evacuations began he left for Halifax with just 'six hours to prepare' in May 1776.[33] Once in Britain Caner continued to maintain his connections with the scattered Anglican community on both sides of the Atlantic, a community that was tied together tightly by familial ties and friendship, and by the insistence of his script.

Writing to Silvester Gardiner in 1777 with news of events – the death of the bishop of London and appointment of Dr. Lowth; the forgery of Dr. Dodd (for which he had been sentenced to death); and sermons preached by acquaintances – the knot of connections seems of a piece with the conversation of an Episcopalian community in exile. Unravelled, however, there is a deeper sense of palpable crisis: trusted sponsors gone, and Church affairs in America consequently in 'stagnation'; the registering of Dodd's counterfeiture and his sovereign punishment curiously symptomatic; sermons by Myles Cooper and East Apthorp (Caner's protégée) causing 'uproar' in the newspapers because of their patriarchalist line on passive obedience rather than compact with the people – criticism 'not altogether without justice', he writes. Caner is careful about what he says: 'I wish I could write you some things wch I know you would be glad to hear, but considering the Danger of Letters being intercepted Prudence thus forbids me to add any thing more than that I am well.'[34]

32   Caner to Reverend Dr. Breynton, Boston, 9 May 1775, HCL.
33   Caner to Dr. Hind, Halifax, 10 May 1776, HCL.
34   Caner to Dr. Silvester Gardiner, London, 25 April 1777, HCL.

Writing could be a zone of jeopardy, as the ex-Governor Thomas Hutchinson also experienced. Bernard Bailyn's biography notes Hutchinson's continual attempt to re-read and re-present the material culture of letters and records, discovering what it was to be at the mercy of a sprawling archive that could not be brought into authoritative control, to speak the loyalist case.[35] Not only was Hutchinson's house burned down, and with it the collected papers and historical record from the time of his ancestor Anne, but his attempts to control the dissemination of his words failed catastrophically. Hutchinson had to counter public versions of himself stalking the land, while opponents excerpted from ransacked letters at will. The 'Misinformation' Caner would expunge from his earlier letter-sending seems endemic in loyalist record, a continuous fear: not only because of the very real repercussions of exposure, but also because of the devastating removal of the sureties that grounded identity, whether in America or the 'mother Country'.[36] Misinformation bred misrecognition, even of the self. For Hutchinson it arrived in a waking dream of depersonalisation. An experience of reverie, he noted, arrived 'the more easily from my situation at this time of life, so unexpected to me, three thousand miles from my country and friends, so that every scene has the appearance of a dream, rather than a reality'. And the dream that haunted him on a January day in 1775 was one of a physical dismemberment, prompted by the loss of a tooth:

> I left a tooth at Whitchurch, which had given me so much trouble that I was glad to part with it, tho' with some additional pain; and I could not help a reflection as I was riding – that part of my body was gone, which I now felt no more affection for, than if it had been the tooth of a stranger. I could easily imagine the case to be the same with a finger, a hand, an arm, and so on to every part of the body, even to the brain, my thinking part still existing, and perhaps assuming some other better form, or the same materials moulded anew.[37]

35 Bernard Bailyn, *The Ordeal of Thomas Hutchinson* (Cambridge, Mass., 1974).

36 A term used by Caner in a letter to the bishop of London, Boston, 27 March 1775, HCL.

37 Thomas Hutchinson, diary entry for 15 January 1775, in *The Diary and Letters of His Excellency Thomas Hutchinson*, ed. Peter Orlando Hutchinson, 2 vols. (Boston, Mass., 1884–86), I, 351.

Hutchinson's hallucinatory dream of his own dismemberment anticipated the imperial fears that others would voice at the loss of America. It is as if his disassociated reverie might reveal a total identification with a state imagining that also took on corporeal dimensions, the familiar metaphor of a balance of limbs. Even his brain, 'my thinking part', might reboot itself somewhere else, alienated by pain. Perhaps that was what the times demanded, a new and traumatic moulding of the self.

There was 'pain in being an Eye witness', Caner wrote to an acquaintance in Maryland in 1775.[38] Beneath the letter-writing was a continuing struggle over political and religious paternal authority that also took private and affective form. His script becomes increasingly palsied as he ages. The time of conflict, for all its intensity, was drawn out, physically deleterious. To think about the violence of shock might be to imagine it as in the shaky fragment of script, arriving 'like a Thunder Clape', rather than something lived out with uncertain duration. It rebounded in unexpected forms, chance stories. The instance I've chosen comes from a reported scene that appears at another remove, but is no less shaped by the shock of circumstances. Arriving in Britain as an evacuee, Caner was accompanied by an ageing housekeeper, and a 'daughter', elsewhere described as a 'niece', and even by some as his 'young wife'.[39] Sally Gore was the daughter of his friend Deacon Thomas Foster. Her husband John Gore, Jr., had died in 1771 soon after their marriage. Caner's attachment to Sally Gore – 'my Sally' – and his makeshift family arrangement is evident. Writing to her father in 1777 to convey the news of her marriage to a 'sober well bred young G̶e̶n̶t̶l̶e̶man', Caner declares she 'has never been from me a Day since we left Boston. She has far'd as well as myself, and has been fully attentive to me as to her Father, having never taken a Step which I did not approve'. And in another note concerning 'your Daughter my dear Child & companion': 'I can't say but it was with reluctance that I consented to part with her.'[40] Yet the news that arrives like a clap of thunder, in a scene worthy of

38   Caner to Mr. Kurnsey, Boston, 16 January 1775, HCL.
39   See Simmons, *A Brief Introduction*, 4, 8–11, for intermittent reference to Sally Gore as Caner's 'ward'. Caner would leave the bulk of his estate to her, with the stipulation that it would not become the property of any husband.
40   Caner to Deacon Thomas Foster, London, 22 April 1777; note dated 25 April, HCL.

a Richardson novel, is that the marriage – which Caner himself con-
ducted – is a bigamous one:

> They had been married but 5 weeks, when Lord Darbrey called upon
> me & acquainted me that Mr Manson had a Wife living in a re-
> mote part of London at the time when he was married to Sally. This
> you may believe was like a Thunder Clape to me. However as soon
> as Manson came home I acquainted him [cursorily?], & turned him
> immediately out of Doors – The same evening I made the matter
> known to Sally in the tenderest Manner I was able; She fainted &
> with much difficulty could we recover her. To be short it went very
> near to cost her her Life.[41]

To read this shock (and its potential pleasures, since the lost 'daughter'
is returned), embedded in a letter copied in a letterbook, is to think
about the private drama of patriarchal authority and its propensity for
failure. Sally Gore remains a cipher in Caner's household, a voice-off
contributing to his correspondence (later: 'She says you may laugh as
much as you please.').[42] To think about sovereign power in the period is
also to address its private and symptomatic manifestations, and the sudden turning counterfeit of bonds that once might have seemed natural,
the living out of artificial ties that are created newly. The presence of
imposture – both real and imagined – in the culture of the period might
thus be symptomatic of the wider experience of social and psychic misrecognition during a time of conflict. This brings me to the place of
women's loyalties in such a climate, and their relation to authority.

Soundings: Women and Sovereign Power

In the introduction to *The Europe of Trusts*, Susan Howe writes of her
experience of her father's absence during the Second World War: 'This
is my historical consciousness. I have no choice in it. In my poetry, time
and again, questions of assigning *the cause* of history dictate the sound
of what is thought.' Watching the newsreels as a child, she writes, '[I]
f to see is to *have* at a distance, I had so many dead Innocents distance

41   Caner to Deacon Thomas Foster, London, 10 January 1778, HCL.
42   Caner to Reverend Mr. Jones, London, 22 April 1778, HCL.

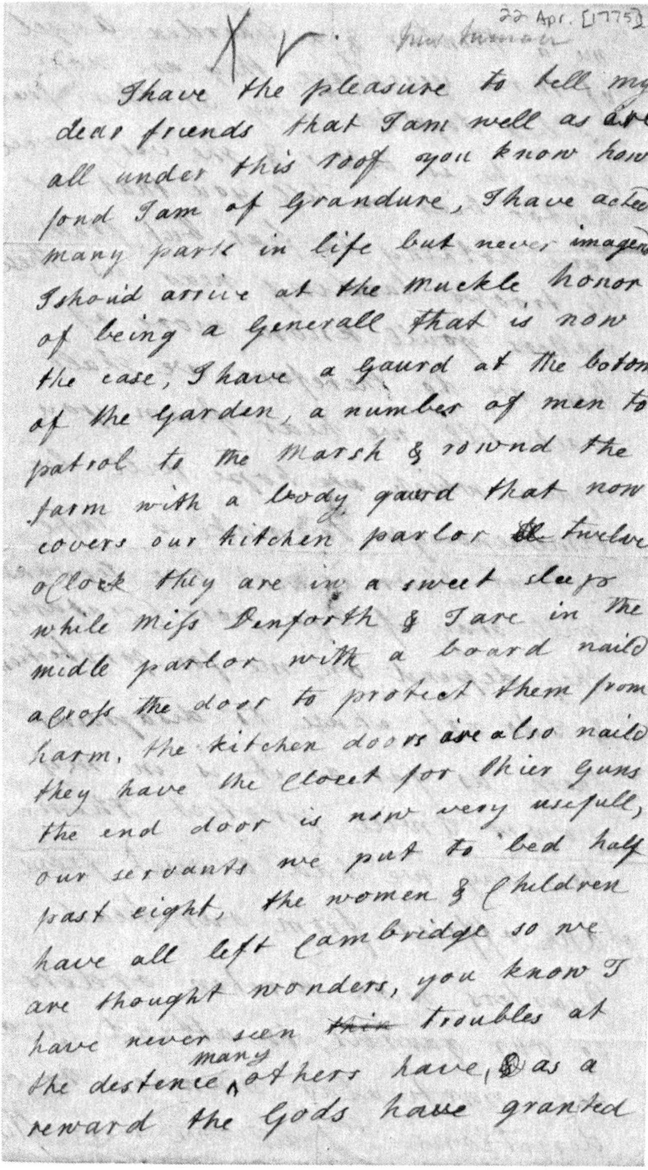

22 Apr. [1775]

I have the pleasure to tell my
dear friends that I am well as are
all under this roof you know how
fond I am of Grandure, I have acted
many parts in life but never imaged
I shou'd arrive at the muckle honor
of being a Generall that is now
the case, I have a gaurd at the botom
of the garden, a number of men to
patrol to the marsh & round the
farm with a body gaurd that now
covers our kitchen parlor & twelve
o'clock they are in a sweet sleep
while miss Denforth & I are in the
midle parlor with a board naild
across the door to protect them from
harm, the kitchen doors are also naild
they have the closet for thier guns
the end door is now very usefull,
our servants we put to bed half
past eight, the women & children
have all left Cambridge so we
are thought wonders, you know I
have never seen troubles at
the destence others have, & as a
        many
reward the Gods have granted

Fig. 2: 'I have the pleasure': Elizabeth Murray Inman to 'dear friends',
Cambridge, 22 April 1775, Massachusetts Historical Society: James Murray
Robbins Family Papers, page 1. With thanks to the MHS and The Elizabeth
Murray Project website (www.csulb.edu/projects/elizabethmurray/EM/index.
html) for permission to reproduce sections of this letter.

was abolished.'[43] The proxemics of witnessing war, the sound of what can be thought: something of the dynamics of the archival pathfinding are suggested in this bind. What happens to assignations of causes when having and losing take place in such close quarters? Or when '[l]aws are relations between individuals', as Howe writes in *Frame Structures*?[44] The dictation of the sound of thought gives way to other acoustics, stuttering against the grain of that collective singularity of historical time – what would become the story of the new nation – with its aligning of the 'passion of individuals' with the narratives of the state.[45]

In the light of these soundings, a loyalist letter from the archive, dated 1775:

> I have the pleasure to tell my dear friends that I am well as are all under this roof you know how fond I am of Grandure, I have acted many parts in life but never imagend I shou'd arrive at the muckle honor of being a Generall that is now the case, I have a Gaurd at the bottom of the Garden, a number of men to patrol to the Marsh & rownd the farm with a body gaurd that now covers our kitchen parlor twelve oclock they are in a sweet sleep while Miss Denforth & I are in the midle parlor with a board nail'd across the door to protect them from harm, the kitchen doors are also nail'd they have the closet for thier Guns the end door is now very usefull, our servants we put to bed half past eight, the women & children have all left Cambridge so we are thought wonders, you know I have never seen troubles at the destence many others have[.]

This hand betrays itself. The 'muckle' is a sign of the writer's immigrant Scots origins. Letters are transposed, vowels follow her tongue: gaurd, rownd, destence. Later in the conflict she will forget what it is to write a letter. The folders will thin. As she keeps watch at this instant, however, her letters are formed bigger and bigger, as if she is drunk. She is writing by candlelight, it is late, she has been keeping watch:

---

43 Susan Howe, *The Europe of Trusts* (New York, 2007), 13, 12.
44 Howe, *Frame Structures*, 6.
45 I am referring here to Paul Ricoeur on Hegel's philosophy of history and its relation to the state, in his *Time and Narrative*, trans. Kathleen Blarney and David Pellauer, 3 vols. (Chicago, 1984–88), III, 197. See John Kraniauskas, 'Difference against Development: Spiritual Accumulation and the Politics of Freedom', *boundary 2* 32.2 (Summer 2005), 53–80: 56.

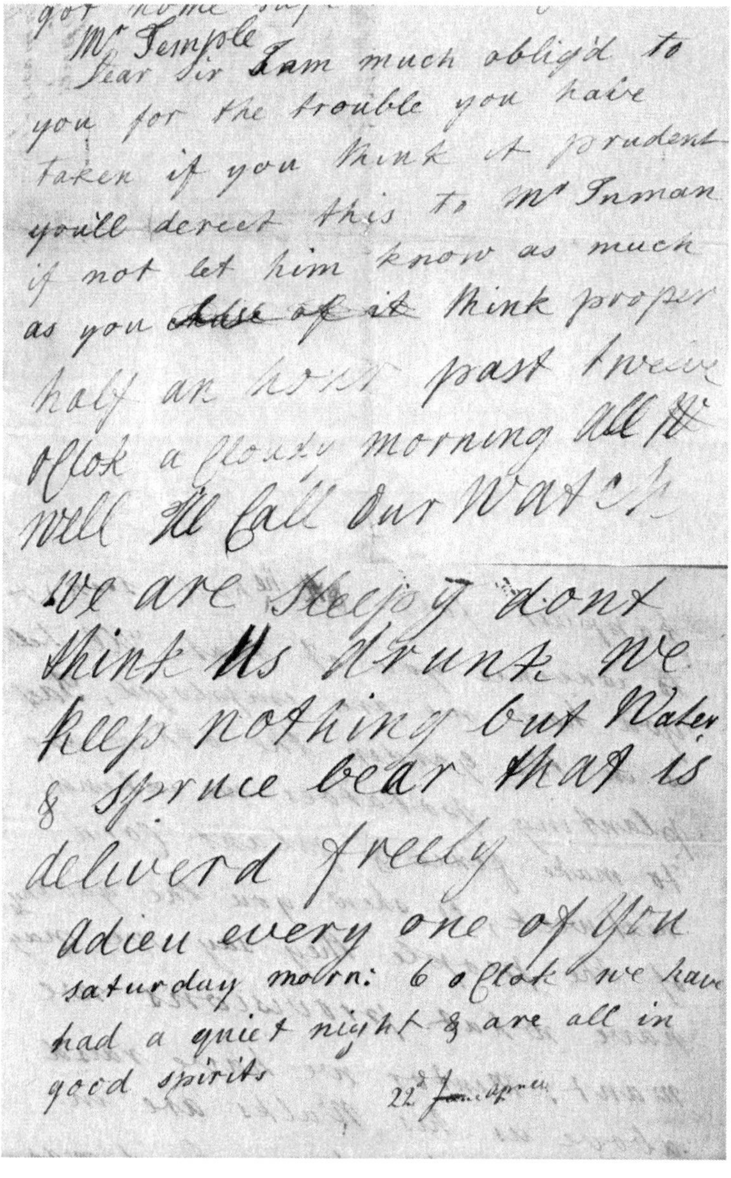

Mr Temple

Dear Sir I am much oblig'd to
you for the trouble you have
taken if you think it prudent
youll derect this to Mr Inman
if not let him know as much
as you think proper
half an hour past twelve
oflok a cloudy morning all Wd
well We call Our Watch

we are sleepy dont
think Us drunk we
keep nothing but Water
& spruce bear that is
deliverd freely

adieu every one of You
saturday morn: 6 oflok we have
had a quiet night & are all in
good spirits   22d

Fig. 3a: 'Dear Sir' and Fig. 3b: 'Dont think Us drunk': Elizabeth Murray Inman to 'dear friends', Cambridge, 22 April 1775, Massachusetts Historical Society: James Murray Robbins Family Papers, pages 3, 4. With thanks to the MHS and The Elizabeth Murray Project website (www.csulb.edu/projects/elizabethmurray/EM/index.html) for permission to reproduce sections of this letter.

Dear Sir I am much oblig'd to you for the trouble you have taken if you think it prudent you'll derect this to Mr Inman if not let him know as much as you ~~have of it~~ think proper half an hour past twelve oclok a cloudy morning all well I'll call our watch we are sleepy dont think Us drunk we keep nothing but Water & spruce bear that is deliverd freely

Adieu every one of You

Saturday morn: 6 oclok we have had a quiet night & are all in good spirits

22nd ~~June~~ April

Elizabeth Murray Inman had been holed up defending her third husband's house in Cambridge, Massachusetts. The Inman house in 1775 had just been taken over as headquarters of the patriot army under General Israel Putnam, who offered her protection, unlike that afforded many loyalist women behind the lines.[46] The house is barricaded, full of guns. She imagines herself with a certain self-mocking hubris as a 'Generall'. There is a part to be played, something larger, as if her gigantic script might be signal. If misrecognition held mortal consequences for loyalists, it also enabled a form of self-fashioning, even a kind of power.

Murray Inman refused to leave for the safety of British lines, continuing to move between the house and her farm at Brush Hill, against the wishes of her husband Ralph Inman (to whom she had been married in King's Chapel by none other than Henry Caner). She follows her own will: 'if I have erred it is in Judgement; and if I did not see a fare prospect of saving you crop, stock &c &c, I would immediately go to town and convince you how ready I was to obey.' Her strong sense of internal authority is pragmatic, grounded in work and commerce. She writes sometimes cryptically – letters can be read, decoded. But also as a woman she is unusually direct: 'I thought, as times were, it was necessary to speak my mind.'[47]

Though the Murray family were loyalists, they were not uncritically so: her eldest brother, John Murray, declared in a letter from England in 1771: 'We have all been slaves to the Government and treated as such. It

46   For an account of this event, and her brief imprisonment by continental troops due to the compromising account given by her husband's slave, Job, see Patricia Cleary, *Elizabeth Murray: A Woman's Pursuit of Independence in the Eighteenth Century* (Boston, Mass., 2000), 174–6. Cleary notes that continental soldiers commonly described their billeting at 'Madam Inman's'.

47   Elizabeth Murray Inman to Ralph Inman, Cambridge, 14 June 1775, *The Letters of James Murray, Loyalist*, ed. Nina Moore Tiffany and Susan I. Lesley (Printed, not published: Boston, 1901), 211–12.

is time to be free'.[48] Her brother James, whom she had first accompanied to America, had presided over the trial of the British soldiers who were held for the Boston Massacre of 1770, and would die a refugee.[49] As in other families riven by the conflict, she struggled with the news of her nephew joining the continental army. For her, freedom of a prosperous kind had come with settling in America, as it had for other immigrants. In 1774 she wrote to her British cousin: 'We make a great noise on your side of the water. Notwithstanding the many bad things they say of us thier is vast numbers of people coming from Cumberland, Yorkshire, Ireland and Scotland to settle here. It is indeed a glorious country and deserves the protection of good people.'[50] Elizabeth Murray Inman's interests underpinned her loyalist position. She had set up shop in Boston at twenty-two, dealing in millinery and indentured servants, and through her second marriage came to run a sugar business with warehouses that served as barracks for British soldiers, bringing in British imports. She had established a school for women apprentices, and believed that women should have access to trades. She was, as her brother wrote and deleted, 'much Respected in Boston, ~~though no Disguiser of her Sentiments~~'.[51]

Boston in Inman's time was not a frontier world any longer, but it knew its methods intimately, and the conflict surrounding the town was as violent: scalping of soldiers, tarring and feathering, expulsions, and twisting logics of exception. 'Tory' women behind the lines were vulnerable to abuse, often remaining behind to keep hold of property while their loyalist men took refuge. Murray Inman trod a line between warring camps – passing letters between patriot friends (for which she was a disobedient wife), visiting British prisoners of war in Concord jail (for which she was named as a traitor in the *New England Chronicle*). She did not believe in predestination, she informed her husband, so there was nothing to fear. 'Tell her friends in England not to lament her being in America at this period, for she is now in her proper element,' wrote

48   John Murray to Elizabeth Smith (later Murray Inman), Norwich, 6 April 1771, MHS: JMR.

49   There is evidence that his Scottish identity played badly among whig radicals, as William Palfrey's comment to John Wilkes might suggest: 'It may not perhaps lessen your opinion of Mr. Murrays good Qualities to inform you that he is a Scotchman and has continually caball'd with his loyal Countreymen in this Town, and the other Governmental tools against the Charter and liberties of this Province.' See George M. Elsey, 'John Wilkes and William Palfrey', *Transactions of the Colonial Society of Massachusetts* 34 (1943 for 1937–42), 411–28: 422.

50   Elizabeth Murray Inman to Mrs. Hope, Cambridge, 24 May 1774, MHS: JMR.

51   James Murray to John Innes Clark, Halifax, 6 January 1779, MHS: JMR.

the niece of her close friend Christian Barnes. 'No (other) woman could do as she does with impunity, for she is above the little fears and weaknesses which are the inseparable companions of most of our sex.'[52]

The shapes of Scottish vowels are sounded on the page. The meaning of Elizabeth Murray Inman's 'muckle honor' would be transformed by what it was to remain in America, her elected 'Native Soil',[53] by the realignment of these individual passions. As she wrote in 1782:

> My attachment to this Country has been violent, but these times and the death of our much loved Brother has wean'd me in such a manner that I am anxious for the sun to rise and the wind to blow that shall clear me of this once happy shore.[54]

The word *muckle* has begun to mutate here perhaps in silent ways: its American meaning is also 'to latch on with the mouth', as in breastfeeding. Elizabeth Inman contemplated her unmuckling – her weaning – from America, but would remain in 'violent attachment' to it until her death.

Loyalties

In what ways then might such a loyalist woman be seen wandering in those same 'Sovreign Woods' that Emily Dickinson imagined in a later time of civil war, where she figures the life of the woman poet as a loaded gun? Is there something heretical about that thought? If a path exists, it is cut by the relation between the state and kinship, the locating of women in sovereign power. There is a unexpected crossing between Emily Dickinson as a poet of war, and Elizabeth Murray Inman the loyalist, both performing as instruments of masculine sovereignty, a master's gun and Generall, called out in the disturbance and catastrophe of conflict, its distance and proximity; both registering, as Howe puts it, that liberty and a certain potency is afforded 'inside the confines of known necessity' defined by paternal law.[55] Inman's 'error' is also her 'Judgement', as she

---

52   E.F. to her aunt Christian Barnes, Cambridge, 17 April 1776, *The Letters of James Murray, Loyalist*, 246.

53   Helen Douglas to Elizabeth Murray Inman, 30 January 1775, entreating her to see the conflict out in England: '[I]t wd be a good time to visit us in the Spring stay wt us till the Blast is over and then return to what you call yr Native Soil when Peace is Established,' MHS: JMR.

54   Elizabeth Murray Inman to John Murray, Cambridge, 22 July 1782, MHS: JMR.

55   Howe, *My Emily Dickinson*, 118.

writes to her husband, refusing obedience. Like Anne Hutchinson, she
sets up a school, listens to the authority of her own mind, stays outside
the patriarchal terms of settlement. She also deals in the unfreedom of
others, believes in work, refuses exile. There is something estranging to be
found in the chance crossings of this landscape – which Howe reads as an
outside, a frontier wilderness – a limit where what is named in women's
terms remains unintelligible, 'not knowing what She', as Howe says in
Thorow.[56] It is this limit I want finally to explore.

What might it mean to be loyal in a time of conflict, behind established lines? In *Europe of Trusts* Howe refers us to *Antigone*: '2,000 years
ago the dictator Creon said to Antigone who was the daughter of Oedipus
and Jocasta: "Go to the dead and love them."'[57] Antigone's is a living
death, one that the law of the state demands because she has given burial
rites to her dead brother, who has betrayed the state in war. One brother
is a hero, the other a traitor. Greater than the designations of the state
are loyalties to the underworld and its laws: Antigone is a loyalist in that
sense, weighing the affinities of kinship even as she uses the vernacular of
the law in its own terms. When Creon asks whether she has dishonoured
her hero of a brother Eteokles by honouring her brother Polyneices, who
died 'ravaging the land', she answers 'he is not his slave, but his brother',
refusing the distinction of friends and enemies: '[M]aybe, down there, all
this is pure.' She will position herself as a continual exile – a stranger to
life and to death – and love both. Creon's demand – 'Go to the dead and
love them' – violently takes Antigone and her rebellion at her word. His
next words are: 'I am alive though, and no woman will rule me.'[58]

Antigone is named as a man by Creon: 'Now I am no man, she is the
man' because, as Judith Butler has argued, she assumes the force of the
law in committing an act against it, finding a hubristic glory – a 'muckle
honor' – in burying her brother and loving the dead. [59] Antigone finds a
liberty in the confines of necessity, but the result is mortal exile. She is a
liminal figure, because her desire is nonetheless unintelligible, not only
in terms of the state but also in terms of kinship: more than the eternal
irony that Hegel laid at her door. Antigone's father is also her brother, her
mother her sister; burying her brother is also implicated in the Oedipal

56 Howe, *Thorow*, in *Singularities*, 40.
57 Howe, *Europe of Trusts*, 13.
58 Sophocles, *Antigone*, trans. Richard Emil Braun (Oxford, 1973), 40–1.
59 Judith Butler, *Antigone's Claim: Kinship between Life and Death* (New York,
2000), 10–11.

curse, a history which may or may not persist. In what sense does she speak that crime, in the aftermath of war – where does she speak from in such ambivalences of kinship? From the midst of the ambiguities of paternal law and fraternal allegiance, which suggests something like the imaginary of the state. For the dictator Creon love only arrives after the safety of the state is secured. Hers, in contrast, is marked by the fatality of contradiction, which Judith Butler probes in the following terms:

> How do we understand the strange place of being between life and death, of speaking precisely from that vacillating boundary? If she is dead in some sense and yet speaks, she is precisely the one with no place who nevertheless seeks to claim one within speech, the unintelligible as it emerges within the intelligible, a position within kinship which is no position. [60]

The experience of the revolutionary war for loyalists and patriots alike generated 'unintelligible' positions and places that were inhabited before they could be known, and given meaning as part of a longer narrative of an emerging republic, or a transforming empire. Some remained unnavigable, even to those living them. The sound of what is dictated in the name of sovereignty is both 'liberty and submission' in Susan Howe's words, but what would this entail?[61] Violence here, as Gillian Rose argues, is in the diremptive 'and':[62] liberty and submission, the state and kinship, freedom and law. Something altogether more equivocal and anxious is here in play, perhaps, beyond the exilic evacuation of the loyal that Elizabeth Murray Inman refused in 1776, and the setting up of oppositional types and histories. If the position of women is central to an exploration of modern subjectivity, in Rose's terms, it is because their condition, 'sovereign and subordinated', is at the hinge of an ongoing scandal: the incommensurability of a posited political universality and equality; citizenship and civil society (with its contradictory forms of loyalty, attachment, love).[63] In that unsettling place, the antinomies of sovereign power continue to stutter in a time of conflict, requiring other soundings.

---

60   Butler, *Antigone's Claim*, 78.
61   Howe, *My Emily Dickinson*, 84.
62   Gillian Rose, *The Broken Middle: Out of Our Ancient Society* (Oxford, 1992), 241–2. Rose's account of the suspension of the ethical is central to what I am beginning to work through here, a suspension which makes it possible to explore 'this diremption in the experience of the individual': 217.
63   Ibid., 185.

Fig. 1: Richard Caton Woodville, *War News From Mexico* (1848). Oil on canvas, 27 × 25 in. (68.6 × 63.5 cm). Crystal Bridges Museum of American Art, Bentonville, Arkansas. Photo © The Walters Art Museum, Susan Tobin.

Proclaiming the War News: Richard Caton Woodville and Herman Melville

TOM F. WRIGHT

How DOES THE ROLE of public speech evolve in an age of technological transformation? Two literary and visual artefacts from the wars of nineteenth-century America pose this question, and offer insights into a chapter of media history that is still poorly understood. In the first, Richard Caton Woodville's *War News From Mexico* (1848), the ambivalent place of wartime voice takes centre stage. This most iconic of genre paintings records a foundational scene of US imperialism, and captures the public drama of national expansion. Its broader subject, however, is the social life of information. Woodville's image depicts news of Mexican surrender to Federal forces processing outwards from the central rectangle of crumpled text, intersecting with the geometry of the porch, the hotel, the post office insignia, the recruitment poster and the canvas itself. Through the isolated female onlooker and African American pair – who are all held, along with the viewer, at one remove from participation – we are shown how information excludes. Through the whisperer who relays the news to one of the hat-wearing men, we watch information being mediated.

But this is an image as much of performance as dissemination: upon the proscenium arch of the 'American Hotel' the public square becomes civic theatre, the setting for a ritual that Woodville wants us to imagine repeated in countless small towns as news of war diffuses through the republic. The waistcoated businessman proclaiming the news becomes a demotic mock orator of the Declaration and his newspaper – tattered from previous readings – is given life, its columns reanimated for the crowd. Speech acts proliferate as members of the group pass on the words of the central figure in both imminent and anticipated repetitions: by the woman to her household, by black father to child, by these townsfolk to those unseen. Above all, we might say, the canvas presents a moment of sound. In a well-known reading of the painting, Bryan Wolf argued that 'the paper provides the centre of the canvas a window of light that organizes the surrounding forces',[1] but we can also see how the rectangle of print interacts with the curve of the opened mouth, an orifice gaping in disbelief but also in power as an instrument with its own organising force. The voice of news arrests eleven varied citizens from the flow of their private pursuits and forms them into a cohesive unit: the listening public, a rural nation integrated by text and voice.

In Herman Melville's collection of Civil War verse, *Battle-Pieces* (1866), the longest poem, 'Donelson', conjured up a strikingly similar scene. A mixed crowd huddles around the post office of a Northern town eager for word from a Tennessee siege:

> The bitter cup
>   Of that hard countermand
> Which gave the Envoys up,
> Still was wormwood in the mouth,
>   And clouds involved the land,
> When, pelted by sleet in the icy street,
>   About the bulletin-board a band
> Of eager, anxious people met,
> And every wakeful heart was set
> On latest news from West or South.
> 'No seeing here,' cries one – 'don't crowd' –
> 'You tall man, pray you, read aloud.'[2]

As the chosen speaker's mouth opens, the margin and typography shifts and the war news is pulled into a poetic hybrid that simulates dispatches being read aloud:

> IMPORTANT.
>   *We learn that General Grant,*
>   *Marching from Henry overland,*
> *And joined by a force up the Cumberland sent*
>   *(Some thirty thousand the command),*

---

1 Bryan Wolf, 'All the World's a Code: Art and Ideology in Nineteenth-century American Painting', *Art Journal* 44.4: *American Art* (Winter 1984), 328–37.

2 Herman Melville, 'Donelson', in *Published Poems: Battle-Pieces; John Marr; Timoleon*, ed. Robert Charles Ryan (Evanston, Ill., 2009), 23, ll. 1–12. Subsequent references to 'Donelson' give line numbers in parentheses.

On Wednesday a good position won –
Began the siege of Donelson. [6–10]

The size of the crowd prevents private reading, the war is channelled
into a communal moment of aural consumption, and 'Donelson' becomes a poem for voices, interweaving media narrative with the inter-
jections from a community of listeners as restive and divided as those in
Woodville's canvas.

These twinned artefacts give imaginative shape to an idiosyncratic
form of social exchange: the oral rendition of printed news. An everyday
phenomenon of social history, that responded to two communications
revolutions: the arrival of mass-market 'penny press' newspapers during
the 1830s, and the widespread adoption of the electric telegraph in the
1850s. Between the two wartime images, important changes in news
standardisation and technology had taken place. Whereas Woodville
could depict the newspaper as a more or less static print artefact, by 1862
habits of print had given way to more fragmentary 'stream-of-news', as
telegraphic communication broke news down into briefer sequential
dispatches.[3] Reading aloud swiftly became part of the communicative
world of these new technologies, but was also bound in powerful ways
to pre-literate habits of association. Painter and poet therefore invite us
to experience the strange persistence of speech in the journey of information, and in doing so, animate the unresolved relationship of vocal
performance to social authority in early America. My response in what
follows fleshes out the historical point that even while the rise of print
and telegraph reworked perception and consciousness it catalysed older
cultures of vocal performance. Rather than becoming diminished, new
styles of orality and new expressive forms emerged from a productive
interplay of voice and literacy technologies. Far from entirely rational
and textual, therefore, the public sphere of this incipient information
age remained embodied, still conditioned to a surprising extent by what
Jay Fleigelman characterised as a potent 'culture of performance'.[4]

Building upon these insights, my argument turns back to canvas
and poem to think about the logic of modernity visible in these acts
of public news reading. If both artefacts are about the emergence of

3 Menahem Blondheim, *News Over the Wires: The Telegraph and the Flow
of Public Information in America, 1844–1897* (Cambridge, Mass., 1994), 132–3.
4 Jay Fleigelman, *Declaring Independence: Jefferson, Natural Language and the
Culture of Performance* (Stanford CA, 1993), 4.

technologies and communication systems that shape new conditions of knowledge, then it seems clear that Melville in particular also points forward in literary history. What Sandra Gustafson has called the 'reciprocal formations of speech and writing' of early American 'emerging media' erupt in his work as an opportunity for expressive innovation.[56] In 'Donelson', I argue, the power and ambivalence of live reading is translated into an aesthetic of fracture, impersonality and ventriloquism that will come to fruition in multiple Anglo-American literary modernisms. Allegories about the social authority of nineteenth-century voice finally force us, I suggest, to reflect on the connection between citizenship and informational literacy, and the roles of wartime audiences as producers in circuits of information.

Forms of the Talking Mind

This historical phenomenon draws us into a classic hierarchical problem of text and voice. As early as 1749, Benjamin Franklin had noted that 'modern political oratory [is now] chiefly performed by the Pen and Press'.[7] The transatlantic Enlightenment's culture of letters had, in this view, supplanted the functions of older forms of spoken interaction. The revolutionary phenomena of the penny press in the 1830s, and telegraph of the following decade, are typically seen as rounding off this process, a deterministic narrative familiar from the work of Walter Ong, who saw in the period 'a new state of consciousness associated with the definite interiorisation of print, and the atrophy of the ancient rhetorical tradition'.[8] But to mid-nineteenth-century Americans, such

5   Sandra M. Gustafson, *The Emerging Media of Early America* (Worcester, Mass., 2006), 3.
6   Sandra M. Gustafson, 'Orality and Literacy in Transatlantic Perspective', *19: Interdisciplinary Studies in the Long Nineteenth Century* 18: *Orality and Literacy*, ed. James Emmott and Tom F. Wright (2014), forthcoming.
7   Benjamin Franklin, 'Proposals Relating to the Education of Youth in Pensilvania' (1749), in *The Papers of Benjamin Franklin*, ed. Leonard Labaree et al. (New Haven, 1959–), III, 412.
8   Walter Ong, *Orality and Literacy: The Technologizing of the Word* (Oxford, 1982), 166. The most authoritative discussion for the communications revolutions of the nineteenth-century United States remains Richard Brown, *Knowledge is Power: The Diffusion of Information in Early America* (Oxford, 1989), 258–83.

claims would have seemed premature. As the New England editor and writer George William Curtis expressed it in 1856:

> a few years since, when the steam-engine was harnessed into the service of the printing-press, we were ready to conclude that oral instruction would have to yield the palm, to written literature . . . but we forgot, in our hasty generalization, how the law of compensation rules everywhere . . . so the new motor, in the service of newspapers and books, would call out other forms of the talking mind.[9]

We might call this 'law of compensation' a governing process of nineteenth-century media life. Whilst the period witnessed substantial erosion of oral modes of thought, in a number of crucial ways technology actually led to more prominence for talking, creating qualitatively different practices of textual interaction, and fostering innovative expressive forms that drew aesthetic power from the interplay of voice, type and wire. Speech texts in the press broadcast newly energised political oratory verbatim throughout the nation in their column inches; promotion in print made cultures of spoken word performance such as the lyceum movement possible.[10] More broadly, as Ronald Zboray has put it, 'pronunciation came to mediate between reading and comprehension, giving the written word in antebellum America a strong oral bias'.[11]

Engaging with Woodville and Melville's scenes therefore means re-connecting to a history of literacy that was as much a social act as it was private. Reading practices went beyond internalised silent contemplation, and as multiple types of records confirm, communal oral consumption in family or other groups was a commonplace.[12] In addition to novels and poetry, newspapers were also part of this culture of recitation, and reading the national and local press aloud became

9   George William Curtis, 'Editor's Table', *Harpers Monthly* 14.79 (December 1856), 125.

10   See Angela Ray, *The Lyceum and Public Culture in the Nineteenth-century United States* (East Lansing, 2005), 2; and Donald Scott, 'The Popular Lecture and the Creation of a Public in Mid Nineteenth-century America', *Journal of American History* 66 (1980), 791–809.

11   Ronald J. Zboray, *A Fictive People: Antebellum Economic Development and the American Reading Public* (New York, 1993), 87.

12   Mary Saracino Zboray and Ronald J. Zboray, 'Nineteenth-century Print Culture', in *The Oxford Handbook of Transcendentalism*, ed. Joel Myerson, Sandra Harbert Petrulionis, and Laura Dassow Walls (Oxford, 2010), 102–14; 103.

a form of sociability that resulted in home and public spaces resound-
ing to the sound of the daily news. As early as 1819, a German visitor
to Pennsylvania, Ludwig Gall, was struck by how people could sometimes not wait to read about current events in private, and 'the few
who cannot read can hear news discussed or read aloud in ale- and
oyster-houses'.[13] This centrality for the newspaper as catalyst and script
for public reading and debate is a major motif in Woodville compos-
itions such as *Politics in an Oyster House* (1848) and *Waiting for the
Stage* (1851), which bear witness to the historical irony of ink and wire
submitting to mouth and ears, with technology reviving older forms of
oral storytelling.[14]

This form of the talking mind produced its own particular scene of
performance and reception at the bulletin board. In 1840s small towns,
newspapers would arrive by mail coach from other places and be pinned
to the front of the building that first acquired the news, whether these
were press and post offices or hotels, a process that the artistic license
of *War News from Mexico* interestingly inverts, with the newspaper held
aloft making the canvas itself a form of pasted board. In the accelerat-
ing 1860s media ecology of 'Donelson', the telegraph dispatch would
come over the wire, and sequential snippets would be fixed to dedicated pasteboards at telegraph hubs from which they could be read to a
waiting crowd.[15] Successive waves of logistical advancement had thus
transformed civic spaces into dynamic scenes of live exchange, performance and social drama. 'The great speed at which these newspapers
are produced', according to Gall, fed 'the excited curiosity with which
the otherwise phlegmatic Americans storm the newspapers office before
the appointed hour and gobble up the produce of the presses.'[16] The urgency of war and the astonishing speed of telegraph communication of
military news exacerbated the importance of these spaces. Upon news
of the Mexican victory in 1847, the *Charleston Courier* recorded 'immense crowds in and around our office, eager to learn the particulars
of the conflict. The news, after being publicly read, flew with rapidity

13   Frederic Trautmann, 'Pennsylvania through a German's Eyes: The Trav-
els of Ludwig Gall, 1819–1820', *Pennsylvania Magazine of History and Biography*
105.1 (January 1981), 35–65; 48.
14   See Justin Wolff, *Richard Caton Woodville: American Painter, Artful Dodger*
(Princeton, 2002), xxiv.
15   David Henkin, *City Reading: Written Words and Public Spaces in Antebellum New York* (New York, 1998), 2.
16   Trautmann, 'Pennsylvania through a German's Eyes', 48.

from mouth to mouth, and was everywhere received with exultation.'[17] Oliver Wendell Holmes wrote during the turmoil of 1861 of how 'men cannot think, or write, or attend to their ordinary business. They stroll up and down the streets, or saunter out upon the public places' await-ing the further vibrations of telegraph wires.[18] One attraction for both Woodville and Melville must have been the temporal disjunction on display in these new communication networks: the anachronism of crowding together to consume information face to face in a world in which information had become largely privatised as an act of individual textual apprehension.[19] Moreover, newspaper and telegraph bulletin boards were unmatched as sites revealing unpredictable public emo-tion, by turn scenes of jubilation and loss, and their particular role in the 1860s was part of a Civil Wartime shift that helped redefine joy and grief as public.[20] The uncertainties of imprecise media reportage were inevitably exacerbated by problems of the crowd, and the fervour that attended this new feature of small-town and urban life was subject to new genres of satirical newspaper coverage that found humour in the naïve enthusiasms, mishearing, and misunderstandings that accom-panied street readings.[21] Nonetheless, to citizen, journalist, poet and painter alike, the bulletin board phenomenon represented something tangibly and ambiguously new in public life, and a primary location of home-front battles for war's meanings.

An Embodied Public Sphere

Just like contemporary observers, historians have been divided on the value of this social and media phenomenon. Richard Brown has seen the text-to-voice process as one simply of the printed message submitting to 'the multifarious networks of face-to-face diffusion. As had always

17 'Glorious News From Mexico', *Charleston Courier* (29 March 1847).
18 Oliver Wendell Holmes, 'Bread and the Newspaper', *Atlantic Monthly* 8.47 (September 1861), 346–52; 348: ebooks.library.cornell.edu/a/atla/index.html.
19 See Alice Fahs, *The Imagined Civil War: Popular Literature of the North and South 1861–65* (Chapel Hill, NC, 2001), 19.
20 See Drew G. Faust, *This Republic of Suffering: Death and the American Civil War* (New York, 2008).
21 See 'Milwaukee Sentinel Reports', *Daily National Intelligencer* [Washing-ton, DC], 21 December 1854. Subsequent reprints include 'A Puzzler', *Colum-bus Enquirer,* 27 January 1857.

been true, nothing could match the speed of face-to-face transmission within a locality.'[22] David Henkin's work has documented the remarkable penetration of display in the urban world of antebellum America, and sees the bulletin board as entirely instrumental. The 'cheers [that] accompanied the reception of the written words' might indicate a role for voice and performance, 'but the posted bulletin remained the centrepiece of the event' and in accounts of bulletin board scenes, the oral 'reading of the news [was] represented, significantly, as a makeshift substitute'.[23] However, Melville and Woodville's representations help us appreciate a key performative aspect at work that goes beyond information transfer. In their depictions, reading the war news aloud facilitates a palpable affective bond, connecting listeners physically not only to the dead and dying but to one another. Far from being a value-free instrument of progress that separated individuals from each other, therefore, live rendering of current events helped to promote a personalised network of human relations.[24] The meaning of *War News From Mexico* and 'Donelson' therefore rests in part in the world of orality that surrounds what Benedict Anderson terms the 'ceremony' of daily newspaper consumption. Hearing the news read aloud alongside other interested citizens might be thought of as an instance of what Anderson calls 'unisonance', through which the sounds of the newspaper becomes 'the echoed physical realization of the imagined community'.[25] And yet, though at the bulletin board the newspaper in one sense becomes the script of an imagined nation brought forth, there is more at work in this process that a simple national imaginary.

As James Carey reminds us, communication processes are always at once instrumental (serving as transmission) and symbolic (a form of ritual). The dissemination of news is a particular case in point. 'Under a ritual view', he maintains, 'news is not information but drama. It does not describe the world but portrays an arena of dramatic forces and action; it exists solely in historical time; and it invites our participation on the basis of our assuming, often vicariously, social roles within it'.[26]

22   Brown, *Knowledge is Power*, 258.
23   Henkin, *City Reading*, 170.
24   Wolf, 'All the World's a Code', 4.
25   Benedict Anderson, *Imagined Communities: Reflections on the Origins of Nationalism*, rev. edn (London, 2006), 148.
26   James Carey, *Communication as Culture: Essays on Media and Society*, rev. edn (London, 2008), 33.

Proclaiming the war news literalises this, as spectators and speakers assume roles within a national story, and become infected with the anxiety of participation and involved in the same episodic narrative that makes manifest subtle and overt power relations.

Read aloud, the newspaper and telegraph press dispatch become a script brought to life for a crowd by an individual player, and information submits to his or her gesture, rhythms and accent, to what Ivan Kreilkampf has called 'the improvisatory re-performance of narrative in public' that characterises Victorian storytelling.[27] Franklin's Enlightenment teleology of print convergence may have imagined a political public sphere of democratic rationality, but the exchange of ideas submitted to the peculiar force of bodily passions. Proclaiming the 'war news' made this prominent. It was not simply an instrumental, functional act, but provided an intermediate space between what Looby characterises as 'the abstract alienated rational *polis* of print culture and the more passionately attached, quasi-somatic experienced nation for which many Americans longed'.[28] As in Samuel Morse's famous vision of how his telegraph would create a national 'network of iron nerves which flash sensation and volition backward and forward to and from towns and provinces as if they were organs and limbs of a single living body', performing the war news at the bulletin board made manifest this somatic rhetoric of the electric sublime.[29]

Two images of war news help to illustrate these paradoxes at work. In her 1866 novel *Sunnybank*, the Southern novelist Marion Harland depicts a domestic scene of reading in wartime Virginia, with a family listening to the war news being proclaimed:

> Papa was reading aloud from a newspaper at the centre-table. The rest were listening. The topic of interest was Lee's march into Pennsylvania, and the probable – or according to the journalist – the certain and overwhelming defeat of the Federals, in a great pitched battle.[30]

27   Ivan Kreilkamp, *Voice and the Victorian Storyteller* (Cambridge, 2005), 101.

28   Christopher Looby, *Voicing the Nation: Voicing America: Language, Literary Form and the Origins of the United States* (Chicago, 1997), 5.

29   Holmes, 'Bread and the Newspaper', 348; see also 'The Magnetic Telegraph: Its Contemplated Extension – Its National Importance', *The Living Age* 4.34 (4 January 1845), 21; 'The Magnetic Telegraph – Some of Its Results', *The Living Age* 6.63 (26 July 1845), 194–5: ebooks.library.cornell.edu/l/livn/index.html.

30   Marion Harland, *Sunnybank* (New York, 1866), 138.

The reading of the war news is presented here as a paternalistic gesture in which the events of conflict unfold for a passive audience, whose scepticism of journalistic accuracy is held at bay by the central force of male voice. A public dimension, however, adds a level of meaning to the events. On 4 July 1862, the *New York Herald* printed the following commentary on the scene outside its offices, whose rhetoric captures the more intricate stakes involved in public reading:

> Thicker and thicker grew the mass of anxious people, until it was impossible for a quarter of them to gain sight of the pleasing transcript. One individual, with the lungs of a Stentor, ventured to act as telegraphic medium to the multitude, and read aloud the following words . . .[31]

The locus of authority in this second depiction is less clear. We have a multitude 'anxious' not only for news but also for a form of shared immersion, and the delegated speaker acts as telegraph, becoming part of a network, embodying the news. The speaker is marked for having 'the *lungs* of a Stentor', and so the news becomes inescapably bound up with the complications of physical attributes (recalling Melville's 'tall man') and the politics of sincerity and authenticity. Yet in ways that seem to anticipate the techno-determinism of Friedrich Kittler the process of reading the news allows the 'individual' to become a technological prosthesis, effacing the human through the 'medium'.[32] We therefore glimpse a tension between two models of communication: the civic resonance of the 'Stentor', the herald of war around whom the multitude can unify; and the competing idea of the 'medium', the bringer forth of distant sounds, possessed of apparent bodily connection with the ethereal voices that threaten social fabric and official narrative. By framing the reading of the news in this way, media accounts became their own rhetorical form, projecting orality through print and affirming an imagined public of fellow listeners and citizens.

But if the need remained for a more psychically compelling mode of attachment to the nation, such desires were met in problematic fashion by bulletin-board proclamations. When a newspaper is publicly read aloud, different traditions of expression mingle, and an older mode of

31 'How the News Was Received', *New York Herald* (4 July 1862).
32 Friedrich A. Kittler, *Gramophone, Film, Typewriter* (Stanford CA, 1999), 130–2.

associating and communicating is brought to bear in unanticipated fashion. When the words of the press are uttered, democratic ideas of the voice of the people – *vox populi, vox dei* – compete and merge uncomfortably with an assumed authority of the technological process, just as in the more technologically advanced Civil War context, popular voice submits to what Oliver Wendell Holmes termed 'the divine right of telegraphic dispatches'.[33] Moreover, through submission to the spoken and unanswerable texts, the public gained an acquiescent and disengaged burlesque of the democratic process, in the place of real discussion. Once news becomes noise and performance, problematic implications arise for any ambitions towards a rational flow of information divorced from affect. These unruly discursive conditions and ideological slippages animate *War News from Mexico,* but are even more pronounced in Melville's dramatization of the ambivalent social and expressive potential of the live reader.

Modernist 'Donelson'

For the Mexican War, Melville had been a provincial observer of the nation's enthusiasms. In a famous 1846 letter to his brother from upstate New York, he was eloquent about the palpable verbal effects of the news, noting how 'people here are all in a state of delirium about the Mexican War . . . nothing is talked of but "Halls of Montezuma"'.[34] Sixteen years later, at the height of the siege of Fort Donelson, Melville had moved back to Manhattan, but was once again experiencing conflict through proxy processes of urban print and speech, of the very type Henkin's work brings so vividly to life.[35] Facing the impossibility of rendering distant carnage in verse, and sharing a collective sense of literary impotence, he rehearsed one compelling solution in 'Donelson' by responding to the home-front phenomenology of telegraph flickers and public debate. The result was a radical, 460-line poem in an unidentified narrative voice that told the story of a hard-won Union victory,

33   Holmes, 'Bread and the Newspaper', 348.
34   Herman Melville to Gansevoort Melville, 29 June 1846, in Herman Melville, *Correspondence*, ed. Lynne Horth (Evanston, Ill., 1993), 40.
35   Hershel Parker, *Herman Melville: A Biography: Vol. 2, 1851–1891* (Baltimore, 2002), 490–5. For Henkin's most relevant discussion of city crowds and oral recitation, see *City Reading*, 170–2.

using the bulletin board to chart the battle and its small-town reception over a course of three days. As we have seen, in attempting to approximate this new fractured miscellany, Melville makes imaginative use of page and form, interspersing headlines and dispatches in jarring manner with the voices of an argumentative crowd. The competing communicative modes of voice and telegraph become at once technique, content and theme.

Thomas Zlatic has seen in the poem affinities with the telegraph-inspired aesthetic of Gerard Manley Hopkins's 'Wreck of the Deutschland' (c.1875), whose form registers a comparable sensitivity to media polyphony.[36] As Ong has noted, the telegraph 'altered human beings' feelings for the world around them and for the presence of themselves in the world'; it seemed set in Hopkins to reconfigure 'the face of poetry as well'.[37] If anything, 'Donelson' makes the formal implications of these cognitive and affective shifts even more pronounced, a stylistic decision that helps explain some of the book's bewildered reception in its own time. Reviews lamented his 'uncouth' and 'epileptic' versification, his 'fearful' rhymes and the intensity of his rhythmic 'convulsions'.[38] However, as Cody Marrs has recently argued, the 'poetics of difficulty' of *Battle-Pieces* might be better seen as a troubled response to conflict, 'enunciated most powerfully on the level of form'.[39] Though Marrs excludes it from his discussion, 'Donelson' was the volume's most radical piece, and in its attempt to capture both national crisis and communicative breakdown in a world of electric and oral voices, it laid bare the capacity of public speech to collaborate in the production of news during wartime.

Written from the perspective of an unnamed observer and listener, the poem largely consists of an incoming torrent of news. Its reportage veers from detailed omniscient description ('*the spaded summit shows the roods | Of fixed intrenchments in their hush*' [25–6]) to vignettes of collective heroism ('*our lads creep round on hand and knee*' [74]); the Tennessee

36   Thomas Zlatic, '"Horned Perplexities": Melville's "Donelson" and Media Environments', *Leviathan: A Journal of Melville Studies*, 13.2 (June 2011), 38–53. Other comparisons have pointed to Robert Browning, and to the Thomas Hardy of *The Dynasts*. See *Selected Poems of Herman Melville*, ed. Robert P. Warren (Jaffrey, NH, 2004), 362.

37   Walter J. Ong, *Hopkins, the Self, and God* (Toronto, 1986), 48–50.

38   Brian Higgins and Hershel Parker, eds., *Herman Melville: The Contemporary Reviews* (Cambridge, 1995), 513.

39   Cody Marrs, 'A Wayward Art: *Battle-Pieces* and Melville's Poetic Turn', *American Literature* 82 (2010), 91–119; 93.

dispatches conjure up both '*a dreamy contrast to the North*' (34) and a grotesque tableau of '*ice-glazed corpses*' (250). The mood rises and falls, from stoic resignation to jubilation; pronouns shift, leaving speakers and perspective unclear. At numerous points the word '*further*' punctuates the text, linking the arrival of information with the theme of military progression. In keeping with his oral theme, Melville's metaphor and lexicon constellate around a linked rhetoric of mouths, digestion and sound: the wartime predicament is repeatedly figured as a 'bowl' or 'cup'; Grant's forces are '*vomited out*' (287); the voices of news and crowd be-come 'different strain[s]' (195). Throughout, Melville makes much of the meta-textual aspects involved in his bulletin board conceit. As the crowd departs the rain-soaked square, the print on the newspaper runs – 'the paper grew | Every shade of a streaky blue' (41–2) – in parallel to the blue of the uniformed Union lines. When '*the earnest North | Has elementally issued forth | To storm this Donelson*' (92–4) readers might al-most conceptualise this as a product of a torrent of vocalised utterance.

The poem's prescience is apparent most obviously in the fractured rendering of this informational tangle, a modernist collage whose jar-ring force enacts a sustained cognitive confusion suggestive of subsequent Anglo-American poetic forms. Like much Civil War poetry this verse sig-nals its own inadequacy, and does so here through confessions of impre-cise composition – '(*Our own reporter a dispatch compiles, | As best he may, from varied sources*)' (196–7). The poem is full of the disconnected voices of observers, journalists, the Lincoln administration, and the listening crowd, full of speculation and unclear facts. Once meaning is mediated by technology, Melville suggests, we risk communication breakdown:

> (*Herewith a break.*
> *Storms at the West derange the wires.*
> *Doubtless, ere morning, we shall hear*
> *The end; we look for news to cheer –*
> *Let Hope fan all her fires.*) [385–389]

As William Dean Howells declared in a contemporary review, the po-ems of *Battle-Pieces* dislocate the reader, 'until you are lost to every sense of time or place', resulting in an aesthetic experience that eludes, repels and undoes the pressures of the material world.[40] The poem is itself a

---

40 'Reviews and Literary Notices', *Atlantic Monthly* 19.112 (February 1867), 252–3; 252.

disjointed stream of news, capturing a kind of knowledge and a category of fact that acquires new meaning due to speed. For a writer so fascinated by repetitions, echoes, rebirths and ironic reflections, we might also trace the chains of equivalence between the older, spoken street-corner ballad form and the fractured news report. Melville's modernism develops into one not only concerned with formal disorder and a sense of lost fixity, but riven with a nostalgia for authentic spoken communication.

There is another conceptual issue that this bulletin-board conceit throws up for Melville, in the symbolic potential of the live reader. In 'Donelson', a world of informational exactitude collides with the unpredictability of larynx, and with the idea of the speaker ventriloquising a multitude of discordant voices. It is a process that involves an interplay of personality and impersonality, the performance of a fractured self. This age of newspaper reading, we should remember, finds its most famous nineteenth-century expression through Sloppy in *Our Mutual Friend*, whose mother tells us he 'was a beautiful reader of the newspaper. He Do the Police in Different Voices,' a phrase which famously reappeared at one of the high points of Anglo-American modernism in the manuscript of T. S. Eliot's *The Waste Land*, as its provisional title.[41] Readers such as Sloppy offer improvisatory performances and draw on mastery of idiom, intonation and rhythm, as they orally interpret texts involving a series of voices, registers and modes. The task demands from the speaker a strange form of embodiment that obscures its origin and its meaning, but also lends permanence to a ritualistic, parodic scene of storytelling, and a disembodied voice of circulating textuality. Eliot saw in this newspaper-reading process the 'poem for voices' aesthetic that he sought, and it is one that Melville was already exploring in 1866. Within technological change and the new public reading habits it brought into being, Melville saw the germs of an invigorating and disorientating form of representation. As Marrs argues, '*Battle-Pieces* not only records the war but also projects and mourns the emergent. In graves and ships it discerns the ascent of mass production and collective labor.'[42] In this light, the experiments of 'Donelson' offer a spirited attempt to dramatise the communicative and social problems of war in an information age. The focus on voice and perspective allows for a far-ranging critique of the ambivalence of mediation, and the ways in which it threatens the relationship of information, narrative and speech.

---

41   Charles Dickens, *Our Mutual Friend* (Oxford, 1997 [1865]), 230.
42   Marrs, 'A Wayward Art', 104.

With its strategies compromised by languid execution and a diffuse imprecision of effect, 'Donelson' seems a strangely muted piece. Perhaps fittingly, at the end of a wilfully oblique poem, the final image is one of a failed quest, as beams of light, 'in vain seek Donelson' (461). At the end of the poem, the narrator's is just another voice embroiled in the attempt to 'seek' and decipher the meanings of crowd, technology, and war, and failure of comprehension and expression becomes the most resonant theme of the poem. Melville's modernism cultivates new tasks for poetry as a form of literary technology that, like the telegraph, relies on the summoning up of sounds and images. As poetic tradition sacrifices its monopoly as a societal form of memory and capture, it faces the challenge and promise of new emergent possibilities. Nevertheless, Melville's innovations come not only from his handling of new telegraphic temporalities, but the emergent epistemological conditions and social dangers that arise from his bulletin-board tableau.

Cacophony and Media Literacy

The most compelling way in which the poem seeks the meaning of 'Donelson' appears through the focus on the bulletin-board crowd. Establishing an elaborate equivalence between front line and home front, the poem presents the social drama of civilian discussion as intrinsic to the conflict itself. The focal point comes in an extended moment as nuanced and carnivalesque as Woodville's canvas:

> 'Ugh! ugh!
> 'Twill drag along – drag along,'
> Growled a cross patriot in the throng,
> His battered umbrella like an ambulance-cover
> Riddled with bullet-holes, spattered all over.
> 'Hurrah for Grant!' cried a stripling shrill;
> Three urchins joined him with a will,
> And some of taller stature cheered.
> Meantime a Copperhead passed; he sneered.
>   'Win or lose,' he pausing said,
> 'Caps fly the same; all boys, mere boys;
> Any thing to make a noise.
>   Like to see the list of the dead;
> These '*craven Southerners*' hold out;
> Ay, ay, they'll give you many a bout.'

'We'll beat in the end, sir,'
Firmly said one in staid rebuke,
A solid merchant, square and stout.
        'And do you think it? that way tend, sir?'
Asked the lean Copperhead, with a look
Of splenetic pity. 'Yes, I do.'
His yellow death's head the croaker shook:
'The country's ruined, that I know.'
A shower of broken ice and snow,
        In lieu of words, confuted him;
They saw him hustled round the corner go,
        And each by-stander said – Well suited him. [152–178]

The dramatis personae – the 'cross patriot', 'Copperhead', naïve 'ur-
chins', and 'solid merchant' – are carefully chosen as a representative
swathe of Northern opinion. Though partly comic, the scene is under-
written by awareness of the real perils of the mob. The oppositional
voice of the 'Copperhead' (salty contemporary slang for a Southern
sympathiser) is 'confuted', a term here stripped of its association with
rational debate and instead bound up with mere elemental force. Just as,
in the stanza to follow, Grant's force will have 'SILENCED EVERY GUN'
(187), the voices here strive for sonic supremacy, and a plurality of wartime opinions is reduced through group coercion to an artificial chorus.
A form of temporal coherence or Anderson's 'unisonance' is imposed
through elemental force, '[i]n lieu of words' (176). Melville's narrator is
careful to distance himself from this mean-spirited scene, framing each
side of the debate in terms of sneering shrillness. But the combination
of pessimism and 'pity' in the anti-war speaker's voice here hints at partial sympathy, as the narrator too seems to attempt to reach beyond the
base pleasures of fresh information.

   This is Melville the satirist, alarmed as much by irrational popular cre-
dulity as by the coercive silencing of dissent, and influenced as much by
his reading of Thomas Carlyle's critiques of democracy as by the anti-hu-
manism of his friend Nathaniel Hawthorne. The bulletin-board scene is
a way of conceiving of both of these strands, and in his hands it becomes
a microcosm of the compromises of the Lincoln administration's wartime
censorship.[43] In finding such meanings in the drama of public reading, we

43   See Christopher B. Daly, *Covering America: A Narrative History of a Nation's Journalism* (Amherst, 2012), 100–3.

can compare this moment in 'Donelson' with another wartime composition on the same theme entitled simply 'The Bulletin Board', originally published anonymously in the Ohio newspaper in June 1864, in which an almost identical anti-war interruption takes place:

> At last a Copperhead comes in the crowd –
> He hears the stories, then laughs aloud!
> Saying: How can sensible men afford
> To be bored by the Journal's Bulletin Board!
> That thunder full, blunder full Bulletin Board!
> Which 'sells' the town in the morning soon,
> That ye Extra may 'sell' in the afternoon.[44]

We find here the same populist voice of scepticism aimed at the curious new prominence of media institutions and practices. But here this is mixed with a sense of the commercial nature of the bulletin-board process, concerned as it is with the novelty of the information rather than its content or validity. And as with Melville's own 'Copperhead', who prefers a straightforward inventory of loss (the 'list of the dead') to any romanticised, gripping narrative, this anonymous poem is a protest against the low motives and social confusion to which the process of war news is often reduced.

If, as Looby argues, public speech retains a 'legitimating charisma' that print lacks, then translating news into voice risks mistaking charisma for sincerity, and substituting performance for fact.[45] In a thematic register that, as elsewhere in Melville, draws upon gothic ventriloquisms of Charles Brockden Brown's fiction, the force of 'Donelson' derives in part from the corrosive social threat of untrusted voices. His fractured narrative poem, in its discord and disunity, in its unseen voice of social authority, and in its new public and potentially deceptive performance, registers his misgivings about the ways in which habits of consumption undermine rational democratic decision-making. Melville's poem warns of the dangers of the wrong kind of over-investment in the news, the risk of losing sight of the realities and real events behind the hue and cry of coercive patriotic kinship. It counsels readers to navigate the competing demands of information and performance, of transmission and ritual. It reminds

44 'The Bulletin Board', *Daily Ohio Statesman* (16 June 1864).
45 Looby, *Voicing the Nation*, 4.

readers how historical change always comes back to the voice, and to the image of the nation condensed into a single mouth – ('wormwood in the mouth' [4]) – with which the poem opened. As in Ralph Waldo Emerson's resonant prophecy that the Mexican war would 'poison' the nation,[46] Melville asks how the war news could not, like 'wormwood', fill the mouth with bitterness, as a cacophony of information and dead language? Melville here shows how conflict intoxicates by imposing artificial 'unisonance' on the national narrative.

'Donelson' thus becomes a parable of citizenship and a cautionary tale about informational literacy, in an age when media developments outstripped ready social comprehension, and when ritualistic scenes could be drastically misleading. For example, on 17 February 1862, halfway through the siege of Fort Donelson, the *Macon Telegraph* in Georgia reported to its readers that the siege was almost won for the Confederates, and carefully noted the following scene of public fervour:

> MORE EXCITEMENT – Late Saturday afternoon, when the telegram announcing the glorious victory at Fort Donelson was placed upon our bulletin board, quite a large crowd soon congregated in front of our office. It was pleasing to witness the crowd, their demonstrations and remarks. One would say, 'glory enough for one day', and go on his way rejoicing. Another thought it was a good offset to Roanoke.[47]

There was clear rhetorical value in affirming this 'pleasing' scene of 'excitement', affirming the enthusiasm and existence of a live 'congregation'. But this Georgia account was tragically premature. At the very moment of these 'demonstrations and remarks', Confederate General Pillow was being forced to surrender by Ulysses Grant; the time-lag in the circuit of information renders such a scene a lesson in the incomplete nature of war news. The provisional nature of this moment can help us to appreciate Melville's message: that technologies such as the telegraph render the conflict sufficiently abstract for it to fall prey to the irrational 'demonstrations and remarks' of group mentality, whose connection to the body and performance make them doubly misleading.

46 Journal entry for May 1846: *The Journals and Miscellaneous Notebooks of Ralph Waldo Emerson*, ed. William H. Gilman (Cambridge, Mass., 1960), 206.
47 'More Excitement', *Macon Telegraph* (Georgia) (17 February 1862).

Conclusion: Voices of War

It is tempting to see the experience of turning from 'Donelson' back to *War News from Mexico* as a retreat from an agonised study of fractured meaning to the vernacular pleasures of a carnivalesque ensemble. But the often-underappreciated ironies of genre painting are one way for Woodville to mediate American democracy for his global audience. The keynote of the image appears as one of seductive momentum, an invitation to vicarious patriotic triumph and collective identity. As the crowd cranes towards newspaper and voice, it is seemingly an icon of assent, and its commercial appeal relied in part upon its being able to be seen simply as a 'victory dance under the safe American hotel'.[48] Its strength, however, lies in the contrary readings it supports, not least that of the grotesque of an ungovernable polity run amok, disrupted by passions and display. Profound unease is written into at least half of the faces of the crowd: anxiety about the Mexican adventure, mob action, callow delusion and the influence of rhetoric. As in the mode of the group portrait associated with the paintings of Joseph Wright of Derby, the meaning of wider social forces can be sought in the exaggerated texture of audience response.

The more ambivalent of these figures, those most clearly implicated as passive audience and mediator, are also the most important. The African American pair and the domestic female worker, for example, are reduced to the status of fearful onlookers to this martial carnival. The black father and child, whose emblematic red, white and blue clothing compels us to invest in them a degree of national symbolism, are spatially the only figures addressed directly. Clothed in almost ecclesiastical white, the child is the figure with the most at stake in this moment of military conflict that might expand or help to destroy slavery, and the one for whom the sound and fury of the bulletin board is the most incomprehensible. Along with that child, we as viewers exist as groundlings in this performance, as we too search the scene anxiously for its elusive meanings. But crucially, the newspaper stands in between the black couple and the sound of the 'news'. And this theme of mediation takes us to the whisperer, the other instrumental figure in the scene, marked as significant for his gestural detachment, refusing to lean towards the voice. As a number of critics have pointed out, this man connects the two generations – the wary veteran of 1776 or 1812,

48   Wolff, *Richard Caton Woodville*, 192.

and the fervent Young American of 1848 – and mediates between their respective military ideals.[49] He also connects their two distinct roles for public speech: the former a heroic age of republican orators imposing civility through reasoned eloquence; the latter a diffuse media ecology of informational exchange. His role as mediator would seem to ask one final question: the role of the artist as teacher of the meanings of public events. In its tapestry of mixed and often uncomprehending responses, the painting presents a group portrait of individuals struggling to work out what public events and rituals mean to them. Woodville asks what any whisperer, printmaker or poet, can truly bring to this journey of national understanding.

Both painter and poet offer studies in reception that force us to contemplate the role of artists and audiences as consumers and producers, asking us to rethink the importance of our role within a ritual of response and reaction. Bulletin-board crowds provide highly evocative microcosmic sites that cast shadows upon national conflict and the social drama of democracy in an age of mass media. As two sceptics using these shadow sites to offer ironic commentaries on the new kinds of public made by modern war and modern media, Woodville and Melville remind us that communications revolutions generate new types of performance and artifice. Whilst media developments might displace the functions of oral poetry or historical painting, they also promise to revitalise its very functions and meanings. Literary and visual art not only chart developing forms of social interaction, but can perceive the new expressive possibilities within emerging media. To think of these scenes as visions of warfare and media that are either wholly damning or wholly affirmative is to miss their instability, and to ignore the prescient problems they pose about visceral forms of nationhood and information exchange. Returning to the problems raised by these proclamations of the war news can help pave the way for fuller accounts of military, literary and media history.

---

49   Bryan Wolf, 'All the World's a Code', 329.

III

Aftermaths

A Feeling for Numbers: Representing the Scale of the War Dead

MARY A. FAVRET

> The purpose of poetry is to remind us
> how difficult it is to remain just one person.[1]

JOSEF STALIN'S CLAIM that 'one death is a tragedy, a million deaths
. . . a statistic' we might take as an aesthetic and moral gloss on another
well-known comment, this one attributed to Napoleon Bonaparte: 'A
man like me does not give a shit about the lives of a million men.'[2]
Stalin's statement makes two assumptions that this essay will question.
It assumes that moral feeling – the sort formalised in tragedy – operates
on the level of the individual, the one, and is not susceptible to multiplication (or, for that matter, division). It assumes additionally that
statistics, the signs for large aggregates of human beings, do not occasion moral feeling. Apparently we do not feel the deaths of a million
men with anything like the force we feel for the death of one, 'a man',
as Napoleon says, 'like me'.

Stalin contributes to an ongoing debate in moral philosophy, set
here in the context of modern mass warfare, a context embracing the
Napoleonic era as well as our own. The terms of the debate and its
governing assumptions were laid out helpfully, if bluntly, by C. S. Lewis
in 1957. Writing in the gloom of the Cold War and against a utilitarian
outlook, Lewis argued that none of us can possibly experience suffering
on a scale other than that of the single person. If two people each feel X
amount of pain, Lewis explained, there is not 2X of pain on hand: '[N]o
one is suffering 2X; search all time and space and you will not find that
composite suffering in anyone's consciousness. There is no such thing as

---

1 C. Milosz, 'Ars Poetica?'
2 David A. Bell, *The First Total War: Napoleon's Europe and the Birth of
Warfare as We Know It* (Boston, Mass., 2007), 25.

a sum of suffering, because no *one* suffers it (emphasis added).'[3] Twenty years later, in a notorious 1977 essay, 'Should the Numbers Count?', John M. Taurek insisted that the value of a human life is not susceptible to addition or multiplication: all things being equal, six humans are not worth six times one human. Therefore, his logic spins out, the death of many can be no worse than the death of one.[4] 'If it were not for the fact that [these six people] were creatures much like me, for [each of whom] what happens . . . is of great importance, I doubt that I would take much interest in their preservation . . . It is the [threatened] loss *to this one person* that I focus on' (307; original emphasis). In other words, as an individual who could lose his own life, Taurek imaginatively sympathises with the man who may lose his one and only life – not as one of some larger group, but simply as one. 'Five individuals losing a life', Taurek determines, echoing Lewis, 'do not add up to anyone experiencing a loss five times greater than the loss suffered by any one of the five' or, for that matter, any one of a million (307). That unique loss is what interests any one of us.

Taurek, and others who follow this anti-utilitarian reasoning, invite us to recall that for the ancient philosophers, Aristotle most explicitly, one is not a number. In his *Metaphysics*, Aristotle explains that '"one" means the *measure* of some plurality, and *number* [means] a measured plurality or a plurality of measures; therefore, of course, *the measure is not plural*.'[5] By this logic, one is not numerous; as the metric or standard, one cannot itself be subject to measure. Because it stands apart from numeracy and plurality, we might say *one alone counts* in these debates over moral feeling.

The representational implications of this approach will be familiar to readers of sentimental and much Romantic literature; they surface repeatedly in the period's wartime writing. In the preface to his 1795 poem 'War: A Fragment', for example, Joseph Cottle, friend and publisher of Coleridge and Wordsworth, insists that war is 'destruction in the vast'. To counter war's devastation, to make it felt, he selects

---

3   C. S. Lewis, *The Problem of Pain*, cited in Derek Parfit, 'Innumerate Ethics', *Philosophy and Public Affairs* 7.4 (Summer 1978), 285–301; 294. Parfit gives an astute repudiation of the arguments by Lewis and Taurek.

4   John M. Taurek, 'Should the Numbers Count?' *Philosophy and Public Affairs* 6.4 (Summer 1977), 293–316; 293.

5   Cited in David Bloor, *Knowledge and Social Imagery*, 2nd edn (Chicago, 1991), 110.

one instance to stand in for the sum total. He believes that 'a detailed account of *one* murder . . . on the field of battle, more interests the heart, and leaves on it a longer impression, than the general account of slaughtered thousands' (emphasis added).[6] In fact, to attempt feeling for the many dead may threaten feeling altogether. In Cottle's poem, Orlando surveys the field of recent battle and finds himself accosted by 'thousands of bloodless trunks', with '[U]nnumber'd eyes' making 'countless claims' that paralyze him: 'The life blood stagnates in [his] heart' (74–5). In this moral universe, one cannot sustain feeling either as or for a human aggregate, for slaughtered thousands. Cottle turns to the sublime here: countless and innumerable corpses send Orlando rushing to find just one dying man – a youth, like him, '[s]ilent and sad, and as the snow-drop pale' (76). Like other contemporary writers, Cottle pulls back from uncountable numbers, settling on the suffering one – the widow, the orphan, the wounded veteran – so as to reboot his hero's own failing heart.

This representational gambit calls upon a familiar understanding – probably most influentially articulated by Adam Smith – that moral sympathy is routed through the experience and imagination of the one. If our brother is on the rack, Smith tells us, we place ourselves in his finite situation: 'By the imagination . . . we conceive ourselves enduring all the same torments, we enter as it were into his body, and become in some measure the same person with him.'[7] Undergirding this concept, and almost too fundamental to be fully articulated by Taurek or Lewis, is the assumption that the feeling *one* must be a living *one*. Like the million disposable men of Napoleon's army, like the man on the rack or Orlando's select youth on the battlefield, the six persons in Taurek's scenario are staring at certain death, but they are not yet dead. The one certain to die attracts the modern philosopher's 'interest' in a way a man already dead cannot. Here again Taurek appears to have adapted but also circumscribed Adam Smith's thought from the *Theory of Moral Sentiments* (1759). Smith's example, a limit case for his analysis of sympathy, makes the dynamic of identification explicit. When we sympathise with the dead, Smith explains, we remain in the realm of the

---

6   Joseph Cottle, *Poems, containing 'John the Baptist', 'Sir Malcolm and Alla, A Tale', . . . 'War: A Fragment . . .'* (Bristol, 1795), i. A similar choice faces poet Joseph Fawcett in the preface to his *War Elegies* (1802).

7   Adam Smith, *Theory of Moral Sentiments*, ed. D. D. Raphael and C. L. Macfie (Indianapolis and Oxford, 1976), 3.

living, 'affected by those circumstances which strike *our* senses, but can have no influence upon *their* happiness' (16). We may sense 'that dreary and endless melancholy, which the fancy naturally ascribes to their condition' (9), but if so, it is a sense unavailable to the dead.[8] Our feeling

> arises . . . from our putting ourselves in their situation, and from our lodging, if I may be allowed to say so, our own living souls in their inanimated bodies, and thence conceiving what would be our emotions in this case. It is from this very illusion of the imagination, that the foresight of our own dissolution is so terrible to us, and that the idea of those circumstances, which undoubtedly can give us no pain when we are dead, makes us miserable while we are alive.[9]

Smith asks us to agree that the dead cannot actually feel. Unless imaginatively reanimated (say, as ghosts) they remain inert matter. This strikes me as a modern, secular thought, its transgressions signalled by Smith's apologetic 'if I may be allowed to say so'.

That said, there remains an implicit logic in this passage that asks us to consider 'the dead' (Smith's consistent phrasing) as moving in their dissolution beyond the measure of the one. One might assume that 'lodging' living souls in dead bodies proceeds on a case by case, casket by casket basis. Such an assumption underwrites claims like Taurek's. Smith's use of plural pronouns in this scenario, however, makes no absolute distinction between individuals: 'our own living souls in their inanimated bodies'. In the waning of person and singularity, 'what', as Smith puts it, 'would be *our* emotions'?[10] As we will see in what follows, the attempt to draw a line between the dead and the living often troubles the contours of the bounded one, and troubles as well the boundaries of identifiable feeling. Note that Stalin refers to a million deaths and Napoleon to a million lives, but we understand them both to be saying more or less the same thing. Facing the countless dead, 'what would be our emotions?'

Though the model of one-to-one correspondence in the working of moral sentiment plays out in much wartime writing, the lines that divide the one from the numerous, or the living from the dead, waver and crack under the pressure of mass killing. For the same years that saw

8   Smith, *Theory of Moral Sentiments*, 9.
9   Smith, *Theory of Moral Sentiments*, 13.
10   Smith, *Theory of Moral Sentiments*, 13.

unprecedented numbers – indeed millions – of persons die from mass warfare, witnessed as well the rise of the science and public implementation of statistics. These numbers accompanied, even provoked what Jacques Rancière has described as 'a revolution in the poetic structures of knowledge', especially historical knowledge, which is also to say, in the structures of feeling.[11]

The scale of the French and Napoleonic wars was unprecedented in many registers (such as its geographical extent and financial cost), but most notably in the destruction of human life: 36,000 died at Austerlitz; 50,000 at Waterloo; 70,000 at Borodino; 380,000 in the Russian campaign. The numbers affix themselves to substantial nouns, proper names; but the series of numbers, the repetitive and ever-increasing zeros, trouble any sense of fixity. Note that these are not the numbers of counted bodies: the large numbers are obvious estimates, rough – or perhaps smooth – approximations. The problem of scale, the sheer number of dead bodies in the Revolutionary and Napoleonic Wars shook nearly every mode and medium of representation in the period. This essay could have included work by William Blake and Anna Barbauld; but also Wollstonecraft, Godwin, Baillie, Byron, Percy Bysshe and Mary Shelley – not to mention Walter Scott or J. M. W. Turner. The numbers of the war dead were as culturally significant as the escalating numbers of the British National Debt or the notorious 'ratio' of food supply to reproductive bodies associated with Thomas Malthus's *Essay on the Principle of Population*.

Other scholars have argued that the value and cultural role of numbers changed significantly in this period, taking on their modern guise; that numbers increasingly became signs of dispassionate, rigorous and scientific truth. If that claim is true, then that transformation flowed alongside the inordinate bloodshed of these first modern wars. This age gave us, as Maureen McLane has put it, the 'emergence and stabilization of a mathesis of persons as . . . reproductive meat'.[12] With the introduction of a national draft and a People's Army, guerrilla warfare and absolute war, the age also had to devise a new way to measure the bio-political opposite: persons converted to cannon fodder and bloody heaps.

---

11 Jacques Rancière, *The Names of History: On the Poetics of Knowledge* (Minneapolis, 1994).
12 Maureen N. McLane, *Romanticism and the Human Sciences: Poetry, Population, and the Discourse of the Species* (Cambridge, 2000), 11.

Within this shifting representational regime, significant literary works tested inherited assumptions about one, about numbers, and their respective capacities to engender moral feeling. At the heart of my examples, stretching from the mid-eighteenth to the mid-nineteenth century, churns an anxiety, a distress: if moral feeling is solely anchored to the standard of the one, how can anyone feel for thousands or tens of thousands? Each of the illustrations to follow imagines numerousness as a quality that seeks expression in a quantity greater or less than one – that tends, in other words, toward values infinitely large or small. As the scale of death rises, these examples exhibit the sense that numbers and the statistics to which they give form cannot be ignored by feeling persons. They appeal to the possibility, as Marjorie Levinson has proposed, of thinking 'singularity as a way of being' – and perhaps feeling – 'numerous'.[13]

These examples are especially interested (to take up Taurek's term) in the large numbers of the war dead during the Napoleonic Wars. Did those numbers elicit a feeling response? Or were the numbers, as Cottle and others suggest, numbing? I will begin on a small scale, in the hope of laying out some of the issues and difficulties in representing persons – even dead persons – by numbers more or less than one. I will proceed to instances of increasing scale, where the numbers lie well beyond the reach of simple counting or empirically verifiable experience. At a certain point I will offer more historical context, though my concerns are less historical than formal and ethical.

Let's begin with the feeling of fear, but a peculiar sort of fear. In his *Treatise of Human Nature*, David Hume offers the following scenario to illustrate his claim that 'all kinds of uncertainty have a strong connexion with fear'.[14] A father receives news from 'a person whose veracity he cannot doubt' that his son has been killed (445). Grief would seem to be the obvious emotion born of the report, but Hume introduces uncertainty: the father has learned that 'one of his sons' has died, 'one of' signalling that he has more than one son, thereby introducing the

13 Marjorie Levinson, 'Of Being Numerous,' *Studies in Romanticism* 49 (2010), 633–57; 634.
14 David Hume, *Enquiries Concerning the Human Understanding and Concerning the Principles of Morals by David Hume*, ed. L. A. Selby-Bigge, 2nd edn (Oxford, 1902), 446: http://oll.libertyfund.org/titles/341, accessed 23 March 2014.

problem of number, or numerousness. The father is told no name, no details that might identify which son; nor is he provided with the presence of his other, surviving sons. 'One of' offers no clear way of distinguishing the dead from the living. ''Tis evident', Hume concludes, that 'the passion this event wou'd occasion wou'd not settle into pure grief till [the father] got certain information, which of his sons he had lost.' In the meantime, Hume tells us, the bereft father's passion 'receives from the imagination a tremulous and unsteady motion, resembling' no single feeling but rather 'the mixture and contention of grief and joy' (445). That unsettled passion, which ranges between possible emotions even as the man's imagination ranges from one son to another, might as well be given the name 'fear', understood now as a composite of various, uncertain feelings (446). Thus the epistemological uncertainty bred of numerousness unleashes fluctuations among a number of emotions.

Several oddities occur in Hume's account, having to do with the problem of numbering persons, and of moving from 1 to more than 1 (n + 1 sons) and from 1 to a fraction of 1 (1 out of n + 1 sons lost).

IF Number of sons killed = 1
AND Number of sons = 1
THEN Certainty = 1/1 → 'pure grief'
IF Number of sons killed = 1
AND Number of sons = n+1 [where n is a whole number]
THEN Certainty = 1/n+1 → 'passion [which] cannot settle'

Among other things, what is lost in Hume's account is the certainty of a one-to-one correspondence, crucial to arguments for moral feeling. This movement in numbers, not unlike the 'tremulous and unsteady motion' of the parent's passion, seems especially onerous when one is called upon to delineate persons dead from persons living.

To grasp these problems, and take them along to later texts, we need to consider the specific language of Hume's illustration. The paragraph begins as the philosopher turns from examples of what he calls 'uncertainty of *existence*' to those illustrating 'uncertainty of *kind*' (445, original emphasis). Hume's terms are not the most straightforward and seem curiously over-determined in this example; but as far as I can make out, they operate in this fashion. In this scenario there is evidently no 'uncertainty of *existence*': it is certain that a son no longer exists. Attention turns instead to 'uncertainty of *kind*': it is uncertain which son, which particular instance of kind or *kin*, has been killed. From this certain non-existence, not yet attached to an identifiable instance of an identified group, Hume unspools a curious formula of number and person: 'Let *one* be told by *a person*, whose veracity *he* cannot doubt of, that *one of his sons* has been killed' (445; emphasis added). Given the kind of uncertainty unleashed here, the 'uncertainty of *kind*', repetition of that generic and impersonal pronoun 'one' provokes only more uncertainty. Doubt is only slightly allayed by the appearance in the middle of the sentence of a certain person, 'a person, whose veracity *he* cannot doubt of'. With the arrival of this indubitable person, 'one' sheds impersonality and is replaced by 'he', only to be told that 'one', that is, 'one of his sons', is no more. 'One' appears, disappears and appears a second time, only to be reported deed. Death does not halt the fluctuation of number and person. 'Here there is an evil certain,' continues Hume, 'but the *kind* of it uncertain: Consequently *the fear we feel* on this occasion is without the least mixture of joy . . .' (445, original emphasis). *One* now gives way to *we*, the first person plural, a pronoun notable for its own uncertainties of number and kind (who exactly and how many are 'we': fathers? parents? readers living and dead?). Death – the death of a person – is certain and fixed; number, by contrast, is moving as with a life of its own. Along with the mobile numbers of persons are movements in feeling: is this a story 'resembling . . . the mixture and contention of grief and joy', or of 'fear . . . without the least mixture of joy'? We learn that 'passion' – of uncertain kind – 'cannot settle' in this uncertainty of persons dead or alive (445). If *one* were the only number, if one had but one son, feeling would be certain (i.e. 'pure grief'). Let the number change (more than one, less than one), and one is launched into uncertain emotional terrain.

This passage in Hume's *Treatise* does not determine how the son died, nor where his brothers might be, but I have been encouraged by Philip Fisher's reading of it, and by previous moments in this section of the *Treatise* which align fear and uncertainty with the figure of the warrior, to understand this as an illustration of a certain kind of death.[15] But the kind of dying here matters less to Hume than these intertwined thoughts: 1) that when numbers move beyond one-to-one certainty; or (as in this case) when numbers straddle the bar separating the living from the dead – call this a fraction or ratio – they send human feeling into restless motion; and 2) as the ratio shifts – from the full certainty of one out of one to the fractional certainty of one out of two or three, or perhaps even one out of ten thousand – feeling alters not in quantity

---

15   See Philip Fisher, *The Vehement Passions* (Princeton, NJ, 2003), 129–33.

or degree (the father of six feels no more or less 'pure grief' than the father of two). Rather, feeling alters in quality: it manifests as unsettled passion. It is important to recognise that Hume's uncertainty 'has a strong connexion' with powerful and turbulent feelings; and that he chooses numbers or numerousness to signal epistemological and moral uncertainty of the most fundamental sort: between living and dead persons.

What if we increased the number of sons dramatically, or even exponentially? What happens to feeling then? Imagine, as Thomas De Quincey does in the finale to the first part of 'The English Mail Coach' (1849) that news of her sons' deaths at the battle of Talavera is brought home 'for thee, O mother England'.[16] Does England respond to this message with the tremulous and unsteady emotions Hume depicts? You will protest, certainly, that England, though addressed in the second person, is merely a figure and hardly a person; but the same could be said of Hume's 'one' in 'Let one be told . . .' We are in a realm – call it wartime – where numbers and persons expand and diminish.

De Quincey gives his first-person narrator the task of answering a mother who has asked for news of 'her only son' at Talavera (1809), a pivotal battle of the Peninsular Wars where many British troops were slaughtered. The situation seems to provide the certainty of empirical singularity – one mother, one son – thus avoiding the problem of moving numbers and the unsettled feelings they elicit. But De Quincey's narrator, the bearer of news, remains unsettled. Unlike Hume's father, he lacks a 'person whose veracity he cannot doubt' (he has been reading dispatches in the newspapers); he recognises in addition the near impossibility of counting, let alone identifying, the dead on the battlefield. Whatever he says will not achieve singular certainty.[17] The trial of number and person slides along a moving scale here, with a range of

16   Thomas De Quincey, *De Quincey's Works*, ed. Adam and Charles Black, 16 vols. (Edinburgh, 1862–71), XVI, 30.
17   On identifying the war dead, see Michael Sledge, *Soldier Dead: How We Recover, Identify, Bury, and Honor Our Military Fallen* (New York, 2007), which deals mostly with twentieth-century warfare; J. M. Winter, *Sites of Memory, Sites of Mourning: The Great War in European Cultural History* (Cambridge, 1995), on World War I practices; Drew Gilpin Faust, *This Republic of Suffering: Death and the American Civil War* (New York, 2008); and less detailed, but more pertinent to the early nineteenth century, David Simpson, *9/11: The Culture of Commemoration* (Chicago, 2006).

emotional effects different in kind, perhaps, from Hume's example, but no less volatile.

The unnamed son was a trooper for the 23rd Dragoons, a regiment whose ordinal number (23rd) functions here as identifier, a name the narrator recognises from recent news reports.[18] If the 'only son' suggests an unnamed and perhaps unidentifiable individual, this particular regiment, the 23rd, provides an identifiable, named entity to which that young man has been assigned.[19] But only for an instant does number furnish secure reference or, for that matter, security. The narrator has read that the men of the 23rd, 'not, I believe, 350 strong' were outnumbered by and yet valiantly resisted French troops '6,000 strong' at Talavera – suffering enormous losses. 'The 23rd were supposed at first to have been barely not annihilated', the narrator recalls, contorted into this triple negative; 'but eventually, I believe, about one in four survived' (30). He presents a series of approximations here, ending with 'about one in four' wrested from the brink of barely nothing. An unknown 'proportion' of the 23rd had fallen in a trench, their corpses mangled with their horses. Elsewhere, the passage continues, 'the large majority' lay 'stretched . . . upon one bloody aceldama' (29, 30). 'The chances' of the son's having perished, our narrator concludes, are, like the dead themselves, 'too many': he takes the son's death as all but certain – as if three in four might as well be rounded up to the certitude of one in one: all dead (30). It is striking that De Quincey never attempts an actual body count, but performs these other mathematical operations.[20] If we want to know how many persons died, we would have to divide and then subtract; and we would not be left with whole

18   On ordinal and cardinal numbers, see Levinson, 'Of Being Numerous'; on numbers as names, see Frances Ferguson, *Solitude and the Sublime: Romanticism and the Aesthetics of Individuation* (New York, 1992), 157–64.

19   Faust explains that in the aftermath of the American Civil War, statisticians relied on the regimental unit, not just for the most accurate and manageable statistics of casualties, but also because the regiment provided 'a more human scale': *Republic of Suffering*, 260.

20   On other occasions, De Quincey shows himself perfectly capable of a body count, albeit of enemy soldiers. In his *Autobiographical Sketches* he reports on the failed French invasion of Ireland in 1798: '[O]n the 8th of September, General Hombert surrendered with his whole army, now reduced to 844 men, of whom 96 were officers; having lost since their landing in Killala exactly 268 men.' Of the loss of British troops, or of local Irish lives, the report remains vague, though we learn that 'fourteen pieces of [British] artillery were lost'. *Works*, XIV, 282–3.

numbers, whole persons. His calculations, which the narrator decides to withhold from the mother, are in fact riddled with wobbly numbers and repetitions of the hardly indubitable 'I believe'.[21] De Quincey's narrator may have the certainty that many men of the 23rd lay dead at Talavera, but driven by the magnitude of the slaughter, his play of proportions, majorities and ratios, and his gestures to statistical probability ('the chances are too many') all admit the failure of full certainty. There is truly no telling if this particular son has died.[22] Consequently, the narrator cannot know for sure the emotional outcome. The passage wavers between enthusiasm, pride and 'peace of mind', as well as horror, fear and a sinking heart.

Balked by the unwieldy number of battle dead, and by the fact that the men of the 23rd are too mutilated in Talavera's 'bloody trench' to submit to a one to one reckoning (these are days well before the use of dog tags) the narrator makes adjustments in scale. Not only does the 23rd regiment stand in as a larger, more identifiable version of the 'only son', but mother England enters to anchor volatile emotion. It is as if both multiplication and magnification are brought in as techniques to bolster a feeling of certainty. We are invited to think

21   Sir William Francis Patrick Napier, in his authoritative *History of the War in the Peninsula and the South of France* (New York, 1855), provides a steadier sense of the numbers: 'Those who were not killed or taken . . . escaped [to the Spanish side] leaving behind two hundred and seven men and officers, or about half the number that went into action': 218. First published in 1831, Napier's account was certainly available to De Quincey.

22   Compare John Wilson Croker's version of this episode in his very popular *Battles of Talavera*, first published in the *Quarterly Review* in 1809, which De Quincey may well have known. In his account, Croker obsessively reiterates the size of each of the armies, and the 'unequal war' in which the British troops were engaged (5, 20). Croker prefers to contemplate the large numbers of dead in battle rather than the individual loss:

> Thousands shall fall of every force . . . .
> Many are doomed to death to-day
> Whose fate shall ne'er at home be told;
> Whose very name the grave shall fold;
> Many, for whose return in vain
> The wistful eye of love shall strain.

> John Wilson Croker, *Battles of Talavera*,
> 6th edn (London, 1810), 10.

of it this way: I do not know if this young man has died, but I believe
that fully three-quarters of the nearly 250 men in that regiment died.
So – given the responsibility of choosing an outcome, I suppose he
must surely be dead. Similarly, I cannot tell how that one mother will
respond, or how I will feel about her emotional response, so I will en-
large her to gigantic, allegorical size and her response will then be clear
to me. That many more than one have died, that this mother England
has not one but countless sons to mourn, functions to make matters
both more certain, and emotionally simpler.

> I told her [the mother he has met] how these dear children of
> England, officers and privates, had leaped their horses over all obsta-
> cles as gaily as hunters to the morning chase. I told her how they had
> rode their horses into the midst of death – saying to myself, but not
> saying to *her* – 'and laid down their lives for thee, O mother England,
> as willingly . . . – as ever, after a long day's sport, when infants, they
> had laid their weary heads upon their mother's knees, and had sunk
> to sleep in her arms.' [30]

The strain of maintaining a stable, feeling 'one' exerts its pressure on
this bizarre scene, where the maternal figure is magnified in order to
absorb the carnage of many, many sons. De Quincey substitutes apostrophe and reverie for actual report; and substitutes a giant, allegorical
second person for the woman, third-person, before him. Numerous sons
– but somehow diminished in size, children, infants! – stand in for that
woman's only son. If they hardly annihilate, these shifts in scale mo-
mentarily divert attention from the bloody trench, the troubling ratios,
and the unanswered questions of war's indiscriminate killings.

It is tempting to think De Quincey is trying out the so-called law of
large numbers, the basis for modern statistics and insurance. 'As a general principle [to quote one definition] the law of large numbers means
that . . . the average (or mean) of a long series of observations', however
compromised in accuracy, may be taken as 'the best estimate of the "true
value" of a variable. In other words, what is unpredictable and chancy
in the case of an individual is predictable and uniform in the case of a
large group.'[23] Increasing the scale of enquiry or investigation allows
the elimination of individual deviations and simplification of findings.

23   www.businessdictionary.com/definition/law-of-large-numbers.html#
ixzz1jqvYhkKI.

Presumably, the law of large numbers would govern one mode of counting the war dead: averaging a series of individual observations from,
say, several surviving officers in a regiment. Before the introduction of
identification tags (in the American Civil War) such averaging was the
standard method for reporting the number of men killed in battle.

Let these two episodes, from the mid-eighteenth and the mid-nineteenth century, frame our thoughts about the problem of numbers and
feeling during the period of the French and Napoleonic Wars, when the
death toll rose at an unprecedented rate. The two passages are not meant
to stand as the beginning and ending of a certain historical narrative;
rather they are meant to introduce characteristic problems to keep in
mind as we proceed. The crucial issues, now somewhat elaborated, are
these: 1) Numbers and the operations of numeracy (e.g. scale, average,
proportion) are called in when one – the singular – is not enough, or too
much, or no more; 2) because numbers are not only used for counting,
they have an equivocal relationship to certainty and empirical verifi-
ability, especially the certainty of person;[24] 3) offering no certainty of
existence or singularity, numbers nonetheless seem capable of generating not simply numbness (Cottle's 'stagnation of the heart') but varied
and active feeling. Finally, following Hume, 4) a move into number
and numerousness yields not an increase (or decrease) in the intensity
of feeling, but rather a difference in its kind; numbers set feeling into
motion. In these instances we might say mathematical figures serve the
aesthetic (they are provocative of emotion); but they also push moral
feeling beyond the bounds of the unitary individual into numerousness.
    Along these lines, we begin to see that much of the writing of the
Romantic period resists Elaine Scarry's claim about numbers and bodies.
Scarry argues that if we want to locate the use of numbers most evacuated
of reference to, or indeed contact with, human form or feeling, we should
look to the 'body count' of war, that 'notoriously insubstantial' figure of
death conjured by modern military institutions.[25] Like Stalin (though in
this way only), Scarry argues that the 'body count' prompts no feeling,
indeed that it is deployed to deny or muffle feeling. Yet the rhetorical
force of the body count seems more robust than she suggests. In this 1988

24   See Mary Poovey, A History of the Modern Fact: Problems of Knowledge in
the Sciences of Wealth and Society (Chicago, 1998), 1–38.
25   Elaine Scarry, Literature and the Body; Essay on Population and Populous-
ness (Baltimore, 1988), viii.

essay Scarry was no doubt reacting to the notorious manipulation of body counts during the Vietnam War. More recently, during the wars in Iraq and Afghanistan, the Pentagon developed a different strategy. In 2003 Secretary of Defense Donald Rumsfeld echoed General Tommy Johns in insisting that 'we don't do body counts' – a *withholding* of numbers which clearly attempts to tamp down a whole range of troubled feelings.[26] Earlier wars only confirm the rhetorical stakes attached to numbers in wartime. In a 1795 pamphlet, the radical journalist James Callendar offers a tirade against the 'war system,' which seethes with numbers. Here is his concluding flourish: 'The question to be decided is, are we to proceed with the war system? Are we, in the progress of the nineteenth century, to embrace five thousand fresh taxes, to squander a second five hundred millions sterling, and to extirpate thirty millions of people?'[27] As when reading De Quincey, it feels counter-productive to ask whether Callendar's appeal to a 'just calculation' of the numbers accompanying the 'war system' ought to be read as irony or complicity (10). In this case, the numbers risk 'insubstantiality' purposefully: rather than documenting what has been, they move into a future, the nineteenth century. Callendar's speculations hover phantasmatically between the already dead and the dead-to-be.

Callendar's outrageously speculative 'thirty millions of people' suggests if not the substantiality of the body count then perhaps the 'substantial dread' – this is Wordsworth's phrase – or volatile fear, in Hume's account – lurking in large numbers, their difficult but productive relationship to an affect that points beyond one, and beyond the line separating the dead from the living (and the yet to come). In response to the vast scale of the wars and in tandem with innovations in political economy, period writers sometimes offer not a mode of resistance, where Imagination sets to work against Calculation, but a coordination of the two that offers a way of thinking through relationships, or even sympathies, between the living and the numerous dead. We might recall the charged role of counting dead and living siblings in Wordsworth's

26   An essay in the *National Review*, written before the Second Gulf War, suggests that the body count then had a very clear affective aim: to build morale among the troops and support for the war effort. Ryan Lizza, 'Numbers Game', *New Republic* (26 July 1999), 16.

27   James Thomson Callendar, *The Political Progress of Britain, or, an Impartial History of Abuses in the Government of the British Empire: In Europe, Asia, and America from the Revolution in 1668 to the Present Time: The Whole Tending to Prove the Ruinous Consequences of the Popular System of Taxation, War and Conquest* (Philadelphia, 1795), 8.

'We Are Seven', or the fifty sheep and six children that dwindle away in his 'The Last of the Flock'. These seem manageable numbers in comparison with the 'heaped up' bodies of 'dead and dying' in Paris, which haunt Wordsworth in Book X of *The Prelude*. The poet searches for some means whereby to 'feel and touch' these slaughtered persons, to experience a 'substantial' rather than purely ideational 'dread'.[28] Most challenging to human emotion and moral response was the threat that in those wars, which extended for at least twenty years and across the globe, the enormous scale of death defied a human standard, the measure given by the individual human body.

What De Quincey understood in his way, Wordsworth recognised in his: that a new ratio had been introduced, where the massive numbers of dead both demanded and produced an oversized, monstrous conception of Man. De Quincey's infants in the mother's arms may be compared with a line attributed to Tsar Alexander after Austerlitz: 'We are babies, in the hands of a giant.'[29]

Like De Quincey, William Wordsworth confronts the escalating numbers of the dead with efforts to hold them within, or return them to, the measure of the individual human form, as if this would provide what Hume calls certainty of *kind*. Wordsworth poses the problem as fundamental to yet separate from the writing of history. If the history of 'calamities, principally those consequent upon war' – this is Wordsworth's phrase – threatens to overwhelm the bounds of the individual body and consciousness, what measures or forms other than the single human could provide an effective ground for historical or moral thinking? And would the human be lost in that recalibration?

Wordsworth's obsessive depiction of 'illimitable waste' in the Salisbury Plain poems provides my last example. As he explains in a retrospective note to 'Guilt and Sorrow,' the last of the Salisbury Plain series, he had travelled across the plain just as British troops set off to war with France in 1793.

> The American war was still fresh in memory. The struggle which was beginning . . . I was assured in my own mind would be of long continuance and productive of distress and misery beyond all possible calculation.

28   William Wordsworth, *The Thirteen Book Prelude*, ed. Mark L. Reed, 2 vols. (Ithaca NY, 1991), Book X, lines 38–82.
29   David G. Chandler, *The Campaigns of Napoleon* (New York, 1995), 411.

In this mood he crossed the plain, home to Stonehenge, ancient bar-
rows, and the ruins of Iron Age forts.

> The monuments and traces of antiquity, scattered in abundance over
> that region, led me unavoidably to compare what we know or guess
> of those remote times with certain aspects of modern society, and
> with calamities, principally those consequent upon war, to which,
> more than any other class of men, the poor are subject.[30]

In these poems Wordsworth tries insistently to fit the human to the
apparently illimitable, to accommodate living Man to the vast waste of
warfare. Even more than in 'The English Mail Coach', this confrontation with the scale of death and suffering in war pushes Wordsworth to
adopt modes of representation favoured by Malthus and the 'Statists',
or statisticians, the poet elsewhere rejects. Though numbers *per se* are
generally absent from the poems in the Salisbury Plain series, the elements of a geometrical formalism – line, point, circle, slope, measures,
ratios – what we might think of as the drawing out or graphing of numbers, the visible form of their operations, are scattered throughout these
works, complicating Wordsworth's commitment to the figure of Man.
But whereas Malthus's graphs were subject to limits and constraints –
such as the law of scarcity – Wordsworth looks on the prospect of total
war and tries to graph something 'beyond all possible calculation'.

Recall the two instances already cited, from Book X of the 1805
Prelude. What press upon Wordsworth's consciousness are not hordes
of the living, but heaped and indiscriminate piles of the dead. These
scenes set up the more substantial and disturbing confrontation with
mass death in Book XII, another element in the Salisbury Plain series.
The writing of this series extends from 1793, when the poet first crossed
Salisbury Plain, through variations in 1798, 1805 and onward to 1842's
'Guilt and Sorrow' – most of the poet's long writing career. Its critical
history is appropriately vast and overwhelming. Here I will focus on just
two constants found in each of the several iterations.

The first is the poet's description of the sacrifice of 'multitudes of
men', warriors, in a gigantic wicker effigy of a Man. The image bluntly
calls up the question of scale, specifically the scale of the human. How

---

30 Advertisement to 'Guilt and Sorrow' (1842), in William Wordsworth,
The Salisbury Plain Poems of William Wordsworth, ed. Stephen Charles Gill
(Ithaca NY, 1975), 216–17.

large does the figure of Man have to be to accommodate this slaughter? Again, we see magnification of the human form, multiplication of the dead. The second constant is the landscape of 'illimitable waste', presented as a nearly two-dimensional plane. Wordsworth's representation of the chalky fields and downs is inscribed with boundless lines, scattered points, circles and other 'traces' or figures. It is as if the desolate plain (erased of its actual topographical features) provided a tentative map or graph of 'calamities, principally consequent upon war'; as if it could supply the terrain of historical geography.

Let me attempt to delineate what is at stake in these two constants. The 'gigantic Wicker,' which Wordsworth would have known from reading Caesar's account of the ancient Britons in his *Gallic Wars*, was a larger-than-life figure of a man fabricated from woven sticks, into which living men were stuffed and burned to death, presumably in ritual sacrifice. Wordsworth's use of this image associates it strongly with the sacrifice of bodies demanded by warfare (his protagonist is a sailor empressed but now released from the navy; the woman he meets is a homeless war widow). The passages that recall this sight repeatedly play with tropes of apostrophe and personification, reminding us of Wordsworth's penchant to 'people the wastes,' but also of the uncertain existence of persons.[31] The passages are marked by a metonymy that might as well be dismemberment: things are made persons as persons disintegrate into things ('spears', or 'arms', or 'mighty bones'). The verse moves with agitation between multiples and singulars and portions of singulars, as if Wordsworth himself has trouble framing the scene: is it about men, or Man, or the fragmented remains of both? For of course it is the human frame that rivets our attention here. The Wicker Man provides the transhistorical vehicle of massive carnage while proving itself, the fascinating figure of Man, impermanent, disposable, about-to-be waste.

Especially in its appearance in *The Prelude*, the 'gigantic Wicker' casts a lurid light on Wordsworth's optimism about his poetic ambitions, announced earlier in the same Book.

> Thus moderated, thus composed, I found
> Once more in *Man* an object of delight,
> Of pure imagination, and of love;
> And, as the *horizon* of my mind enlarged,
> Again I took the intellectual eye

31   Ferguson, *Solitude and the Sublime*, 117.

> For my instructor, studious more to see
> Great Truths, than touch and handle little ones. [XII, 53–9]

This self-congratulation apparently distinguishes the poet from the 'modern Statists' or political economists he deplores a few lines later: those who, like Malthus, are deceived by the 'utter hollowness,' the 'Idol' otherwise known as the 'Wealth of Nations' (1805 XII, 77, 78; 1850 XIII, 77).[32] Their minds are guided by calculations drawn from populations, aggregates, averages and ratios (the 'one of four' of De Quincey's narrator). Their approach threatens to eradicate what the poet will go on to celebrate: 'The dignity of Individual Man, | Of Man no composition of the thought' (XII, 83–4).[33] Given these lines, we might read the Wicker Man not simply as a prehistoric leviathan, but precisely the 'hollowness', the 'dire thing' or 'Idol' born of the aggregated and thus discounted lives of modern political economy.[34] Yet there is something more to say. The desire to see 'Great Truths' rather than 'touch and handle little ones' should alert us: Wordsworth is no stranger to abstraction, and his generic 'Man' may be hard to pry apart from the 'dire thing' of economic calculation, the horrifying Wicker Man. The poet confesses in startlingly economic terms, 'I could not but inquire, | Not with less *interest* . . . | But greater . . . | . . . Why is this glorious Creature [Man] to be found | One only in ten thousand? What one is | Why may not many be?' (XII, 87–91). At the heart of *this* awful ratio, we find a wartime anxiety about the very possibility – and consequence – of framing history or poetry on the human scale. What Wordsworth calls here the 'true proportion' of 'the promise of the present time' remains elusive: is it one to ten thousand? If so, what promise can we extrapolate from these numbers when we arrive at the scene in Salisbury Plain (64–5)? 'What one is' – one Man, larger than life, burning – 'why may not many be'?

The Salisbury Plain poems might be understood as a series of half-hearted, or perhaps broken-hearted, maps or graphs, where the 'illimitable wastes' entailed by 'certain aspects of modern society, . . . principally

32 William Wordsworth, *The Fourteen Book Prelude*, ed. W. J. B. Owen (Ithaca NY, 1985).
33 In 1850, these claims grow stronger: 'Life, human life, with all its sacred claims | Of sex and age, and heaven-descended rights' (*Fourteen Book Prelude*, XIII, 70–8, and *passim*).
34 See also 1805, XII, 205–19.

war' are plotted onto other 'illimitable wastes', 'the wastes interminably spread', the 'bleak domain' (*SP* I, 423) of the plain. For as Wordsworth *first* lays it out, this barren plain, bereft of signs of the human, is void of the markers of particular place. Salisbury Plain, Geoffrey Hartman determines, 'undermines the very idea of place. It is a "no-place", an inhuman plane, hardly part of Nature, on which Wordsworth's traveller wanders lost.'[35] Hartman pinpoints the 'horror of horizontality' that governs the scene, especially in the earliest versions. 'The starker the horizontal' in the poem, he finds, 'the stronger [its] anticipation of a static point, and vice-versa. Neither extreme is free of horror' (120). (We recall, grimly, the poet's claim in Book XII that 'the horizon of my mind [had] enlarged'.) In pursuing the 'horror of horizontality' evident in the '[l]engthening . . . dreary line', the 'measuring . . . painful steps', the stretched horizons and scattered static points of Salisbury Plain, Hartman hints at the workings of a dark geometry. Even the vertical pile of Stonehenge is flattened to a 'circle', eventually vanishing altogether into *The Prelude*'s vague 'mystery of shapes'. The 'horizontal infinity' and bleak purity of form increases the traveller's sense of vulnerability; it extends scale beyond the human, beyond even the mediations of Nature (119). Here 'place . . . is powerfully reduced to its essence of spot' (or, we might say, point) without the familiar Wordsworthian compensations of renovation or sustenance.[36] Indeed as the series progresses, the scattered 'spots' of each poem become increasingly fatal to men and Man – not just the concentered site of mass sacrifice but, later, the hangman's gibbet. ('The law', we are told, 'must weigh him' – the traveller, the individual man – 'in its scale,' thus offering another scalar option [*SP* II, 809].) Geometrical figures – this collection of lines, circles and spots or points, and the unbounded 'horizon' – threaten to obliterate the human and substitute the 'mystery of shapes' for his mortal frame. They remain in the end disturbingly unresolved: remote from any human measure or any fixed bound or framing, they do not cohere (as Malthus's graphs would) to give meaning and permanence to human history.

Without such coherence, without solution, the blasted graphics horrify as much as the burning, giant Man. Yet how else, but through these

35 Geoffrey H. Hartman, *Wordsworth's Poetry, 1787–1814* (New Haven CT, 1964), 120.
36 Hartman suggests the 'death of nature' is implicit here: 'imagination in its withdrawal from nature first withdraws to a single point': Ibid., 122.

stark visualizations of the infinite, to capture what Wordsworth understood to be the prospect of war's 'distress and misery beyond all possible
calculation'?

Coda

Since 1898, Salisbury Plain has served as a training ground for the British
military, the largest Defence Training Estate in the United Kingdom.
Nearly half the plain has been permanently restricted or closed to the
public; one hundred and fifty square miles are marked off and reserved
for manoeuvres and weapons testing. The Royal School of Artillery re-
sides there; signs along the perimeter of the estate warn trespassers that
the terrain could be fatal. The ground is seeded with 'live' mines and
mortar bombs. The Defence Training Estate at Salisbury Plain served as
a training ground for the Allied invasion of Normandy in 1944, which
sent nearly 160,000 troops across the English Channel on 6 June, and
hundreds of thousands more throughout that ferocious summer. We
know with some certainty that two months later, by the end of August,
36,976 Allied soldiers had died, 153,475 had been wounded and 19,221
were missing. An additional 16,714 Allied airmen were killed or missing. Estimates of German casualties are less certain: they range from
210,000 to 450,000. Somewhere between 13,632 and 19,890 French
civilians were killed during the campaign; but just as many – 11,000
to 19,000 – died from pre-invasion bombing, and continued dying for
years afterward, the victims of bombs planted in the landscape, yet to
be exploded.[37]

  The area of Salisbury Plain also includes two National Nature
Reserves. Large populations of botanical and animal species – notably birds and butterflies – flourish there, in the near absence of human
beings.

37 For statistics on Operation Overlord, see Edward R. Flint, 'The Development of British Civil Affairs and Its Employment in the British Sector of Allied
Military Operations during the battle of Normandy, June to August 1944', un-
publ. Ph.D. thesis (Cranfield University Defence and Security School, 2009);
and Niklas Zetterling, Normandy 1944: German Military Organization, Combat Power and Organizational Effectiveness (Winnipeg, 2000).

The Guilt of the Noncombatant and W. H. Auden's 'Journal of an Airman'

RACHEL GALVIN

W. H. AUDEN WROTE that the Great War was 'the decisive experience' of Wilfred Owen's life.[1] In the absence of such experience, Auden and his generation struggled to find grounds from which to write during the 1930s. In the present essay, I show that Auden's 'Journal of an Airman', which is Book II of *The Orators* (1932), reflects the legacy of the Great War for interwar English writers and 'the guilt that every noncombatant feels',[2] as he calls it. This guilt is a manifestation of a larger cultural turn that military historians have traced back to the Enlightenment, in which non-transmittable knowledge is understood to be gained exclusively through sensory experience on the battlefield. That knowledge grants combat veterans the 'authority of flesh-witnessing'.[3] After discussing this cultural turn and how it affected Auden and his generation, I explore how positions of optical dominance inform the 'Journal of an Airman' and the text's concern with the idea of the poet as wartime orator – elements that presage Auden's World War II poetics. I conclude by considering an often-overlooked episode in Auden's life, when he was sent to assess the effects of air bombing on German morale as part of the 1945 US Strategic Bombing Survey.

The Authority of Witnessing in the Flesh

Going to war in the twentieth century has been described as 'a definitive coming to manhood for the industrial age'.[4] In an article published

---

1 'Poet in Wartime', W. H. Auden, *Prose and Travel Books in Prose and Verse*, ed. Edward Mendelson, 4 vols. (Princeton, 1996–), II, 73.

2 Ibid., II, 74.

3 Yuval Noah Harari, *The Ultimate Experience* (New York, 2008), 1–25, 231–40.

4 James Scott Campbell, 'Combat Gnosticism: The Ideology of First World

in 1940, George Orwell noted that his generation 'grew up in an atmosphere tinged with militarism'.[5]

> As the war fell back into the past, my particular generation, those
> who had been 'just too young', became conscious of the vastness of
> the experience they had missed. You felt yourself a little less than
> a man, because you had missed it. I spent the years 1922–7 mostly
> among men a little older than myself who had been through the war.
> They talked about it unceasingly, with horror, of course, but also
> with a steadily growing nostalgia. Besides, the pacifist reaction was
> only a phase, and even the 'just too young' had all been trained for
> war. Most of the English middle class are trained for war from the
> cradle onwards, not technically but morally.[6]

Many men who were 'just too young' to fight but old enough to remember the Great War's aftermath experienced a thirst for heroism that colours their writing. Following the logic according to which masculinity is defined through military service, the interest in heroism led not only to the veneration of T. E. Lawrence, 'the last of the romantic military heroes',[7] but also to the glorification of adventurers – pilots, mountain climbers, and feature journalists. 'The World War had destroyed the traditional British ideal of heroism in battle, but there was still the air, there were still mountains, and these offered metaphors for the challenge and danger of individual action, and the possibility of heroism,' as Samuel Hynes observes.[8] Between 1920 and 1939, seven British expeditions were launched to climb Mount Everest, and others explored other Himalayan and Alpine mountains; these efforts received avid press coverage.[9]

War Poetry Criticism', *New Literary History* 30.1 (Winter 1999), 203–15; 204.
5   George Orwell, 'My Country Right or Left', in *The Collected Essays, Journalism, and Letters of George Orwell*, ed. Sonia Orwell and Ian Angus (New York, 1968), 540.
6   Ibid., 537–8.
7   Samuel Hynes, *The Auden Generation: Literature and Politics in England in the 1930s* (London, 1976), 190–191, 238–41.
8   Ibid., 189.
9   Ibid., 236–7. For discussion of the homosexual dimension to the culture of hero-worship among Auden and his friends, see Richard R. Bozorth, *Auden's Games of Knowledge: Poetry and the Meanings of Homosexuality* (New York, 2001), 117–18, 155–8.

The desire for heroism Orwell describes pervaded the poetry published during this time. Wilfred Owen famously declared in the preface to his poems that '[t]his book is not about heroes. English poetry is not yet fit to speak of them'; [10] but the anticipation carried in the word 'yet' tells its own, contradictory, story. Stephen Spender writes that even the political poetry of what was technically an interwar period had a 'temporary, "for the duration" look' that might be called 'a variety of war poetry'.

In the event, what they wrote was anti-fascist poetry which was profoundly influenced by the diction and attitudes of Wilfred Owen – a kind of anti-fascist pacifist poetry. Examples of this are Auden's sonnets from China and my own poem, 'Ultima Ratio Regum'.[11]

Spender notes that Owen himself was in fact 'made a hero' by poets of the period.[12] This glorification went hand in hand with a corresponding sense of guilt at having missed the chance to test one's own mettle. Christopher Isherwood observes in *Lions and Shadows* (1947), 'We young writers of the middle 'twenties were all suffering, more or less subconsciously, from a feeling of shame that we hadn't been old enough to take part in the European war.'[13]

Like most of my generation, I was obsessed by a complex of terrors and longings connected with the idea 'War'. 'War', in this purely neurotic sense, meant The Test. The test of your courage, of your maturity, of your sexual prowess: 'Are you really a Man?' Subconsciously, I believe, I longed to be subjected to this test; but I also dreaded failure. I dreaded failure so much – indeed, I was so certain that I *should* fail – that, consciously, I denied my longing to be tested, altogether. I denied my all-consuming morbid interest in the idea of 'war'. I pretended indifference. The War, I said, was obscene, not even thrilling, a nuisance, a bore.[14]

---

10   Wilfred Owen, *The Collected Poems* (London, 1963), 31.
11   Stephen Spender, *The Thirties and After: Poetry, Politics, People 1933–1970* (New York, 1978), 7.
12   Ibid., 7.
13   Christopher Isherwood, *Lions and Shadows* (New York, 1947), 55.
14   Ibid., 56.

Isherwood goes on to explain that in writing *Lions and Shadows*, he turned his desire for the 'Test' of war into a fantasy of public-school heroism, since the idea of war 'needed a symbol – a symbol round which I could build up my daydreams about "The Test"' and through which his main character could emerge "'a Man"'.[15] Auden's *The Orators* is structured very much along the same lines. As I will elaborate below, it too conflates public-school pranks and war games with a narrative of 'mobilisation' in the Airman's journal.

Auden referred to himself and his generation as 'a sort of poor relation | To that debauched, eccentric generation | That grew up with their fathers at the War' in his 1936 poem 'Letter to Lord Byron'. He described the guilt experienced by civilians in an article of 1940, which reviewed new translations of the poems of Rainer Maria Rilke and an edition of Rilke's wartime letters.[16] For Rilke, Auden wrote, the four years of the Great War were 'a negative and numbing horror that froze his poetic impulse, a suspension of the intelligible'. The implicit parallels are rife between Rilke's wartime experience and Auden's own during the Spanish Civil War, the Sino-Japanese War, and the first stages of the Second World War. Auden defends Rilke's refusal to be a 'newspaper reader' and his choice to spend his time 'waiting . . . not understanding, not understanding'. He claims that to call such an attitude 'ivory-tower' would be 'a cheap and wicked lie', defending an ethics of civilian inaction against the trap of patriotic emotion.

> To resist compensating for the sense of guilt that every noncombatant feels at not sharing the physical sufferings of those at the front, by indulging in an orgy of patriotic hatred all the more violent because it is ineffective; to be conscious but to refuse to understand, is a positive act that calls for courage of a high order. To distinguish it from selfish or cowardly indifference may at the time be difficult for the outsider, but Rilke's poetry and these letters are proof enough of his integrity and real suffering.[17]

Auden provides a category name for a pervasive phenomenon that has persisted since the eighteenth century: 'the guilt of the noncombatant'.

---

15 Ibid., 57.
16 'Poet in Wartime', *The New Republic* (8 July 1940), in Auden, *Prose and Travel Books*, ed. Mendelson, II, 74.
17 Ibid.

He describes the same notion again four years later, in a 15 October 1944 review of Marianne Moore's *Nevertheless*, praising her poem 'In Distrust of Merits':

> There have been surprisingly few good poems about the present war; no new Wilfred Owen has appeared among the armed forces to describe their experiences, and most of the civilians who have tried have fallen into the old snare laid by the guilt which every civilian must feel at not being in the fighting line, i.e. instead of writing about that guilt or what the war requires of *them*, they have flourished self-induced, hectic and fake emotions about fox-holes.[18]

The guilt Auden refers to in these two passages is not 'survivor's guilt'. Rather, it is a structure of feeling conditioned by the conviction that combat veterans possess a non-transmittable knowledge, which endows them with special and unassailable authority concerning war.

The epistemological and socio-historical bases of the crisis in poetic authority that post-First World War poets experienced is rooted in the valorisation of witnessing 'in the flesh'.[19] The basic assumption is that 'words go only a short distance and that sensations must play a crucial part in the production and transmission of knowledge'.[20] The military historian Yuval Harari has called this 'the authority of flesh-witnessing' in his cross-cultural study of military history.[21] He borrows the term from Hynes, who in *A Soldier's Tale: Bearing Witness to a Modern War* cites a French soldier's remark that the person 'who has not understood with his flesh cannot talk to you about it'.[22] But such remarks – and this

---

18   Auden, *Prose and Travel Books*, ed. Mendelson, II, 235.

19   Yuval N. Harari, *The Ultimate Experience: Battlefield Revelations and the Making of Modern War Culture, 1450–2000* (Basingstoke, 2008), 32 and *passim*.

20   Yuval Noah Harari, 'Scholars, Eyewitnesses, and Flesh-Witnesses of War: A Tense Relationship', *Partial Answers: Journal of Literature and the History of Ideas* 7 (2009), 213–28; 224.

21   Eric J. Leed has called this special knowledge 'disjunctive knowledge', likening it to that of ritual initiations: *No Man's Land: Combat and Identity in World War I* (Cambridge, 1979), 74. See also Campbell, 'Combat Gnosticism', 207: '[T]he experience of fighting provides a connection to Reality, an unmediated Truth to which only those who have undergone the liminal trauma of combat have access.'

22   Samuel Hynes, *The Soldiers' Tale: Bearing Witness to a Modern War* (New York, 1998), 2.

genre of claim – are pervasive in war literature from at least the eighteenth century, as Harari has documented. Combat veterans are believed to have privileged access to a visceral knowledge that is not verbally transmittable. The seat of knowledge is located in the body, and the experience of war is ineffable, a version of the sublime. The authority of flesh-witnessing, Harari explains, is based in an experiential truth, the 'extreme sensory and emotional conditions of war', the very conditions that 'the uninitiated cannot grasp'.[23] Its authority is 'not squandered by usage', as is the authority of eyewitnesses:

> whereas a person who hears many eyewitnesses gets a good factual understanding of battle, a person who hears many flesh-witnesses gets only a good understanding of his or her own ignorance. The more fleshwitness accounts civilians hear, the *less* authority they have. This means that, in contrast to eyewitnesses in a murder trial, the flesh-witnesses of war must be witnesses *and judges* rolled into one. Nobody else is eligible for the role of judge.[24]

This set of beliefs was renewed in the Great War's literature of disillusionment, and later bolstered in the literature of the Second World War. It has direct ramifications for Auden and his generation. The poets of the trenches (Owen, Siegfried Sassoon, Isaac Rosenberg, Ivor Gurney) certainly made significant formal innovations in their poetry, but they occupied a position of authority because of their experiences as soldiers.

This background offers important context for Auden's interwar texts, such as the experimental volume *The Orators*, as well as his subsequent writing during the Spanish Civil War and Second World War. Part of my aim in the larger project from which the present essay is drawn is to broaden the canon of what is considered 'war literature' to include civilian writing of the 1930s and 1940s that has not often been read as such. I wish to respond to critiques levelled against Modernist writing for its 'oblique thematics', which is to say that Modernist literature is not sufficiently about war, by arguing that texts such as *The Orators* (as well as *Journey to a War* and *Another Time*) should be read as war literature.[25] In civilian writing of this period, poets responded to the

---

23 Harari, 'Scholars, Eyewitnesses, and Flesh-Witnesses of War', 220.
24 Ibid., 221. Campbell makes a similar point about the 'exclusionary activity' of combat veterans talking about war in 'Combat Gnosticism', 209.
25 In this I expand on the recent work of scholars such as Marina McKay,

tendency to represent war as 'an agent of revelation'[26] to which they do not have access. This archive reflects socio-historical factors such as the civilian experience of asynchrony and dislocation: belatedness with regard to the Great War, which they had missed, and dislocation with regard to their mediated relationship to violence. Civilian poets were keenly aware of their distance from war – the lapses, uncertainties and abstractions in news reports were constant reminders. Their poetics therefore often critiques the pitfalls inherent in patriotic oratory of all kinds – newspapers, advertising, politics and war-speak,[27] as well as inflated poetic language. A broader definition of 'war literature' permits study of the full effects of war upon cultural forms, and recognises that in the age of modern warfare, when acts of violence are not at all contained, war itself is a form of everyday experience. Wartime has become a condition rather than an event, as Mary Favret writes, so that it 'translates war from the realm of sublime event to an underlying situation or condition of Modernity'.[28] One of my points of departure in reading *The Orators* is the assumption that the experience of war is a version of the everyday, rather than a state of exception.

Optical Dominance in the 'Journal of an Airman'

'The closest modern equivalent to the Homeric hero is the ace fighter pilot,' Auden wrote.[29] An aerial perspective implies domination, literally providing the hero with a privileged viewpoint. This convergence has a long history. An ocular 'watching machine' has always existed alongside the 'war machine', Paul Virilio argues: 'From the original watch-tower through the anchored balloon to the reconnaissance

who 'urges a reshaping of what counts as the literature of war, in order to include authors who were not combatants, and texts that are not "about" war in any straightforwardly mimetic way': Marina MacKay, *Modernism and World War II* (Cambridge, 2007), 6–7.

26   Harari, *Ultimate Experience*, 22.

27   Peter Nicholls, 'Wars I Have Seen', in *A Concise Companion to Twentieth-century American Poetry*, ed. Stephen Fredman (Malden, Mass., and Oxford, 2005), 14.

28   Mary A. Favret, *War at a Distance: Romanticism and the Making of Modern Wartime* (Princeton, 2009).

29   'Introduction to *The Portable Greek Reader*', in Auden, *Prose and Travel Books*, ed. Mendelson, II, 365.

aircraft and remote-sensing satellites, one and the same function has been indefinitely repeated, the eye's function being the function of a weapon.'[30] But since the First World War, 'the story of military technology has been one of prosthetic extension, especially that of sight'.[31] During the Great War, despite the realities of the trenches, the image gained precedence over the object in the course of the 'derealisation' of military engagement resultant from technologies of representation. Strategic and political interpretations of the 'picture of reality' established the conditions for a 'logistics of military perception', Virilio explains, 'in which a supply of images would become the equivalent of an ammunition supply'.[32]

Auden and his generation were 'airminded', and references to an aerial view, Patrick Deer writes, 'tap into the futuristic imaginary of a modernizing official war culture reinventing itself by projecting strategic fantasies of air power'.[33] But a pilot's-eye view is also desirable for the writer, as Auden commented in a letter of 28 July 1932 to the poet John Pudney. The writer may be something of an airman in his distance from social groups: 'There are some, poets are generally such, who will always be a little outside the group, critical, but they need the group to feel a little out of just as much as they need it to be at home in.'[34] His 1930 poem 'Consider this and in our time' satirises the English middle class by taking a bird's – or an airman's – eye view: 'As the hawk sees it or the helmeted airman | The clouds rift suddenly – look there | At cigarette-end smouldering on a border | At the first garden party of the year.'[35] From the perspective of a winged predator or flying ace, bour-

30 Paul Virilio, *War and Cinema: The Logistics of Perception* (London, 1989), 3.
31 Ryan Bishop and John Phillips, *Modernist Avant-Garde Aesthetics and Contemporary Military Technology: Technicities of Perception* (Edinburgh, 2010), 26.
32 Virilio, *War and Cinema*, 1.
33 Patrick Deer, 'Auden and Wars', in *W. H. Auden in Context*, ed. Tony Sharpe (Cambridge, 2013), 150–9; 153.
34 Cited in Edward Mendelson, *Early Auden* (New York, 1981), 23.
35 *Southern Review* (Summer 1940), in W. H. Auden, *Prose and Travel Books*, ed. Mendelson, II, 46. Auden wrote in 1940 of Thomas Hardy: 'What I valued most in Hardy, then [in 1923], as I still do, was his hawk's vision, his way of looking at life from a very great height, as in the stage directions of *The Dynasts* or the opening chapter of *The Return of the Native*.' *Southern Review*, Summer 1940, cited in John Fuller, *W. H. Auden: A Commentary* (London, 1998), 74.

geois neuroses, mania and 'classic fatigue' are comically both magnified and diminished.[36]

Throughout his work, Auden was interested in finding ways to take an aerial view of matters, to step back and survey human life: whether through theories borrowed from psychology or religion, or the extensive, schematic graphs and charts with which his notes, manuscripts and notebooks are peppered. This tendency became particularly urgent in the 1930s, as he weighed the writer's role in society in light of the legacy of the 'greatest war in history'[37] and the threat of the next war, which was commonly taken to be imminent. *The Orators* was written at a moment when Auden felt the public's trauma had advanced to a new stage: 'The wound is healing and we can now look back to the war, not forgetting a sacrifice, and all the miseries which it caused, but without such very painful memories.'[38] Written between March and November 1931 and published in 1932, *The Orators* 'set the seal' on his reputation.[39] Auden writes 'as a domestic anthropologist', satirising the English ruling class.[40] Although he later criticised the book with some severity, he maintained from first to last that its key concern is hero worship: 'The central theme is a revolutionary hero. The first book describes the effect of him and of his failure on those whom he meets; the second book is his own account; and the last some personal reflections on the question of leadership in our time.'[41]

Although titled *The Orators*, the book displays a discursive field that is far from finely wrought rhetoric, and not at all monological. The first section is made up of a set of rhetorical exercises in prose: an address, an argument, a statement and a letter addressed to a wound. The second section, Book II or the 'Journal of an Airman' – by far the longest section, at forty-one pages – is generically hybrid. Book III consists of six odes. Fuller writes that the 'English study' portion of the title suggests that the book is 'a portrait of a culture sketched both by social

---

36 For discussion of the aerial viewpoint in Auden's work, see Nicholas Jenkins, 'The "Truth of Skies": Auden, Larkin and the English Question', in *The Movement Reconsidered: Essays on Larkin, Amis, Gunn, Davie and Their Contemporaries*, ed. Zachary Leader (Oxford, 2009), 34–61.

37 W. H. Auden, *The Orators: An English Study* (London, 1966 [1932]), 66.

38 Auden, *The Orators: An English Study*, 1st edn (London, 1932), 74.

39 Fuller, *Auden: A Commentary*, 85.

40 Ibid., 95.

41 This prefatory note, dropped from the first edition, is cited in Mendelson, *Early Auden*, 96.

and political allusion', as well as a 'self-referential display of literary
and verbal forms', and 'a quasi-anthropological analysis of a variety of
socially embedded rites of initiation, conflict and sympathetic magic'.
He describes the orators as 'compulsive verbalisers, all with some apprehension of the malaise, some with a felt need for spiritual leadership; but all bound by their own social and psychological conditioning,
and all doomed to failure'.[42]

The 'Journal' opens with a startling hodgepodge of forms and voices
separated by rows of three stars. In just the first twelve of the forty-one
pages the reader finds a pseudo-scientific voice – detached, objective,
'above' the proceedings – that draws from psychology, physics and biol-
ogy. It incorporates Gestalt psychology diagrams, a sestina, starkly juxtaposed observations in Imagist style, an extended, notational set of remarks on 'The Enemy as Observer', and an abecedarian 'The Airman's
Alphabet' structured through Icelandic rhymes. The opening engages in
a series of riffs on Wolfgang Köhler's 1930 *Gestalt Psychology*, rephrasing
his comments on introspection and the 'optical illusions that we accept
as real', thus extrapolating from visual perception to social perception.[43]
The Airman offers a series of six diagrammatic figures, instructing the
reader-turned-detective to 'give the party you suspect' one of the figures,
and, based on the forms your suspect perceives in the figure, either to
'accept him as a friend' or 'shoot at once'.[44] The issue of perception is
immediately made as humorous as it is grand. 'Day-dreams of victory'
are enumerated: an aerial photograph ('of earth-works in a harvest sea-
son'), a bomb shard on a mantelpiece – and self-mocking progress in the
drafting of a monograph 'on Professional Jealousy'.[45] 'Complete mastery
of the air' is one of the three 'counter attacks' against the enemy that
are proposed by the Airman – along with practical jokes and ancestor
worship.[46]

The Airman is a neurotic, intellectual, homosexual hero, likely modelled on T. E. Lawrence, whose main question, according to
Auden in 1934, is 'How shall the self-conscious man be saved?'[47] It
becomes clear in the first few pages that the author of the journal –

42   Fuller, *Auden: A Commentary*, 86.
43   Ibid., 100.
44   Auden, *The Orators* (1966), 42–3.
45   Ibid., 72.
46   Ibid., 56.
47   Hynes, *The Auden Generation*, 191.

the Airman – may be the embodiment of 'the armoured masculinity
and panoramic gaze', a 'Truly Strong Man', but he is also is metaphorically a 'surveyor': 'Organization owes nothing to the surveyor. It is in
no sense pre-arranged. The surveyor provides just news.'[48] His role is
thus played down, and his optical position reduced to that of humble
reporter, rather than the commanding perspective of the fighter pilot.
The surveyor merely has a bird's-eye view over a public school. Yet the
school will soon be transformed into a battleground, and the Airman
must also be read as a would-be dictator or 'Surveyor-in-Extraordinary,'
a term Isherwood coins in one of his short stories, 'The World War'.[49]
(In Isherwood's story, the newly proclaimed 'generalissimo' of the vic-
torious forces claims a motley array of titles, including 'Prime Minister,
Surgeon-in-chief, Viceregent, President of the Academy of all arts and
sciences, Supervisor of Customs and Sanitation, Censor, Surveyor-in-
Extraordinary and Grand Patriarch'.)[50] Nonetheless, *The Orators* is
marked by pervasive self-deprecation amidst the carnivalesque scenes of
'battle'. Mendelson notes that it is a work 'of a subversive writing from
within: the grand-guignol quality of some of its details, its wild violence
against the established order, may reflect Auden's sense that he could
accomplish nothing more practical than this in reality'.[51]

The 'Journal' contains letters folded into it, such as this one from the
Airman's Uncle Henry, which is likened to a call for help 'scribbled on
the walls of public latrines':

Some people say 'Why does anyone want to think about the war at
all?' and accuse those who do of militarist ideas. We weren't thinking
about war in 1914, except for a small body of thinking soldiers and
statesmen, who saw it inevitably approaching. The British nation as
a whole had no thought or idea of war – and yet in a matter of days
it was upon us, and we entered it as thoughtlessly and light-heartedly
as we would send off a team for a contest match. I must say that the
team – in this case the British Expeditionary Force – went into the

48   Auden, *The Orators* (1966), 41.
49   One of Isherwood's 'Mortmere stories', a literary project conceived with
Edward Upward to be a 'satirical portrait of English society as anatomized in [a]
small, highly eccentric village where moral anarchy secretly reigned and the inhabitants were all a bit mad'. Katherine Bucknell, 'Introduction' to Christopher
Isherwood, *The Mortmere Stories*, ed. Katherine Bucknell (London, 1994), 14.
50   Isherwood, *Mortmere Stories*, 116.
51   Mendelson, *Early Auden*, 95.

game just as cheerfully and light-heartedly, if not more so – but that
was their job as soldiers. The people who committed them to the
greatest war in history, and who afterwards backed them up and took
their turn so nobly, were the British public, the British nation.[52]

This letter contains two central ideas: the constant imminence of war,
and the similarity between war and sports matches, which are integral
to the overarching premise in *The Orators* of the similarity of the social
and psychological structures that support both boys' schools, and the
British nation at large. But this letter is also the note Uncle Henry
left when he killed himself with an air gun. The document intimates
the veteran's first-hand experience of war, and bitter knowledge of the
deceptions that had facilitated the nation's mobilisation – which grants
him the right to criticise the state's claims to authority. This is precisely
the kind of knowledge, gained through flesh-witnessing, that Auden
and his generation felt themselves to be lacking. The last few pages of
the 'Journal' feature a letter that replies to Uncle Henry. The letter,
labelled '*To begin at once*', provides a portrait of the Airman, the poet's
proxy, in the form of a self-mocking psychological assessment. Writing
and action are pitted against each other, and writing is condemned as
useless nonsense.

> *To begin at once.*
>   To my Uncle, perpetual gratitude and love for this crowning mer-
> cy. For myself, absolute humility.
>   I know that I am I, living in a small way in a temperate zone,
> blaming father, jealous of son, confined to a few acts often repeated,
> easily attracted to a limited class of physique, yet envying the simple
> life of the gut, desiring the certainty of the breast or prison, happiest
> sawing wood, only knowledge of the real, disturbances in the general
> law of the dream; the quick blood fretting against the slowness of
> the hope; a unit of life, needing water and salt, that looks for a sign.
>   What have I written? Thoughts suitable to a sanatorium. Three
> days to break a lifetime's pride.[53]

The last line refers to the time remaining until mobilisation occurs:
three days in which to take stock and humbly prepare his soul for

52   Auden, *The Orators* (1966), 72–3.
53   Ibid., 81.

battle. The letter is self-deprecating, as is most of the 'Journal', and makes a conventional gesture of poetic humility ('What have I written? Thoughts suitable to a sanatorium.'). But it also describes the Airman's sense of his own ordinariness, his failure to commit heroic deeds, and his sense of shame ('make me worthy'). This effect is reinforced by the syntax, with phrases that concatenate like a liturgical confession of sins. Implicitly, 'the simple life of the gut' and 'a few acts oft repeated' – mundane tasks, possibly neurotic tics – are unfavourably compared to heroic action. The Airman's 'only knowledge of the real', which is precisely what the authority of flesh-witnessing is rooted in, are brief epiphanies within a ploddingly unmindful life ('the general law of the dream'). The letter, although framed as the journal of a flying ace, encapsulates the guilt of the noncombatant.

The following section, titled '*First Day of Mobilisation*', is a page-long exercise in high camp and public-school hilarity. 'Stink-bombs' are thrown, and accusations of 'onanism, piracy on the high seas' bandied about. It is a mock war story. Its paratactic parody of a dispatch's objective tone is in each line undercut by the absurdity and puerility of the events it reports.

> At the pre-arranged zero hour the widow bent into a hoop with arthritis gives the signal for attack by unbending on the steps of St. Philip's. A preliminary bombardment by obscene telephone messages for not more than two hours destroys the *morale* already weakened by predictions of defeat made by wireless-controlled crows and card-packs. Shock troops equipped with wire-cutters, spanners and stink-bombs, penetrating the houses by infiltration, silence all alarm clocks, screw down the bathroom taps, and remove plugs and paper from the lavatories.[54]

This section of the Journal draws from Ludendorff's 1931 *The Coming War* ('a very dotty semi-autobiographical book') and Baudelaire's *Intimate Journals* (which Isherwood had translated two years previously),[55] and features details from Auden's experience in a scout camp during two weeks of the summer of 1930.[56] It is also bears a relation to Isherwood's story 'The World War', in its 'Bosch-like apocalyptic turn', as Fuller

54   Ibid., 77.
55   'Foreword', Auden, *The Orators* (1966), 7.
56   Mendelson, *Early Auden*, 95.

has noted.[57] It is hard to miss the similarities in the humorous friction between jocular tone, silly scenario, concern with bathroom functions, intimations of homosexuality and the mock-grave circumstances staged by both Auden and Isherwood. Both texts are furthermore concerned with positions of optical dominance. In the climactic scene of the enemy's retreat in 'The World War', a menacing voice – perhaps issuing from the radio – speaks in the protagonist's ear, 'hoarsely, with the urgency of a maniac: ". . . crossed the frontier. The *swine*. An hour and a half and they will be here."'[58] Isherwood's protagonists select an observation perch in a small café that offers a position of surveillance: 'The position was a suitable one for watching everything which would happen.' The scene resembles that of the 'Journal' quoted above, though it is more deeply marked by bitter black humour:

> In a room at the back of the counter we found . . . a terrified old woman, who, taking us for more of the enemy hussars, began at once to undress. A squadron of them had been there two hours ago, buying Vichy water for their horses; and now the maidservant was upstairs, giving birth to twins. We asked whether there was anybody else in the house. The old woman led the way into the bathroom. A pair of boots projected from the bowl of the water-closet. Our united strength disengaged the body of the unfortunate Charles. He was in a sorry condition, but not much worse for his adventure.[59]

In the 'Journal', the humour turns specifically around communications technology, parodying the strategic and political use of images. An ostensibly devastating newspaper article distributed 'in time for a late breakfast' is the 'first objective':

> A leading article accusing prominent citizens of arson, barratry, coining, dozing in municipal offices, espionage, family skeletons, getting and bambling [sic], heresy, issuing or causing to be issued false statements with intent to deceive, jingoism, keeping disorderly houses, mental cruelty, loitering, nepotism, onanism, piracy on the high seas, quixotry, romping at forbidden hours, sabotage, tea-drinking, unnatural offences against minors, vicious looks, will-burning, a yel-

---

57   Fuller, *Auden: A Commentary*, 111.
58   Isherwood, *The Mortmere Stories*, 115.
59   Ibid.

low streak, is on the table of every householder in time for a late breakfast.[60]

Psychological failures, possibly inebriated spelling ('getting and bambling'), snippets from boys' adventure tales, and accusations of cowardice mix in a frenzied and hilarious enumeration that has the effect of flattening any seriousness possessed by items such as 'sabotage' and 'unnatural offences against minors'. In the conclusion of this section, noncombatants are subject to a mass of corrupted information, and the act of reading the newspaper morphs into taking a test: 'At 6 p.m. passages of unprepared translation from dead dialects are set [sic] to all noncombatants. The papers are collected at 6.10. All who fail to obtain 99% make the supreme sacrifice. Candidates must write on three sides of the paper.'[61] There is no clear boundary between the world of public school and boys' nonsense, the bourgeois domestic sphere and the arena of war.

At the close of the 'Journal', when combat is imminent, the hyperverbal text subsides into a set of statistics. As the Airman prepares to mobilise, terse instrument readings are offered, along with one oblique reference to the Airman's physique and state of mind. In this passage, the Airman is preparing for his 'Test', as Isherwood would have said, his earlier subversion having subsided. It resembles Isherwood's line in 'The World War': 'Several minutes passed. I felt no terror. My pulse was regular. The sound for which I had been listening began to grow upon my senses, thin as a fretting of a gnat.'[62]

28th.
3.40 a.m. Pulses and reflexes, normal.
Barometric reading, 30.6.
Mean temperature, 34° F.
Fair. Some cumulus cloud at 10,000 feet. Wind easterly and
    moderate.
Hands in perfect order.[63]

This schematic notation is in the register of technical competence or authority, avoiding sentiment, and suggesting a heroic stoicism.

60   Auden, *The Orators* (1966), 77.
61   Ibid., 77–8.
62   Isherwood, *The Mortmere Stories*, 123.
63   Auden, *The Orators* (1966), 74.

Whatever tension, anticipation or fear the Airman is experiencing, it evades verbal description. The structure of language has buckled under this expressive burden, leaving only figures of objective scientific assessment to communicate in a laconic fashion. The Airman has transcended the fray of the public school, its pranks and ruckus, and achieved a 'manly' calm. The instruments are probably not wrong when they agree that the outlook is clear, but they are only instruments, and they offer no existential truths; nor does the Airman really need them for the simple act of dying – which it is probable that he will do, given that the 'Journal' concludes with this passage. Like W. B. Yeats's 'The Irish Airman Foresees His Death', which prophesies the Irish Airman's self-sacrifice, the final page of the 'Journal' invokes the Airman's 'balanced', rational evaluation of 'this tumult in the clouds'.

The 'Journal' closes by indicating that the Airman's otherwise kleptomaniac and onanistic (and writerly) hands have quieted: 'Hands in perfect order.' The line makes reference to Owen's assertion (ironic though it may have been) that his nerves were in perfect order in letters he wrote to his mother and to Sassoon shortly before he died: 'The Battalion had a sheer time last week. I can find no better epithet; because I cannot say I suffered anything, having let my brain grow dull. That is to say, my nerves are in perfect order.'[64] The reference makes clear how thoroughly tied up with Auden's thinking about the previous generation – and how engaged in working through the guilt of the noncombatant – his 'Journal' is.

As the Hawk Sees It: The Late 1930s and 1940s

How was the noncombatant English poet to gain objective distance from the tumultuous events of the 1930s, and yet at the same time write authentically, that is, from personal experience, with the authority of the flesh-witness? Achieving both would seem to be impossible, no matter how ethically urgent. Auden wrote to his friend E. R. Dodds at the onset of the Spanish Civil War:

> I am not one of those who believe that poetry need or even should be directly political, but in a critical period such as ours, I do be-

64   Fuller, *Auden: A Commentary*, 113; Mendelson, *Early Auden*, 109.

lieve that the poet must have direct knowledge of the major political events.

It is possible that in some periods, the poet can absorb and feel all in his ordinary everyday life, perhaps the supreme masters always can, but for the second order and particularly to-day, what the poet knows, what he can write about is what he has experienced in his own person. Academic knowledge is not enough.

I feel I can speak with authority about la Condition Humaine of only a small class of English intellectuals and professional people and that the time has come to gamble on something bigger. I shall probably be a bloody bad soldier but how can I speak to/for them without becoming one?[65]

Becoming a soldier was a potential solution, but it was not a commitment that Auden was able to fulfil. Many otherwise authoritative records of Auden's life are vague on Auden's doings in Spain; but the majority concur that he never served as soldier, stretcher-bearer or even ambulance driver, as he had wished.[66]

Auden continued to write with concerted preoccupation about positions of optical dominance that is the hallmark of *The Orators*. In his famous poem about the Spanish Civil War, 'Spain, 1937', the last generation of military power is compared to 'a motionless eagle eyeing the valley'. In *Journey to a War*, Auden and Isherwood stand in Liu Chan, looking down the slope to Li Kwo Yi and the Grand Canal:

From here we looked down on War as a bird might – seeing only a kind of sinister agriculture or anti-agriculture. Immediately below us, peasants were digging in the fertile, productive plain. Further on there would be more peasants, in uniform, also digging – the unproductive, sterile trench. Beyond them, to the north, still more peasants; and, once again, the fertile fields. This is how war must seem to the neutral, unjudging bird – merely the Bad Earth, the tiny, dead patch in the immense flowering field of luxuriant China.[67]

---

65   Mendelson, *Early Auden*, 195–6.
66   'The Good Comrade', 259–61, Jan Kurzke Papers, Archives of the International Institute for Social History, Amsterdam, cited in Paul Preston, *We Saw Spain Die: Foreign Correspondents in the Spanish Civil War* (London, 2008), 145.
67   W. H. Auden and Christopher Isherwood, *Journey to a War*, in Auden, *Prose and Travel Books*, ed. Mendelson, I, 547.

Auden's trips to Iceland, China, and Spain in the 1930s were a way of
bridging the private self and the public event, and intervening in the
world without becoming a soldier; and further, a way of turning the
sedentary, solitary exercise of writing into a kind of action, since this
style of reporting is predicated on a variety of heroic travel. In addition
to permitting him to don a heroic persona, such travel allowed him to
write a '*poésie de depart*', a parable of escape, emigration, or release.[68]

Auden's only dispatch from Spain, 'Impressions of Valencia', first appeared in the *New Statesman and Nation* on 30 January 1937.[69] It points
to the *mise-en-scène* that is part of all textual representations of war, be
they journalistic or poetic. Each of the first five of the six paragraphs
features at least one mode of symbolic representation. The first three
showcase positions of optical dominance: the map and the comic strip;
the poster (and constituent photomontage); the daily papers and the
'huge black arrow' on the Ministry, indicating that the front at Teruel
lay 150 kilometres away. Next, a variety show that includes 'an extremely sinister dance of the machine-guns' and foreign correspondents
who 'come in for their dinner, conspicuous as actresses'; and finally, in
contrast to the 'blood-thirsty and unshaven Anarchy of the bourgeois
cartoon', enter the people, the main actors, 'in corduroy breeches with
pistols on their hip, in uniform, in civilian suits and berets'. The per-
formativity and self-consciousness of the foreign correspondents, with
their bourgeois rituals and passivity, is feminised in contrast with the
masculinised partisans, who are associated with action, practical garb
and phallic weapons. The dispatch is aware that its own process is as
iconic and reductive as that of a comic strip or poster, and as dramatising as that of a theatre piece.

At the dispatch's midpoint, Auden theatrically names the nation
that he has thus far been describing, citing the reports of English airmen: 'This is the Spain for which charming young English aviators have
assured us that the best would be a military dictatorship backed by a
foreign Power.' While contradicting the supporters of the Nationalist
cause with a rhetorical flourish – and dethroning the pilots with their
ostensibly masterful vantage point – Auden sets himself as master of
ceremonies, revealing to the readership of the *New Stateman and Nation*
what the Spanish situation is 'really' like, on the ground. Yet against

68   Hynes, *The Auden Generation*, 228.
69   'Impressions of Valencia', *New Statesman and Nation*, 30 January 1937, in
Auden, *Prose and Travel Books*, ed. Mendelson, I, 384.

this concluding gesture of naming, the dispatch as a whole mixes popular culture with military imagery, as a way to indicate the reduction inherent in mass depictions of military manoeuvres. His flippant tone (for example, 'Altogether it is a great time for the poster artist' – a sarcastic warning against artistic opportunism in wartime, about which Auden often wrote) is amplified in the description of the tasteless photomontage of 'a bombed baby' that 'lies couchant upon a field of aeroplanes', as stylised and emblematic as a lion recumbent upon a heraldic crest. These contrasts also serve to indicate Auden's own role as eyewitness and recorder of the scene: but in essence, on holiday, as he had been in Iceland. The dispatch compares the sins of journalism to those of stage acting and advertising, which, in its political incarnation, becomes propaganda. Ultimately, the dispatch sets aside the politically wrongheaded opinions of 'charming English aviators' in favour of a first-hand, ground-level view. But the reporter is not a participant: his position as interloper is made clear in the piece's very opening line: 'The pigeons fly about the square in brilliant sunshine, warm as a fine English May.' The Civil War map, likewise, is 'rather prettily illustrated after the manner of railway posters urging one to visit Lovely Lakeland or Sunny Devon'. The points of reference familiar to the reader situate the reporter as 'one of us', an Englishman with an English eye, surveying the Spanish conflict from a distance.

Coda: Major Auden and the Morale Division of the US Strategic Bombing Survey

In February 1940 Auden sent a letter-questionnaire to E. R. Dodds, in which he cross-examines himself regarding his decision to stay in the United States, where he had emigrated the previous year. The dialogic format recalls 'The Public v. the Late Mr. William Butler Yeats', as Auden takes on the personae of both interviewer and interviewee. On being asked *'On what conditions would you come back to England?'* he replies that he might do so only '[i]f anyone can convince me that there is something that has to be done, by a writer with my kind of gifts that can only be done in England and is so important that it justifies smashing his private life (which also has certain responsibilities)'. He adds, 'I am neither a politician nor a novelist, reportage is not my business.'[70] A

---

70   Humphrey Carpenter, *W. H. Auden: A Biography* (New York, 1981), 290.

biographical irony is that as the Second World War was ending, Auden did indeed have the chance to travel abroad to gather facts and 'reportage' in the form of oral testimony, and 'Not only to write well but be | Of some use to the military'.[71] He travelled through post-war Germany in the employ of the US government, as a surveyor who 'looked down on War as a bird might'.[72]

While he was teaching at Swarthmore, Auden was contacted by the Pentagon to participate in a six-to-twelve-month mission in Germany, to assess the effects of bombing on morale through interviews with the civilian population. It is not clear why Auden was selected, although at the time he thought it was because of his knowledge of German language and culture.[73] Auden was assigned to the 'Morale Division' of the US Strategic Bombing Survey as a 'Bombing Research Analyst', and given a major's rank and military uniform (of which he was very proud).[74] His biographer reports that he quipped to a friend, 'My dear, I'm the first major poet to fly the Atlantic'.[75] He arrived in Germany on 5 May 1945, before the war was over, and shortly thereafter began interviewing civilians to ascertain the effects that bombing had on morale, 'a kind of low-level spying'.[76] About collecting oral testimony, he noted tersely, 'We got no answers that we didn't expect,' and wrote to several correspondents that the work was interesting but that sometimes he found himself crying.[77] He objected to the idea of 'morale' itself as quantifiable, terming it 'psycho-sociological nonsense' (and the final 'e' in 'morale' 'illiterate and absurd'): 'What they want to say, but don't say, is how many people we killed and how many buildings we destroyed by that wicked bombing.'[78] Auden's identification with the American military in his use of the first-person plural is noteworthy, implying a willingness to close the distance between himself and those who carried out the bombing.

Unfortunately, little has been preserved regarding Auden's experi-

71 W. H. Auden, *The Double Man* (New York, 1941), 83–4.
72 Auden and Isherwood, *Journey to a War*, in Auden, *Prose and Travel Books*, ed. Mendelson, I, 547.
73 Carpenter, *Auden: A Biography*, 333.
74 Ibid., 333–4.
75 Ibid.
76 Peter Edgerly Firchow, *W. H. Auden: Contexts for Poetry* (Newark, NJ, 2002), 68.
77 Quoted in Carpenter, *Auden: A Biography*, 335.
78 Ibid., 334.

ences working for the Morale Division. The reports he filed, along with those of his colleagues, were compiled in a two-volume book for the Division, *The Effects of Strategic Bombing on German Morale*.[79] One characteristically Audenesque remark was recorded: 'None of us could have imagined that [the Germans] could go that far . . . They applied to it the same pedantic organization skills a piano-tuner does when he tunes a virtuoso's concert piano grand.'[80] But afterward he barely spoke or wrote of his experiences – just as he hardly remarked on his much-trumpeted visit to Spain.

Only one of Auden's poems, 'Memorial for the City', an elegy written for Charles Williams in 1949, makes mention of what he had seen in Bavaria. It does so through a relatively unsentimental description of destroyed institutions: 'burnt-out Law courts' and a 'Cathedral far too damaged to repair'. The press, Auden drily notes, receives better accommodations than that of a governmental initiative: 'Around the Grand Hotel patched up to hold reporters, | Near huts of some Emergency Committee, | The barbed wire runs through the abolished City.'

Nicolas Nabokov (first cousin of the novelist Vladimir), also working for the Bombing Survey, recorded a few of Auden's comments in his diary. They were previous acquaintances, and met by chance near Frankfurt in July 1945:

'I know that they had asked for it,' [Auden] would say, 'but still, this kind of total destruction is beyond reasoning . . . It seems like madness! . . . It is absolutely ghastly . . . [I]s it justified to reply to *their* mass-murder by *our* mass-murder? It seems terrifying to me . . . And I cannot help ask myself, "Was there no other way?"'[81]

In his correspondence Auden also made several statements about the human cost of war. Of Munich, he wrote to Elizabeth Mayer, 'The city as a whole is gone. The towers of the Frauenkirche remain and half the nave, but why go on.'[82] To Tania Stern he wrote of the bombing of Darmstadt, but instead of describing the actual wreckage, he turned to a statistic: 'The town was ninety-two per cent destroyed

79   Vol. II was published in December 1946; vol. I in May 1947.
80   Carpenter, *Auden: A Biography*, 336.
81   Nicolas Nabokov, *Bagázh: Memoirs of a Russian Cosmopolitan* (London, 1975), 221.
82   Quoted in Carpenter, *Auden: A Biography*, 334.

in thirty minutes. You can't imagine what that looks like unless you
see it with your own eyes.'[83] The latter remarks invoke the authority
of the eyewitness, drawing on *adynaton*, the impossibility trope. Kate
McLoughlin has identified this device as the 'mother of all diversion-
ary tactics', and calls its use a 'distress-flare declaring a representational state of emergency'.[84] This is a key rhetorical strategy in wartime
texts written by both eyewitnesses and flesh-witnesses alike,[85] and it
stems from the cultural turn toward valuing sensory experience as a
crucial grounding for the acquisition of knowledge. In his few written comments about what he saw while interviewing noncombatants
during the US Strategic Bombing Survey, Auden drew on the same
epistemological matrix that in the early 1930s had caused him 'the
guilt of the noncombatant', spurred doubts about the social role of the
writer, and fuelled texts such as *The Orators*. To witness the aftermath
is not the same as to experience the bombing in the flesh, but it can
spur a similar claim of inexpressibility.

According to the logic of the cultural turn toward authority rooted
in experience, the eyewitness may report observable facts, but he is
never in the position of judge. And once an eyewitness has recounted
what he has seen to an audience (or historian, or journalist), his authority is 'squandered by usage'.[86] The authority Auden gained through his
work as Bombing Research Analyst was never expended, however: the
compilation of information was not especially generative of literary expression. The poet's silence, rather than a text, is the trace of his survey.
Although he had planned with his colleague James Stern to collaborate
on a book about their experiences in the Morale Division, afterwards
Auden was reluctant to discuss the survey, and Stern ultimately wrote
The Hidden Damage by himself.[87] Auden's choice not to communicate

83   Ibid.
84   Catherine Mary McLoughlin, *Authoring War: The Literary Representation
of War from the Iliad to Iraq* (Cambridge, 2011), 157. Paul Fussell writes, 'Whatever the cause, the presumed inadequacy of language itself to convey the facts
about trench warfare is one of the motifs of all who wrote about the war': *The
Great War and Modern Memory* (London, 1975), 170.
85   Rachel Galvin, '"Less Neatly Measured Common-Places": Stevens' Wartime Poetics', *Wallace Stevens Journal* 37 (2013), 38–41.
86   Harari, 'Scholars, Eyewitnesses, and Flesh-Witnesses of War', 216–22.
87   Claire Seiler argues that Auden's 1947 *Age of Anxiety* emerged from his
experiences in the Morale Division, since there are significant parallels between
the poem and Stern's *The Hidden Damage*: Claire Seiler, 'Auden's War Book

his experience in Germany had the effect of conserving it. By cordoning it off from the possibility of transmission, he archived the experience, and did not pass on to his readers the authority he had accrued. It left him with a set of untold stories, as veterans may have. But by refusing to trade in those stories, he avoided placing himself in an authoritative position from which he might judge or interpret. Rather than become a 'Surveyor-in-Extraordinary' as Isherwood satirically had it, Auden chose to file his reports and fall silent. His decision recalls the opening of the Airman's Journal: 'Organization owes nothing to the surveyor. It is in no sense pre-arranged. The surveyor provides just news.'[88]

Manqué', forthcoming in *Auden at Work*, ed. Bonnie Costello and Rachel Galvin (New York, 2015). I am grateful to Seiler for her generous response to the present essay.

88   Auden, *The Orators* (1966), 41.

Does Tolstoy's War and Peace Make Modern War Literature Redundant?

MARK RAWLINSON

> People who have read *War and Peace* more than once, and enjoyed it immensely, can often scarcely remember a thing about it.[89]

THE CONCEPT OF REDUNDANCY employed in this essay is the one used in mathematics and linguistics to designate symbols that do not add information to a sequence. One of the hazards of teaching twentieth-century war literature is the tacit inference of redundancy by readers, namely that the representational conventions as well as the facts and values represented are 'predictable from . . . context'.[90] The claim that twentieth-century war writing is made superfluous by *War and Peace* (1869) is polemical, but it is also intended to do serious work: to draw attention to representations of war which are not predictable from context, and to renew questions such as why representing war as irrational, murderous activity is unefficacious, and why we would imagine otherwise.

The designs of *War and Peace* as war writing can be recognised as early as 1853, when Tolstoy published a story drawing on his own military experience in the Caucasus:

> War always interested me: not war in the sense of manoeuvres devised by great generals – my imagination refused to follow such immense movements, I did not understand them – but the reality of war, the actual killing. I was more interested to know in what way and under the influence of what feeling one soldier kills another than to know how the armies were arranged at Austerlitz and Borodino.[91]

---

89 John Bayley, *Tolstoy and the Novel* (London, 1966), 98.
90 *OED*, *s.v.* 'redundant', A.I.6a.
91 Leo Tolstoy, 'The Raid', in *The Raid and Other Stories*, trans. Louise and Aylmer Maude (Oxford, 1982), 1–28; 1.

The insistence that there is a 'reality of war', that that reality is occluded or camouflaged by discourses which choreograph military violence at the macroscopic level of generals, armies and battles, and that this reality consists in nothing but 'the actual killing', reads like a template for twentieth-century English culture's discovery of war (it might be better to call it an invention).[92] English literary culture was quarantined from many of the nineteenth century's developments in warfare, its prototypes of modern mass destruction, for they were proven in continental Europe or in North America.[93] John W. De Forest, an officer of the Union and author of *Miss Ravenel's Conversion from Secession to Loyalty* (1867), acknowledged that Tolstoy led the way in deconstructing the heroic ethos:

> Let me tell you that nobody but [Tolstoy] has written the whole truth about war and battle. *I* tried, and I told all I dared, and perhaps all I could. But there was one thing I did not dare tell, lest the world should infer I was naturally a coward, and so could not know the feelings of a brave man. I actually did not dare state the extreme horror of battle, and the anguish with which the bravest soldiers struggle through it.[94]

In the twentieth century it has become customary to ground apprehensions of the 'whole truth about war' in combatant experience – James Campbell has even dignified this presumption with a name, 'combat gnosticism'.[95] Tolstoy, the beginning of whose career as a writer is coterminous with his military experience in the empire's as-yet-unpacified Caucasian conquest, then during the Crimean War (his *Sebastopol Sketches* appeared in 1855), appears to be the archetypal modern war writer, converted to anti-militarism by his encounter with the reality of combat.[96] But in the following extract from Vassily Grossman's novel *Life and Fate* (first published in Switzerland in 1980), which vies with

---

92   As narrated, for instance, in Paul Fussell's influential study *The Great War and Modern Memory* (Oxford, 1975).

93   See Daniel A. Bell, *The First Total War: Napoleon's Europe and the Birth of Modern Warfare* (London, 2008).

94   John W. De Forest to William Dean Howells, quoted in Edmund Wilson, *Patriotic Gore: Studies in the Literature of the American Civil War* (London, 1987 [1962]), 684.

95   Campbell, 'Combat Gnosticism', 203–15.

96   Rosamund Bartlett, *Tolstoy: A Russian Life* (London, 2010), 106.

Solzhenitsyn's novel-sequence *The Red Wheel* (1971 onwards) for the status of the 'War and Peace' (or big war novel) of the era of world war, Tolstoy's combatant status provokes a crisis:

> 'Those sons of bitches never see any action themselves. They just sit on the other side of the Volga and write articles. If someone gives them a good dinner, then they write about him. They're certainly no Tolstoys. People have been reading *War and Peace* for a century and they'll go on reading it for another century. Why's that? Because Tolstoy's a soldier, because he took part in the war himself. That's how he knew who to write about.'
>
> 'Excuse me, comrade General,' said Krymov. 'Tolstoy didn't take part in the Patriotic War.'
>
> 'He didn't take part in it – what do you mean?'
>
> 'Just that,' said Krymov. 'He didn't take part in it. He hadn't even been born at the time of the war with Napoleon.'
>
> 'He hadn't been born?' said Guryev. 'What do you mean? How on earth?'
>
> A furious argument then developed – the first to have followed any of Krymov's lectures. To his surprise, the general flatly refused to believe him.[97]

In contrast to the English paradigm of subalterns faulting rear-echelon staff officers (a partisan view of the correlation of rank and risk dramatised in the character of Williams in the eve of Agincourt scenes in Shakespeare's *Henry V*), Grossman has a general criticise the newspapers and the commissariat for neither fighting nor being Tolstoy. These are the same thing in the view of General Guryev, who will not renounce the inferences he has made in his reading of *War and Peace*. A crisis of *mimesis* lurks behind this concept of the authority of experience:

> [Plato] despises the poet's ability to construct convincing representations of those possessed of genuine knowledge and understanding (generals, kings, even philosophers) without himself being in possession of the comprehension he counterfeits.[98]

---

97 Vasily Grossman, *Life and Fate*, trans. Robert Chandler (London, 1986), 239–40.

98 Stephen Mulhall, *Wounded Animal: J. M. Coetzee and the Difficulty of Reality in Literature and Philosophy* (Princeton, 2010), 15.

In *War and Peace*, Tolstoy promotes the imaginative writer's ability to represent a comprehension which generals and kings themselves cannot attain, even in the privileged field of their own supposed agency. He would also insist on the literary sources of his own knowledge of war, declaring in 1901 that 'all he had learnt about war he had learnt from Stendhal's description of the battle of Waterloo in *La Chartreuse de Parme*, where Fabrizio wanders about the battlefield "understanding nothing"'.[99] Tolstoy would later assume a Platonic distrust of the aesthetic in *What is Art?* (1897), but in the 1860s the novel still had potential as a cognitive and moral instrument.

Tolstoy's historical precedence was not exhausted by England's encounter with mass, popular warfare in 1914–18. Introducing a wartime radio adaptation of *War and Peace*, E. M. Forster specified that Tolstoy's scepticism about the origins of wars was the most contemporary aspect of his book:

> Tolstoy is describing an international upheaval, such as we are facing to-day . . . Does he think anyone is to blame? To Tolstoy, both people and events are floating on a stream . . . We waste our time if we try to guide the stream or even to understand it . . . There is something very modern in his attitude here, and this is a reason why *War and Peace* seems so up-to-date.[100]

Forster's position on the war against Nazi Germany is on one level strikingly heterodox, but on another the quietism he commends chimes with a more widespread lack of enthusiasm for the coercions experienced living in a state at war. Tolstoy's critique of military reason becomes counsel for survival. More recently, *War and Peace* has been seized upon as providing a pre-formed analogy for the hubris of the US campaigns in Iraq and Afghanistan.[101]

The foregoing are some of the reasons I want to argue that Tolstoy's *War and Peace* makes modern war literature redundant, by which I mean

99 Isaiah Berlin, 'The Hedgehog and the Fox: An Essay on Tolstoy's View of History', in *The Proper Study of Mankind*, ed. Henry Hardy and Roger Hausheer (London, 1997), 436–98; 472.

100 E. M. Forster in *Tolstoy's 'War and Peace': Introduction to the Series of Broadcasts* (The British Broadcasting Corporation, 1943), 8.

101 Michael R. Katz, '*War and Peace* in our Time', *New England Review* 29.4 (2008), 185–95; 186.

that writers coming after Tolstoy have told us nothing we do not find in
Tolstoy. The Second World War poet Keith Douglas worried that, writing after Owen, Sassoon and in particular Isaac Rosenberg, he might
only be tautological, and this is the sense of my contention: not that the
local and temporal inflections of the literatures of the Western Front, or
Vietnam, are not real, but that their articulation involves the restate-
ment of Tolstoyan forms and perspectives.[102] My argument is clearly
over-stated in the significance it gives to Tolstoy's writing, but it may
not be such an over-statement to claim that war writing consists in a finite set of tropes – which evidence suggests may be discovered over and
over by each new generation of warriors (thus confounding both Whig
and Russian Formalist accounts of literary history) – rather than a series
of particularised military-historical contexts.[103]

    Some of the ways in which *War and Peace* prevents, but does not
preclude, twentieth-century war writing are apparent in Tolstoy's defence of the work on which he had spent five years during the 1860s,
and in particular the way in which he ranges his achievement against
the then hegemonic discourses of war. Again, we might be reminded
of a long-serving orthodoxy about the literature of the Great War,
namely that, after 1916, a new kind of war writing protested both the
prosecution of war and the representation of war as heroic and pur-
posive: '[o]nce the solider was seen as a victim, the idea of a war hero
becomes unimaginable' (and Samuel Hynes underlines this historical
event with a nod to Robert Graves, 'the First World War changed all
that').[104] First of all, Tolstoy makes the claim that *War and Peace* was
generically unconventional, though he argues that this 'departure from
European forms', like the novel, was a characteristic of Russian writing from Gogol to Dostoyevsky, not a consequence of writing about
warfare.[105] The force of this claim lies in Tolstoy's contrast between his
work and historical writing. In an argument which seems to anticipate
Hayden White's deconstruction of the boundary between historiography and narrative fiction, historical writing is alleged to be formally de-

102   Desmond Graham, ed., *Keith Douglas: A Prose Miscellany* (Manchester,
1985), 120.
103   See Kate McLoughlin, *Authoring War* (Cambridge, 2011).
104   Samuel Hynes, *A War Imagined: The First World War and English Culture*
(London, 1990), 215.
105   Leo Tolstoy, 'A Few Words Apropos of the Book *War and Peace*' (1868),
in *War and Peace*, trans. Richard Pevear and Larissa Volokhonsky (London,
2007), 1217.

pendent on reductive symbols of agency, such as the figure of the hero. Tolstoy is far from equating different modes of discursive power, which is one way of reading White: Tolstoy's critique of historiographical representations is intended to be fatal to the truth-claims of historians. He excoriates battlefield description, a representational project which, he argues, necessitates falsehood: the 'clear and always flattering picture' is homologous with the rhetoric of the official reports from which they derive – a simplification of action which reproduces the discipline of drill in choreographing the movement of thousands as one – and which produces the same psychological relief in substituting order for chaos.[106] In *War and Peace*, the disparity between how things were, and what they will become in historiographical retrospect, is presented as a paradox about the inefficacy of the general officers to whom greatest agency is attributed.[107] Late-twentieth-century Memory Studies has caught up with Tolstoy's insights into chains of perceptual command, noting how official or hegemonic popular symbols and narratives may usurp experience in personal memory, a hypothesis explored in the research of the oral historian Alistair Thomson, who has analysed private forgetting under the pressure of public remembrance.[108] In order to be about 1812, Tolstoy's book has to be unlike historical accounts of war, and this also means not being like a novel.

The critic Gary Saul Morson has pointed out how deliberately this has been forgotten in the creation of a canon of European realism. Tolstoy's contrariness was repressed in the twentieth century, as *War and Peace* was installed as the ideal type and classic instance of the historical novel, a process which Morson tellingly calls 'the pacification of *War and Peace*'.[109] This has included abridgements which cut the epilogues and other direct authorial addresses seen as 'perverse interruption[s] of narrative'.[110] Drawing on the implications of Bakhtin's theory of fictional narrative, Morson proposes that Tolstoy's scepticism about historical

106 Tolstoy, 'A Few Words', 1220.
107 Berlin, 'Hedgehog and Fox', 448–9.
108 See Alistair Thomson, 'Anzac Memories: Putting Popular Memory Theory into Practice in Australia', *Oral History* 18.1 (Spring 1990), 25–31.
109 Gary Saul Morson, *Hidden in Plain View: Narrative and Creative Potentials in 'War and Peace'* (Stanford, 1987), 78.
110 Nicholas Rzhevsky, 'The Shape of Chaos: Herzen and *War and Peace*', *Russian Review* 34.4 (October 1975), 367–81, 367; Berlin, 'Hedgehog and Fox', 439.

and psychological explanation is really scepticism about narrative *in toto*, a scepticism which is enacted in the novel's narrative heterodoxy:

> [*War and Peace*] questions the validity of all narrative forms and [. . .] satirizes the concealed assumptions of all available genres [. . .] it satirizes all historical writing, and all novels.[111]

I have argued elsewhere that while singular literary narratives of war cannot be taken as historically representative, they may well reveal the assumptions on which more representative (i.e. more conventional, more widely read or imitated) narratives are founded.[112] Tolstoy's novel is the *sine qua non* of such laying bare of the devices of war representation. As Morson shows, it is Tolstoy's insistence in foregrounding this intellectual and artistic activity which shatters the novel – for earlier critics '[i]t was the experience of reading that was devastated' – though the latter-day recuperation of a 'transparent' Tolstoy has disguised this.[113] Features of *War and Peace* which drew uncomprehending responses from contemporary reviewers and early critics include: 'non-novelistic', proverbial or 'absolute language' and 'dogmatizing'; 'essays and lectures on narratology'; encyclopaedism; irrelevant or irregular incidents, 'redundancy, a ponderosity of petty details'; the absence of connections between incidents, or between thoughts and actions.[114] We can try to imagine how perplexing was the experience of the earliest readers of the serialised work (as we might imagine the first readers of *Ulysses*): who are the protagonists? How long will this work be? What is its theme?[115] Victor Shklovsky, picking up on Tolstoy's own diagnosis of Russian antinomianism, asserted that Tolstoy had designed his work so that it did not cohere, that a rage for 'formal anomaly' characterised an imperial literature which was historically belated, and which therefore proceeded by 'rejection and parody'.[116]

111   Morson, *Hidden in Plain View*, 80 and 83.
112   Mark Rawlinson, 'Memory and Nation in British Narratives of the Second World War after 1945', forthcoming in *Memories of World War II in Post-War Europe: Redefining the Self and the Nation*, ed. M. Bragança and P. Tame (Oxford and New York, 2015).
113   Morson, *Hidden in Plain View*, 54 and 2.
114   Ibid., 10, 18, 39, 45, 53, 55. See also A. V. Knowles, 'Tolstoy's Literary Reputation before *War and Peace*', *Modern Language Review* 72 (1977), 627–39.
115   Morson, *Hidden in Plain View*, 57–60.
116   Ibid., 74.

The novels of Tolstoy will be incomprehensible if we come to judge them according to the norms of the old poetics, which would be like judging Kutuzov's actions according to Clausewitz's rules of war.[117]

Tolstoy refuses to judge Kutuzov, or war, by Clausewitz; indeed *War and Peace* is a partial refutation of Clausewitz's *On War* (posthumously published in 1832). This might appear surprising, because both authors saw themselves as philosophers of war, clearing away the deceptive assumptions attached to the terms employed to prosecute and to commemorate war. Thus, in his first chapter, 'What is War?', the Prussian general who, unlike Tolstoy, was a veteran of the Napoleonic Wars (1803–15), stripped war back to its essence:

> I shall not begin by formulating a crude, journalistic definition of war, but go straight to the heart of the matter, to the duel. War is nothing but a duel on a larger scale. Countless duels go to make up war, but a picture of it as a whole can be formed by imagining a pair of wrestlers. Each tries through physical force to compel the other to do his will; his *immediate* aim is to *throw* his opponent in order to make him incapable of further resistance.
>
> *War is thus an act of force to compel our enemy to do our will.*[118]

On War is apparently distinguished by its author's determination to provide an objective account of military conflict: the deep structure or logic of war, its practical nature, and its relationship to policy. The interwar tactician and historian Basil Liddell Hart may have viewed Clausewitz as 'the Mahdi of mass and of mutual massacre', but to Tolstoy the Prussian's conception and discourse of war constituted another falsehood.[119] The foundational definition of war as duel is directly parodied in Tolstoy's treatment of Austerlitz, the last battle of the 1805 section of *War and Peace*, and the one at which, in an earlier version of the narrative, Prince Andrei was to have been killed.

Prince Andrei and his battalion were now twenty paces from the cannon. Above him he heard the unceasing whistle of bullets, and

---

117   Victor Shklovsky, quoted in Morson, *Hidden in Plain View*, 75.
118   Carl von Clausewitz, *On War*, ed. and trans. Michael Howard and Peter Paret (Princeton, 1976), 75 (original emphasis).
119   R. M. Gallie, *Philosophers of Peace and War* (Cambridge, 1978), 37.

soldiers ceaselessly gasped and fell to right and left of him. But he
did not look at them; he looked fixedly only at what was happening
ahead of him – at the battery. He clearly saw the figure of a red-
haired gunner, his shako knocked askew, pulling a swab from one
side, while a French soldier pulled it towards him from the other
side. Prince Andrei saw clearly the bewildered and at the same time
angry expression on the faces of the two men, who evidently did not
understand what they were doing.

   'What are they doing?' Prince Andrei wondered, looking at them.
'Why doesn't the red-haired artillerist run away, since he has no
weapon? Why doesn't the Frenchman stab him? Before he runs away,
the Frenchman will remember his musket and bayonet him.'

   In fact, another Frenchman with his musket atilt ran up to the
fighting men, and the lot of the red-haired artillerist, who still did
not understand what awaited him, and triumphantly pulled the swab
from the French soldier's hands, was about to be decided. But Prince
Andrei did not see how it ended. It seemed to him as though one of
the nearest soldiers, with the full swing of a stout stick, hit him on
the head. It was slightly painful and above all unpleasant, because
the pain distracted him and kept him from seeing what he had been
looking at.[120]

The long-windedness of this account is a consequence of a reiterative
insistence on epistemic conditions. The repetition of verbs denoting
Andrei's looking and seeing is not redundant: it registers the moment-
by-moment sustaining of the Prince's perceptual orientation to battle as
it is immediately manifest in the disposition of a Russian and a French
soldier tugging at a swab (the out-sized cotton bud of the Artillery).
Their incomprehension is clear to Andrei's eyes, but their behaviour
remains inexplicable. This is a microcosm of Tolstoy's critique of causal
explanations which hinge on heroes or great actors of history, which
gives the lie to Clausewitz's definition of war as 'duel' and 'an act of force
to compel our enemy to do our will'. In the parody duel taking place before
Andrei's eyes, neither 'wrestler' possesses volition; they appear to the
prince to be captives of their antagonistic relation.

   It is quite typical of Tolstoy's art of interruption, and his suspicion
of narrative closure, that this bathetic rewriting of On War is incomplete as a perception – Andrei 'did not see how it ended' – but also

---

that Andrei's wounding is experienced as a perceptual interruption, not as an act of violence with potentially fatal consequences (and this is the wound that will bring Andrei, one body amongst a myriad strewn on the battlefield, to look up at 'the figure of the little, insignificant Napoleon, and the lofty sky over it all').[121] No more did Tolstoy know how it would end.[122]

In the 1812 section of *War and Peace*, when Tolstoy has resurrected Andrei to serve on Kutuzov's staff at the battle of Borodino, he and his friend Pierre Bezukhov cross paths with the historical General Clausewitz, and 'involuntarily' overhear his exchange with Walzogen:

> '*Der Krieg muss im Raum verlegt werden. Der Ansicht kann ich nicht genug Preis geben,*' said one.
>
> '*O ja,*' said the other voice. '*Da der Zweck ist nur den Feind zu schwächen, so kann man gewiss nicht den Verlust der Privatspersonen in Achtung nehmen.*'[123]

Andrei reacts with growing anger to these conceptions of war. The abstract space (*Raum*) into which it is urged war should be extended is the real home of the Bolkonsky family. Forster observed that

> After one has read *War and Peace* for a bit, great chords begin to sound, and we cannot say exactly what struck them [. . .] They come from the immense area of Russia over which episodes and characters have been scattered [. . .] Many novelists have the feeling for place [. . .] Very few have the sense of space [. . .] Space is the lord of *War and Peace*, not time.[124]

This is the hinterland to battle (encompassing the Rostovs as well as the Bolkonskys, and the whole of the civil life of Russia) which Andrei instinctively opposes to the theoretical extension of the abstract space

121   Ibid., 293.
122   Bayley, *Tolstoy*, 76.
123   Tolstoy, *War and Peace*, 774: 'The war must be extended widely. I cannot commend this view enough,' said one. 'Oh yes,' said the other voice. 'Since the point is only to weaken the enemy, one certainly cannot take into consideration the loss of private individuals.'
124   E. M. Forster, *Aspects of the Novel*, ed. Oliver Stallybrass (Harmondsworth, 1979), 51.

of the battlefield. The second assertion overheard, that there is no need
for attention to the loss of private persons, is the occasion of a fantasy
of total, un-hypocritical, war. Pierre is shocked by Andrei's counsel of
unlimited violence:

> Take no prisoners . . . That alone would change the whole war and
> make it less cruel. As it is, we've been playing at war – that's the
> nasty thing, we act magnanimously and all that. It's like the mag-
> nanimity and sentimentality of the lady who swoons when she sees
> a calf slaughtered; she's so kind, she can't bear the sight of blood,
> but she eats the same calf in sauce with great appetite. We're told
> about the rules of war, about chivalry, about parleying, sparing the
> unfortunate, and so on. It's all nonsense. I saw chivalry and parleying
> in 1805: they cheated us, we cheated them. They loot other people's
> houses, spread false banknotes, and worst of all – kill my children
> and my father, and then talk about the rules of war and magnanim-
> ity to the enemy. Take no prisoners, but kill and go to your death!
> Whoever has come to this, as I have, through the same sufferings.[125]

The analogy between prisoners of war and the swooned-over calf is bril-
liantly subversive: soldiers are meat, and this breath-taking proposition
makes every other representation look like a lie. But Andrei's reaction
to staff-talk is more significant for its disproportionateness than for its
clear-sightedness. If war is structurally a reality-contest, the term into
which Elaine Scarry translates Clausewitz's duel to propose a homology
with torture, we should not be surprised that reactions to it take on
something of the partiality, the situatedness, of the discourse of adversaries.[126] Great War writing is structured adversarially, as Fussell pointed
out, and the impress of these binaries and dualisms can be traced in the
writing of the aftermath.[127] Andrei's jeremiad reads like Sassoon's poems for C. K. Ogden's *Cambridge Magazine*, which from 1915 provided a
weekly digest of the European press, to liberate its readers from the myo-
pia of English war reporting, but which, in giving Sassoon a platform,
promulgated a partisan poetic view of the war which, as Orwell would

---

125   Tolstoy, *War and Peace*, 775.
126   Elaine Scarry, *The Body in Pain: The Making and Unmaking of the World*
(New York, 1985), 62.
127   See Fussell, *Great War*, and Valentine Cunningham, *British Writers of the
Thirties* (Oxford, 1988).

later conceptualise it in 'Inside the Whale', presented a 'passive, negative angle'.[128] The exorbitance of Andrei's view is evident if we compare it with the passage from Clausewitz's *On War* which is its intertextual occasion:

> If then, civilised nations do not put their prisoners to death or devastate cities and countries, it is because intelligence plays a larger part in their method of warfare and has taught them more effective ways of using force than the crude expression of instinct.

But Clausewitz is too intelligent not to immediately qualify this point about the disciplining of instinct with an acknowledgement of the counter-effect of more 'productive' technologies of death which save his own thesis:

> The invention of gunpowder and the constant improvement of firearms are enough in themselves to show that the advance of civilization has done nothing practical to alter or deflect the impulse to destroy the enemy, which is central to the very idea of war.[129]

On War fails to keep its object in view. Clausewitz cites what would later be called 'body-counts' to measure relative forces, but the conventions of this battlefield arithmetic – Tolstoy calls it a 'game of checkers' – occult the marks of violence on flesh.[130] René Girard writes that Clausewitz 'had a stunning intuition about history's suddenly accelerated course, but he immediately disguised it and tried to give his book the tone of a technical, scholarly treatise'.[131] When it suits him, Tolstoy, too, employs this algorithm to scorn the 'reason' of and for the battle of Borodino: it is 'mathematically clear' that the actions of Kutuzov and Napoleon are 'involuntary and senseless', and the battle 'took place not at all as it is described'.[132] Baudrillard's once-scandalous diagnosis that Bush 41's Second Gulf War (1990–91) 'did not take place' – that

128 George Orwell, 'Inside the Whale', *The Collected Essays, Journalism and Letters*, ed. Sonia Orwell and Ian Angus, 4 vols. (Harmondsworth, 1970), I, 574.
129 Clausewitz, *On War*, 76.
130 Tolstoy, *War and Peace*, 753; see also Mary Favret's essay in the present volume.
131 René Girard, 'On War and Apocalypse', *First Things* 195 (Aug/Sept 2009), 17–22; 18.
132 Tolstoy, *War and Peace*, 753–6.

information invented the event – no longer appears to be a critique but has been normalised in a permanent twenty-first century state of war.[133] Tolstoy's reading of Borodino had a comparable reception – what was initially viewed as nonsensical or unethical was subsequently recognised as a kind of common sense – because it presented a comparable insight into a representational regime. The cognitive challenge has, in each instance, proved the more indigestible element.[134]

Military mathematics – war as enumeration, attrition, body counts – is likely to strike us as an abstraction of the embodied facts of war's violence, and as a complement to the grand reduction involved in the figure of the wrestlers. It is nevertheless to mathematics that Tolstoy turns in order to defend his challenge to battlefield description, that genre of narrative that falsely imposes causal determinism and sense-making devices onto the violence of war. (It was Baudrillard's fantasy that the televised war pundits of 'Desert Storm' would 'die' on screen, 'that some event or other should overwhelm the information').[135] Tolstoy writes that

> [f]or human reason, absolute continuity of movement is incomprehensible. Man begins to understand the laws of any kind of movement only when he examines the arbitrarily chosen units of that movement. But at the same time it is from this arbitrary division of continuous movement into discrete units that the greater part of human error proceeds.[136]

The 'immense movements' which Tolstoy's imagination rejected in 'The Raid' (and throughout *War and Peace* these diagrammatic dispositions of force are presented as fatal illusions of the staff) must be substituted with an 'infinitesimal unit', a 'differential of history', mass individual will. Tolstoy is likely to have derived the mathematical metaphor from his friend Sergei Urusov, who published on 'military-mathematical

133   Jean Baudrillard, *The Gulf War Did Not Take Place* (Sydney, 2000), 50.

134   See Dominic Lieven, 'Tolstoy on War, Russia, and Empire', and Dan Ungurianu, 'The Use of Historical Sources in *War and Peace*', in *Tolstoy on War: Narrative Art and Historical Truth in 'War and Peace'*, ed. Rick McPeak and Donna Tussing Orwin (Ithaca NY, 2012), 12–25; 12 and 26–41; 36–41.

135   Baudrillard, *Gulf War*, 50; see Mark Rawlinson, 'After War: Writing about World War in a Post-War Era?' in *Literatures of War*, ed. Eve Patten and Richard Pine (Newcastle-upon-Tyne, 2008), 381–400; 385.

136   Tolstoy, *War and Peace*, 753–6.

problems' of the 1812–13 campaign in 1868, when Tolstoy was finishing his book.[137] In the second Epilogue to *War and Peace*, he prophesies that if history is to be sociological rather than biographical, it will 'set aside causes' and seek laws common to 'all the equal and inseparably bound together infinitely small elements of freedom'.[138] It is not a failure on the part of Tolstoy that these laws are not expounded here, but one on the part of the reader who has forgotten that this historical calculus is a metaphor with which the author schools us in reading his non-novel. If the fundamental error of historical explanation is the attempt to render what is continuous in nature by 'arbitrary division', then this is also a bias that afflicts imaginative narrative. As the evolutionary psychologist John Tooby argues, citing *War and Peace*, a 'cartoon of single causes' is part of our conceptual toolkit.[139]

Daniel Kahneman's grand synthesis of the psychology and economics of human sense-making presents us with a counter-intuitive, and Tolstoyan, lesson – we are enslaved, despite our Prufrockian protestations of failure, by our undaunted facility in sense-making. Kahneman spells out the significance of the idiom to 'pay attention'; 'cognitive work' is often aversive because it is so costly in energy terms: the default is a cognitive system which minimises effort.[140] This gullible, sense-making system of the mind 'appears to have a special aptitude for the construction and interpretation of stories about active agents, who have personalities, habits and abilities', a bias which is amplified by the weakness of statistical inference, a 'belief in the law of small numbers'.[141] The fallacies of Tolstoy's military historians, and novelists, are under this description reduced to a neurophysiological substrate which best explains the irrationality and poor risk calculation of American college students (who happen to constitute the experimental subjects in the largest number of psychology papers). Contrary to persuasive arguments, ranging from Lukács's realism to Nussbaum's pedagogic humanism, about the cognitive power of fictional narrative, and their extension in recent

137   Stephen T. Ahearn, 'Tolstoy's Integration Metaphor from *War and Peace*', *The American Mathematical Monthly* 112.7 (Aug-Sept 2005), 631–8; 635–6.
138   Tolstoy, *War and Peace*, 1213.
139   John Tooby, 'Nexus Causality, Moral Warfare, and Misattribution Arbitrage', in *This Will Make You Smarter: New Scientific Concepts to Improve your Thinking*, ed. John Brockman (New York, 2012), 33–6; 34–5.
140   Daniel Kahneman, *Thinking Fast and Slow* (London, 2011), 23, 43.
141   Ibid., 29, 113.

years to practices such as medicine,[142] story in this domain is evidence
of a cognitive vacuum.

> Paradoxically, it is easier to construct a coherent story when you
> know little, when there are fewer pieces to fit into the puzzle. Our
> comforting conviction that the world makes sense rests on a secure
> foundation: our almost unlimited ability to ignore our ignorance.[143]

Modern war literature is incontestably a literature of disillusionment (in this it refracts the effects of both realism and modernism),
though there has to be a point at which the repetition of the drama
of innocence and experience, and the attendant jeremiads, require us
to think harder about the relationship of literary traditions to social
and biological generations, and about the covert militarism in our civil
culture. Tolstoy's presentation of the education of the young Hussar
Nicolai Rostov is as much an act of homage to Stendhal as a reworking of the *Sevastopol* material, though *War and Peace* claims a kind of
chronological precedence. Comparison with the narration of Waterloo
in *The Charterhouse of Parma* (1839) reveals shared themes (ignorance,
embarrassment, idealism, fear of cowardice) as well as devices (making
strange, realism): Nikolai is a relay for Fabrizio's question, 'Is this a real
battle?' But Tolstoy is more generous to his protagonist, which accounts
for the more complex registration of war:

> Some of his writings are bitter attacks on war; in others he has de-
> scribed as no one else the beauty and the thrill of a cavalry charge
> and the spectacular and alluring sides of army life, even during a
> campaign.[144]

That Tolstoy includes war's affirmations (or the values and symbols with
which war is affirmed) will be relevant to the conclusion of this essay,
namely that the utility of *War and Peace* lies in its variousness, its internal tensions.

---

142 Trisha Greenhalgh and Brian Hurwitz, 'Narrative Based Medicine:
Why Study Narrative?', British Medical Journal 318.7175 (2 January 1999),
48–50.
143 Kahneman, *Thinking*, 201.
144 Clarence A. Manning, 'The Significance of Tolstoy's War Stories', *PMLA*
52.4 (December 1937), 1161–9; 1161.

Tolstoy takes Pierre Bezukhov, apparently a wiser man than Fabrizio del Dongo, to Borodino in order to further prove Stendhal's image of battle: the 'non-military figure in a white hat' is a spectator or witness rather than combatant, and promises a different perspective to the combatant's, a proximity to the reality of battle which is nevertheless qualified by the distance of dispassion.[145] Pierre's act of witness is consistent with the narrative of disillusion, beginning with aesthetic apprehensions – 'delight in the beauty of the spectacle [. . .] Everywhere – ahead, to the right, to the left – troops could be seen. It was all lively, majestic and unexpected' – and ending with horror.[146] It also conforms to the inscrutability of the battlefield as a system of forces, at least in prospect: Pierre thinks the Raevsky battery is an insignificant location, though it will come to dominate retrospective accounts. But it is the site of a reorientation of Pierre's vision, as he finds himself attending more closely to the 'family animation' of the gunners.[147] Pierre is put through another bathetic reprise of von Clausewitz's duel when he collides with a French officer:

> For a few seconds the two men looked with frightened eyes into their mutually alien faces, and both were perplexed about what they had done and what they were to do. 'Am I taken prisoner, or have I taken him prisoner?' each of them thought.[148]

Tolstoy's collision will be reprised in the writing of the Great War with leaps into occupied shell-holes or other spaces out of battle (Owen's in 'Strange Meeting' is the most mystical, Remarque's in *All Quiet on the Western Front* the most pedagogic, James Hanley's in 'The German Prisoner' the most unremitting in its obscenity). What these writers share with Tolstoy is a sense of the monstrosity of 'mutually alien', of the triumph of the structure of war over common humanity. Pierre has had enough, seen enough, and assumes everyone else has too: 'now they'll stop it, now they'll be horrified at what they've done'.[149] The sensory registration of wounding in the novel is a proportionately minor element, but Tolstoy's attention to the hurt body is always amplified by

---

145   Tolstoy, *War and Peace*, 793.
146   Ibid., 789.
147   Ibid., 793.
148   Ibid., 797.
149   Ibid., 798.

its place in those networks of perceptions and relations which are the source of the undidactic resonance of Tolstoy's great fiction.

The wounded are often apprehended by a person in the story, rather than by an undeluded narrator. The 'painful work' of Rostov's coming to doubt his conception of imperial warfare – in Tilsit, at the time of the alliance of the former adversaries Napoleon and Alexander I (1807) – might now be diagnosed as a traumatic recurrence (as in Pat Barker's *Regeneration*), but Tolstoy wants to insist on the cognitive coincidence of military display and military violence in Rostov's consciousness: '[H]e imagined so vividly now that hospital stench of dead flesh that he looked around to see where the stench could be coming from.'[150] Andrei's apprehension of his regiment bathing is knowingly proleptic: 'All that naked, white human flesh [. . .] flopping about in the dirty puddle like carp in a bucket [. . .] Flesh, the body, *chair à canon*.'[151] Held in reserve at Borodino, they are laid waste like the 'trampled oat field' in which they are ranked under artillery fire.[152] It is witnessing his rival Anatole Kuragin's amputation that provides the mortally wounded Andrei with access to experiences of compassion, amplifying his demystification of Napoleon as he lay wounded at Austerlitz. The matrix is extended by the way the 'dreadful sight' of the wounded has 'an unexpected impression on Napoleon, who ordinarily liked to survey the dead and wounded' (as he did at Austerlitz when he interrogated Andrei).[153]

Pierre's story is picked up again twenty thousand words further on, when we meet him desiring to return 'to the ordinary conditions of life' in order to understand what he has seen.[154] The battle returns unbidden in another traumatic symptom, a war nightmare, but Tolstoy attaches to this residue an altogether more literary dream or vision (like Andrei in hospital, he recalls antagonists from his past) in which he receives an injunction to unite 'the meaning of all things', or as he recalls it, in the daily residue of the noise of breaking camp, to 'hitch' things together.[155] It is a dream in the manner of the oneiric prolepsis in *Anna Karenina*, foreshadowing what the narrative will bring to our attention by more prosaic means, namely the Russian soldier epitomised

150   Ibid., 416.
151   Ibid., 703–4.
152   Ibid., 808.
153   Ibid., 814.
154   Ibid., 840.
155   Ibid., 843.

by Platon Karataev. Like Pierre a prisoner of the French in retreat from Moscow, Platon Karataev is a veteran of many campaigns but 'talked reluctantly about his time as a soldier'.[156] The war stories in Michael Herr's *Dispatches* (1977) or Tim O'Brien's *The Things They Carried* (1990) communicate what war *is* to the extent that they fail as stories. Like Marlow's stories in Conrad's *Heart of Darkness*, their meaning is not extractable but auratic; the nod to Walter Benjamin at this point would take in the counsel that 'it is half the art of storytelling to keep a story free from explanation', and his thesis that the novel is a symptom of the decline of storytelling.[157] Platon Karataev's discourse is even more spare and numinous than the post-Vietnam examples of war story I have cited: 'He often said something completely opposite to what he had said before, but both the one and the other were right.'[158] It is also resistant to repetition or interpretation – to mechanical reproduction and to philosophical analysis:

> When Pierre, sometimes struck by the meaning of what he said, asked him to repeat it, Platon could not remember what he had said [. . .] Each of his words and each of his acts was the manifestation of an activity he knew nothing about, which was his life. But his life, as he looked at it, had no meaning as a separate life [. . .] He was unable to understand either the value or the meaning of a word or act taken separately.[159]

It would be convenient to see Platon Karataev, in his role as Pierre's guru, as a fictional embodiment of Tolstoy's anti-historiographical thesis, a man incapable of levering himself out of the continuity of existence with discrete concepts. Like Kant in *The Critique of Pure Reason* (1781), or Freud in his *Introductory Lectures* (1916–17), Tolstoy declared that his reorientation of thinking about causation should have the impact of a Copernican revolution, that it is as if his opponents 'maintained that the earth stood still'.[160] But, to reiterate the question posed by Tolstoy's metaphor of a historical calculus, is there a constructive as

---

156 Ibid., 973.
157 Walter Benjamin, 'The Storyteller: Reflections on the Work of Nicolai Leskov', in *Illuminations*, ed. Harry Zohn (London, 1973), 89.
158 Tolstoy, *War and Peace*, 973.
159 Ibid., 974.
160 Ibid., 987.

opposed to negative continuation of the analogy with heliocentrism? Platon Karataev's speaking in contradiction (an existence Levin strains to live up to at the end of *Anna Karenina*) is contrasted with Andrei's desperation in the face of the contradiction which he defiantly brings to light in his equation of prisoners and veal. Neither of Tolstoy's aristocrats, Andrei and Pierre, succeeds in his projects of intellectual transcendence, though the narrative grants each embodied episodes of compassion or understanding. The novel seems to weary readers who recall this defeat of the intellect in the triumphalist tones of the author (here the generic heterogeneity of the work is significant); it inspires those who can remember how the frustration of a transcendent perspective is ubiquitous in the quiddity of the novel's details of perception, speech and behaviour, and in the weave of relationships and viewpoints.

Isaiah Berlin's 'solution' to the problem posed by Tolstoy's philosophy of war and of history in *War and Peace* is to displace it. Taking Tolstoy seriously as a theorist, Berlin nevertheless argues that the contradiction in the novel between the author's denial of free will and the readers' conviction that the fictional characters exhibit it in abundance is the literary form taken by a fundamental tension in Tolstoy's personality. According to this argument, Tolstoy's most significant denial was a denial of the tension between his experience and his vision of what life should be, between 'the immediate data, which he was too honest and too intelligent to ignore, and the need for an interpretation of them'.[161] Berlin notes Boris Eikhenbaum's contribution to our understanding of Tolstoy, that he had an incomparable capacity to recognise singularities, but he longed for synthesis.[162] The philosopher Thomas Nagel has written illuminatingly on the consequences of this division – '[h]ow to combine the perspective of a particular person inside the world with an objective view of that same world, the person and his viewpoint included' – as a fundamental property of consciousness, noting that 'the difficulty of reconciling the two standpoints arises in the conduct of life as well as in thought'.[163] This could stand duty as a description of the moral and aesthetic challenges which result in the nineteenth-century novel, and of the genre's thematic and formal responses to the negation of traditional world-views. The sociologist Norbert Elias addressed a comparably 'absurd' opposition between involvement and detachment,

161   Berlin, 'Hedgehog and Fox', 463.
162   Ibid., 464.
163   Thomas Nagel, *The View from Nowhere* (Oxford University Press, 1986), 3.

but in a way which recognised the epistemological problem as a moral and a political problem. Thus an issue in the methodology of the social sciences was of the greatest social urgency because the detachment that had produced control over nature (science) had made much less headway in human affairs which are characterised by an imbalance of involvement and detachment, a 'high affectivity of ideas and low ability to control dangers coming from men to men'.[164] Both Nagel and Elias make the opposition – between subjective and objective, involvement and detachment – structural, and this suggests that characterising it in *War and Peace* as biographical, as Berlin and Eikhenbaum do, is another form of resistance to the novel, or to pick up Morson's suggestive term, another act of 'pacification'.[165]

A final perspective on the themes of this essay – the idea that Tolstoy's *War and Peace* is out of sync with prevailing histories of war representation, and that the book continued to provoke resistance after its time in this sequence had come – is provided by the English novelist Henry Williamson (1895–1977). Williamson's narrative of the World Wars, *A Chronicle of Ancient Sunlight* (1951–69) dwarfs *War and Peace* in the scale of its composition, but in a number of senses it exists in Tolstoy's shadow. The sense of Tolstoy's exemplary precedence is coded into the protagonist Phillip Maddison's development as a veteran war-writer. As a subaltern in 1917 he is enjoined to read *War and Peace*, as an inoculation against both ignorance and dogma:

> Even we see only a fractional aspect of the war. It will take thirty years before anyone taking part in this war, or age, will be able to set-tle down enough to write truly about the human beings involved in this war, let alone what really happened on the battlefield, and in the council chambers [. . .] I once had ambitions to write a *War and Peace* for this age [. . .] Have you read Tolstoi? Then you haven't begun to live clear of the crowd.[166]

But when Maddison does read *War and Peace*, some seven volumes later, he finds 'the entire motive for the Napoleonic War was missing from the work'. Tolstoy's failure to understand Napoleon is Williamson's way of

164   Norbert Elias, 'Problems of Involvement and Detachment', *The British Journal of Sociology* 7.3 (Sept 1956), 226–52; 252.
165   Morson, *Hidden in Plain View*, 78.
166   Henry Williamson, *Love and the Loveless* (London, 1963 [1958]), 191.

signalling the stakes involved in Maddison's projected 'comprehensive novel' of 1914–18, which hinges on the controversial representation of Hitler as an agent of a spirit of 'reconstruction' born out of the brotherhood in suffering of the Western Front.[167] This critique of *War and Peace* places a limit on the book's scepticism (permitted with respect to military hierarchies of command), in order to save the idea of the veteran-as-hero.

167   Henry Williamson, *Lucifer Before Sunrise* (London, 1967), 206.

Index

Woolpit, Green Children of, 67
Wordsworth, William, 186, 198–201
Wright, Joseph, of Derby, 181
Wyndham, John, 57

Yeats, W. B., 220, 223

Zboray, Ronald, 167
Zlatic, Thomas, 174